Verena Schmidt
Gender Mainstreaming—
an Innovation in Europe?

Verena Schmidt

Gender Mainstreaming— an Innovation in Europe?

The Institutionalisation
of Gender Mainstreaming
in the European Commission

Barbara Budrich Publishers, Opladen 2005

A CIP catalogue record for this book is available from
Die Deutsche Bibliothek (The German Library)

© 2005 by Barbara Budrich Publishers, Opladen
www.barbara-budrich.net
ISBN 3-938094-28-1   **paperback**
ISBN 3-938094-29-X   hardcover

Die Deutsche Bibliothek – CIP-Einheitsaufnahme
Ein Titeldatensatz für die Publikation ist bei Der Deutschen Bibliothek erhältlich.

Verlag Barbara Budrich 🅑 Barbara Budrich Publishers
Stauffenbergstr. 7. D-51379 Leverkusen Opladen, Germany

2963 London Wall. Bloomfield Hills. MI 48304. USA
www.barbara-budrich.net

Zgl. Diss. Ruhr-Uni Bochum, Germany
Jacket illustration by disegno, Wuppertal, Germany – www.disenjo.de
Typeset by Andres Friedrichsmeier
Printed in Germany on acid-free paper by
DruckPartner Rübelmann, Hemsbach

Contents

1. Introduction and Methodological Approach

2. Definition and Evolution of Gender Mainstreaming

3. Organisational Theories and Gender Mainstreaming

4. Organisational Innovation

5. Role and Function of the European Commission

6. The Environment of the European Commission

7. The Construction and Implementation of Gender Mainstreaming within the European Commission

8. Conclusion

9. Annexe

10. Bibliography

Figures

Tables

Abbreviations

CEEP	Centre Européen des Entreprises à Participation Publique et des Entreprises d'Intérêt Économique Général (European Centre of Enterprises with Public Participation and of Enterprises of General Economic Interest)
COPA	Committee of Agricultural Organisations
COPEC	Comité Paritaire pour l' Egalité des Chances (Joint Committee on Equal Opportunities for Women and Men)
DECODE	Dessiner la Commission de Demain (Literally translated: 'Designing the Commission of Tommorow'. Plan on the Reform of the Commission)
DG	Directorate General
DNE	Detached National Expert
ECJ	Court of Justice of the European Communities
ECSC	European Coal and Steel Community
EP	European Parliament
ESF	European Social Funds
ETUC	European Trade Union Congress
EU	European Union
Eurostat	Statistical Office of the European Commission
EWL	European Women's Lobby
IGC	Inter-governmental Conference
ILO	International Labour Organisation
MAP 2000	Modernisation of Administration and Personnel Policy
MEP	Member of the European Parliament
NGO	Non-Governmental Organisations
SEM 2000	Sound and Efficient Management
TFAR	Task Force for Administrative Reform
UN	United Nations
UNICE	Union of Industrial and Employers' Confederations of Europe
UNIFEM	United Nations Development Fund for Women
WID	Women in Development

Acknowledgements

This book is a slightly revised version of my doctoral dissertation which was submitted to the Faculty of Social Sciences at the Ruhr University Bochum in 2003.

I owe an enormous debt of gratitude to a considerable number of people who have contributed directly or indirectly to the production of this book. First of all I would like to recognise the continuous caring, advice and encouragement by Prof. Ilse Lenz and Prof. Heiner Minssen to which I am very grateful and for which I would like to thank them very much. The graduate research team of the Hans Böckler Foundation and the Ruhr University Bochum "Innovation from and within Organisations" run by Prof. Heiner Minssen and Prof. Uwe Wilkesmann and in which I was a scholar for three years, was a place of many stimulating research debates. I would also like to thank the research colloquium of Prof. Ilse Lenz, and in the beginning of my work also that of Prof. Ulrike Liebert for many important ideas and constructive criticisms. I would like to particularly thank Dr Rüdiger Piorr, Magnus Rodrigues, Kohei Sawabe, Helen Schwenken and Dr. Michelle Westerbarkey who have supported me in friendship and professionally. I would also like to thank Prof. Cilja Harders, Prof. Prof. Ulrike Liebert, Prof. Amy Mazur, Prof. Theresa Rees, Freya Schwarzbach, Pamela Wehling, Prof. Alison Woodward and Susanne Zwingel for important advice and input. My appreciation also goes to Andres Friedrichmeyer for the support in making the manuscript. I am also very grateful to Natalia Tari for her continous and much appreciated proofreading. Martin Budich and Gabriele Riedl provided advice and important diversions during my times of writing.

The Hans Böckler Foundation enabled this study through a generous scholarship and through an excellent ideational support for which I am very grateful. I would like to particularly thank Werner Fiedler who is the head of the unit of the doctoral scholarship section of the foundation. I received tremendous cooperation and support from staff of the European Commission and beyond who shared their time and expertise with me in in-depth interviews. The empirical part of this book would not have been possible without their time and efforts.

In closing, I wish to express my deep gratitude and affection to my parents Hartmut and Sybille Schmidt for their continous support and encouragement.

Preface by Ilse Lenz
A new Perspective on Gender Mainstreaming in the European Union

Globalisation has been associated with economic neoliberalism and deregulation. It has propelled the reorganisation of the gender division of labour in various ways: Women leave the fields and work at assembly lines in the South. In the North, they leave the household and go increasingly into irregular flexible work, but they also climb up the hierarchies of global corporations and enter the ranges of middle management. Gender relations become more complex. But globalisation also has the effect of a levelling or downgrading of former privileges of male core workers. Former employment security and wage advantages are also often levelled downwards.

But in globalisation, new 'soft forms of regulation' towards gender equality also have emerged (cf. Lenz 2005). The most important are the UN norms established during the UN decade of women and the EU directives on gender equality at work as well as the gender equality goal in the Amsterdam treaty of 1997. Gender mainstreaming is a key concept which plays a central role in the UN declarations as well as in the EU norms.

The EU has been as a pace setter and model for global governance as being the single supranational institution which can agree on legal rules and procedures for its member states. The signal role of the Commission, of the Parliament and of the Europeans Women's Lobby (EWL) have been highlighted. But while there are a lot of policy papers and prognosis, empirical research on the challenges and problems of institutionalising and implementing gender mainstreaming is only beginning.

In this context, Verena Schmidt's work is highly innovative and important: She starts from organisation theory especially variants of neo-institutionalism (DiMaggio, Powell). She combines this with theories of modernisation and structuration (Giddens) in a new and fruitful research perspective. Her innovative approach enables a major new departure from the present concentration on policy and policy network research. For organization research is the touchstone for the implementation and efficacy of gender policies: It can show whether gender mainstreaming is an innovation in the organisation and thus supported (and maybe also ignored or doubted). It can look at the differential strategies of actors – the top management, male and female femocrats, feminist networks – around this innovation. The people who argue for gender mainstreaming and their motivations become visible as well as the ones who ignore gender mainstreaming or who are dismissive or hostile. Moreover, it can demonstrate, if a program like gender mainstreaming is simply a new organisational fashion or whether it has been institutionalised and thus become part of core routines of the EU and the EU Commission.

Verena Schmidt starts with these issues and concludes with innovative results which are highly relevant for future research as well as for practitioners and activists in gender politics. Gender mainstreaming has proved to be an innovation for the European Commission and it has gone through institutionalisation processes. But how far does this change lead? Verena Schmidt combines organisation and structuration theory which asks how actors use the rules and resources of an organisation in their strategies. Her results point to a differential innovation and institutionalisation of gender mainstreaming which is characterized by different groups of actors: The European Commission has committed to the concept of gender main-streaming as a leading principle and has established organisational depart-ments responsible for implementation. But it is mainly the gender main-streaming network in and around the European Commission which is well informed and acting on this idea of gender mainstreaming; for them it is rele-vant in knowledge and practices in organisational institutionalisation. Their male and female colleagues in the Commission have diffuse information and limited interest in gender mainstreaming. Following neoinstitutionalism, Verena Schmidt interpretes this as decoupling of gender mainstreaming knowledge and practices in the organisation and not as resistance or hostility. Gender is not a division line in these decoupling processes: Men and women are committed and active – or indifferent. Rather boundaries are observed between commitment and interest for equality of certain policy networks and diffuse information and indifference in other parts of the organisation. The support of the top EU management was crucial; feminist networks are committed as well as a (smaller) group of men. But incentives and rules supporting men's commitment are lacking.

The in-depth organisational analysis of the Commission shows patterns of a decoupled or split innovation and institutionalisation of gender main-streaming. The research approach and this result have far reaching relevance beyond research on the European Commission. Organisations are crucial actors in globalisation and the future of gender equality is linked to the issue how far they will integrate gender justice as an innovation and institution.

This study unfolds an innovative theoretical framework and far reaching results on gender mainstreaming in the European Commission as one of the most important International Organisations. I hope it will find many readers within academia, administrations, social groups and from politically interested citizens.

1 Introduction and Methodological Approach

1.1 Introduction

Since the United Nations World Conference of Women in Beijing in 1995, the concept of gender mainstreaming has experienced an unexpected boom in the European Union (EU) and beyond. Gender mainstreaming was included as a strategy in the Platform for Action which emanated from this conference (UN 1995). In 1996 gender mainstreaming was transposed into a Commission Communication, thereby establishing the principle of gender mainstreaming within the European Commission. In 1999 gender mainstreaming became an integral part of the Treaty of Amsterdam which entered into force that year (European Council 1997). Despite its early limited success, discussions on equal opportunities between men and women and on positive action, had mostly declined. Since 1995, however, gender mainstreaming has become an important issue for discussion at European, national and local levels.

The general idea of gender mainstreaming is to alter what are often marginalised 'women's concerns' into the mainstream of the analysis by ensuring that the effects of all policies and organisational processes on both genders are taken into account. Gender mainstreaming is often regarded as a new paradigm compared to previously used concepts of equal treatment and positive action programmes (Rees 1998).

Starting from the evolution of gender mainstreaming, this book examines the extent to which gender mainstreaming can be regarded as an innovation and institution in a complex organisation like the European Commission. The book has three aims. Firstly, from a policy analysis standpoint I shall examine to what degree the definition and interpretation of gender mainstreaming by the European Commission can be seen as a policy innovation. Secondly and thirdly, from an organisational point of view I shall study to what extent the implementation of gender mainstreaming in the European Commission can be seen as an organisational innovation and organisational institution. These are crucial points regarding the current state of the art in organisational studies as well as in EU policy analysis.

In the European Commission's key document on gender mainstreaming (i.e. the Communication 'Incorporating Equal Opportunities for Women and Men into all Community Policies and Activities'), gender mainstreaming is defined as:

not restricting efforts to promote equality to the implementation of specific measures to help women, but mobilising all general policies and measures specifically for the purpose

15

of achieving equality by actively and openly taking into account at the planning stage their possible effects on the respective situation of men and women (gender perspective). This means systematically examining measures and policies and taking into account such possible effects when defining and implementing them (The brackets were added in the original text; European Commission 1996).

It might seem surprising that gender mainstreaming, which is an interventionist measure, is part of the Commission's[1] political agenda (European Commission 2002c), and that at a time of increasing deregulation of economic markets and economic stagnation, the Commission has chosen to stress its importance. Indeed, equal treatment and positive action policies have been traditionally framed as social policies due to their perceived economic cost. However, gender mainstreaming is often framed as being in the EU's economic interest and therefore the emphasis on it is consequently less surprising.

Within implementation studies, it is feasible to some extend to judge from the implementation of a policy by the political élite in a particular area under its control, how seriously that political élite might take it in other areas (Meuser 1989: 2). However, it is important to take various context indicators into account when analysing this. Taking the concrete example of the Commission, it would thus be partly possible to judge from the Commission's own implementation within the different Directorates General (DGs), whether it in general takes seriously the implementation of gender mainstreaming in policy-making and programme management. In addition, the level of implementation of gender mainstreaming also illustrates the general difficulties and internal power struggles that organisations, in particular public administrations, face, when introducing change.

The Commission is seen as a melting pot of European ideas: Jean Monnet, one of the founding fathers of early European integration, once called it 'the laboratory of Europe' where people 'work together'. In a manner, that attests to the birth of the 'European spirit' (Monnet 1976: 208). Indeed, the French anthropologist Irène Bellier stated: 'Hence, the Commission is one of the best places to understand how changes take place in the context of the European Union' (Bellier 2002: 207). Adopting Bellier's point of view, the examination of gender mainstreaming in the Commission can be seen as a test case for the implementation of gender mainstreaming in the Member States of the European Union[2], which form part of the 'context

---

1   The terms 'Commission' and 'European Commission' are used interchangeably.
2   Legally, the term 'European Union' only denotes the three 'pillars' which were created by the Treaty of Maastricht (European Council 1993). Pillar one incorporated the three founding treaties now forming the 'European Community', pillar two established the Common Foreign and Security Policy, pillar three created the Justice and Home Affairs policy. It has become common practice among scholars writing on European integration to use the term 'European Union' for the 'European Community' and 'European Economic Community', this practice will be followed in this book.

16

of the European Union' Bellier mentions as cited above. The Commission will be viewed primarily as an administrative organisation[3] and thus the implementation of gender mainstreaming will be analysed from an organisational perspective.

There are a wide variety of publications on gender mainstreaming. Many have been written by consultants or scholars at requests of governments or government agencies. Such studies are normally produced under enormous time pressure. Many are limited to best practice studies where 'best practice' sometimes means any element of gender mainstreaming practice, as the implementation of gender mainstreaming in most Member States remains meagre. This book will provide an in-depth study into the construction and implementation of gender mainstreaming in the European Commission. It is founded in organisation sociology and European integration research. Gender studies will be pursued as an integral perspective.

In the assessment of the implementation of gender mainstreaming in the Commission, I shall analyse different frame alignment processes (based on Snow et al. 1986) to discover whether it can be seen as a policy innovation. The term innovation will be considered according to Hauschildt's definition (i.e. from a subjective, processual and normative dimension) because this approach allows to see gender mainstreaming as a potential innovation in a recursive way (Hauschildt 1993).

The innovative element in this book is that for the elaboration to what extent gender mainstreaming can be seen as an organisational innovation and institution, I shall combine elements of the theory of structuration by Giddens (1984) and neo-institutionalism by DiMaggio and Powell (1991a and 1991b [1983]), Zucker (1988 [1977]); Jepperson (1991) and Oliver (1991). Neo-institutionalism enables us to examine how institutions develop as a result of isomorphic processes. Structuration theory is largely an interior view since it studies internal confrontations and structuration processes within the organisation. It enables us to assess the recursive processes between structure and action with regard to gender mainstreaming. The theory of structuration facilitates to focus on the dynamics by which institutions are reproduced and altered.

In this book, I argue that gender mainstreaming was implemented in the Commission due to the norms bestowed upon it by the United Nations and European Women's movements and that their actual activities on gender mainstreaming are decoupled from the structure. This is based on Meyer and Rowan's (1991 [1977]) concept of decoupling and confidence, which means that organisations attempt to fulfil norms expected from them by the outside world, by decoupling elements of structure from activities. For examining the decoupling process further, it is important to adopt an exterior and interior

---

3   For a detailed study of the policies of different DGs refer to Pollack/ Hafner-Burton 2000.

view on the European Commission in order to examine its structure, activities and outside pressures.

Neo-institutionalism permits an exterior view on organisations by making it possible to study the connection between the organisation and society. Structuration theory can be used as an interior view since it studies processes within the organisation. Based on DiMaggio's (1998) differentiation of previous neo-institutionalist accounts, I study institutionalisation as a process which allows bringing agency and interest back into the research. This allows us to reflect the power structures within the Commission and among actors who mobilise around gender mainstreaming. Neo-institutionalism enables us to examine how institutions develop as a result of isomorphic processes. Neo-institutionalism moves away from the previously dominating view that organisations take rational decisions despite being bounded by limited information and resources. Rather, neo-institutionalism argues that organisations take the decisions they take, because they believe them to be regarded as rational and that the main aim of the organisation is to increase social legitimacy by these decisions.

Structuration theory facilitates to examine the recursive processes between structure and action. Giddens' (1984) concept of rules and resources will be used to examine the modification of actions and structures, which are necessary for the implementation of innovations. Structuration theory enables us to examine the emergence of particular organisational structures and to examine internal power dynamics within organisations further.

European women's movements such as the European Women's Lobby and academic scholars have criticised the concept of gender mainstreaming as being only weakly supported by the Commissioners and top civil servants when it comes to actually implementing it. This view is critically evaluated in this book. However, even policies that were initially intended as mere rhetoric, can turn into effective policies (Ritti and Gouldner 1979; DiMaggio and Powell 1983). Once a problem is treated as politically relevant, even if only at a rhetorical level, political groups can mobilise around it. This mobilisation and lobbying can prevent the policies from continuing to be treated as merely rhetorical.

For the understanding of this book it is important to briefly describe how the key terms of this study will be used. These terms will be further developed in chapter 3. The terms actors, organisation, institution and institutionalisation for the framework of this book will be defined based on neo-institutionalism and structuration theory. This book will examine to what extent the implementation of gender mainstreaming in the European Commission can be regarded as an innovation and/ or institution. The European Commission will be analysed as an organisation which consists of different sub-organisations or Directorate Generals (DGs), of which two DGs will be examined in an exemplary way. The institutionalisation or structuration of gender mainstreaming will be studied with special emphasis on the actors within the organisation. It will be elaborated which rules and resources they possess and which strategic reactions they pursue relating to the implementation of gender mainstreaming.

Outline of this Book

Gender mainstreaming is a complex issue. This is partly demonstrated by the mass of definitions and interpretations of gender mainstreaming. For this reason, chapter 2 examines the evolution of the concept and the interpretation of gender mainstreaming by the European Commission. I shall argue that gender mainstreaming was strategically framed by the European Commission to fashion 'shared understandings of the world' (McAdam et al.1996) that legitimate the Commission. I shall also argue that the framing of gender mainstreaming in the European Commission can be regarded as a policy innovation.

Chapter 3 considers the implementation of gender mainstreaming within the European Commission on the basis of organisational theories. The isomorphic model of neo-institutionalism will be used to assess why gender mainstreaming was introduced in the Commission. Structuration theory will be utilised to explain the power struggle inside the Commission when implementing gender mainstreaming. Both theoretical strands will be combined in order to thoroughly examine the implementation of gender mainstreaming in the European Commission. Meyer and Rowan's (1991 [1977]) model of decoupling and confidence will be further illustrated and applied to gender mainstreaming. The aim of this is to analyse whether the Commission merely attempts to fulfil norms with regard to gender mainstreaming expected from them by the United Nations by decoupling elements of structure from their actual activities on gender mainstreaming.

In this book, gender mainstreaming will be examined with regard to Hauschildt's definition of innovations (Hauschildt 1993) which will be elaborated in chapter 4. The subjective dimension of Hauschildt is particularly important for the research on the implementation of gender mainstreaming, that is, the issue of to whom the innovation is new. For the introduction of gender mainstreaming, the European Commission adopted a top-down perspective. It is thus important to take the individualistic perspective into account, i.e. whether individual actors are familiar with gender mainstreaming, whether they regard it as something new and whether they intend to actively implement it. In transferring the other aspects of Hauschildt's subjective dimension to the case of the Commission, the micro-economic aspect will be interpreted to mean whether gender mainstreaming is new to DG Employment and Social Affairs and DG Administration and

Personnel. The third and fourth perspectives, i.e. the sectoral economic aspect and the macro-economic perspective will correspond to the relations of the European Commission to other International Organisations. Hauschildt's processual dimension of innovation with regard to the boundaries of an innovation is particularly important to make a distinction between gender mainstreaming and equal treatment and equal opportunity policies. Throughout the book, the 'interactive process perspective' (Slappendel 1996: 118) will be used. This implies taking structures and actions into account and, in particular, examining the dynamic nature of the innovation process, i.e. that gender mainstreaming is continually transformed by the process of implementation.

The fifth chapter assesses the role and function of the European Commission. It places particular emphasis on the administrative traditions and administrative cultures that constitute the background of the Commission. The legitimacy of the European Commission was seriously challenged at the time of the corruption scandal in the late 1990s, which led to the resignation of the entire Commission in March 1999. As a result, a fundamental administrative reform has been brought forward. I shall argue that with regard to equal opportunities and gender mainstreaming, some important changes are envisaged in the suggested reform package. I also bring forward the argument that the Commission used the policy of equal opportunities to increase its own competencies and power.

Chapter 6 examines the environment of the European Commission and looks at the interplay between European institutions and social movements. Within neo-institutionalism, the environment plays an important role. I follow Meyer and Rowan's (1991 [1977] and DiMaggio and Powell's (1991b [1983]) contention that the organisations can become isomorphic with their environments. I shall argue in this chapter that the interplay between the international women's movement, the UN and the Commission were of utmost importance for the introduction of gender mainstreaming. The introduction of gender mainstreaming in the European Commission can be regarded as an example of mimetic and coercive isomorphism. Partly gender mainstreaming was implemented in the Commission because the environment created uncertainty (mimetic isomorphism), partly it was implemented because of pressure from the UN level (coercive isomorphism).

The empirical chapter (chapter 7) analyses the construction of gender mainstreaming within the Commission. I shall argue that gender mainstreaming has become an institution for those who are part of the gender mainstreaming advocacy-network. For them, gender mainstreaming has led to standardised interaction sequences and these are clearly self-reproducing. However, the institutionalisation of gender mainstreaming has not spread beyond the relatively small group of gender experts and thus the institutionalisation of the concept remains limited.

20

In the conclusion, the theoretical questions will be assessed with the findings of the empirical chapter. Summarising the results of the first research question, i.e. the extent to which gender mainstreaming can be seen as a policy innovation, we can conclude that gender mainstreaming was strategically framed by the Commission in Adams et al.'s (1993) definition to fashion 'a shared understanding of the world'. All four frame alignment processes that were initially developed theoretically by Snow et al. (1986) for Social Movement Organisations and which were transposed to public administrations by Rein and Schön (1993) took place with regard to gender mainstreaming in the European Commission. With regard to the second research question, i.e. examining the extent to which gender mainstreaming can be seen as an innovation, the subjective dimension of Hauschildt (1993) is particularly important as it allows to distinguish between the actors who are part of the gender mainstreaming advocacy-network and those who are not. Those actors who are members of the gender mainstreaming advocacy-network generally see gender mainstreaming as an institution and an innovation, while the others usually only have limited knowledge on gender mainstreaming.

It is first of all important to explain the methodological approach and the operationalisation of the research undertaken for this study. This book is based on triangulation, i.e. quantitative elements combined with qualitative elements. Expert interviews were conducted with actors within the Commission and in the environment of the Commission. This will briefly be elaborated in the following.

1.2 Methodological Approach

This part focuses on the research methodology and procedures used in this study. While the late 1960s and 1970s were characterised by a fundamental dispute between positivists and proponents of qualitative research, there are now few who see quality and quantity as the fundamental dichotomy in social science research (Robson 1993: 303). Recently, attempts have been made to build bridges and seek a rapprochement between the respective approaches (e.g. Westie 1957; Denzin 1989 [1970]). In this study, quantitative and qualitative elements will be combined in order to match the strengths of qualitative approaches to the weaknesses of quantitative approaches and vice versa by means of triangulation.

The benefits accrued through the use of triangulation both as design strategy and as an analytical tool are considerable since they allow for the clustering and organisation of disparate yet related data. No single research method will ever capture all of the changing features of the social world under study (Robson 1993). While triangulation is not an end in itself, with any approach based upon a singular methodology some unknown part or aspect of the results obtained may be attributable to the method used (Macauley 2001: 82).

The implementation of gender mainstreaming within the Commission is elaborated in a twofold way: The processes and changes are examined in a qualitative analysis by means of expert interviews. The situation in the Commission is also examined quantitatively by looking at gender differences between different grades of personnel. This is important since one indicator of gender mainstreaming is positive action, which includes balanced decision-making by women and men. The methodology for this quantitative part is explained within the quantitative section in chapter 7 since it is closely linked to the data.

Definition of Experts

In a modern knowledge-based society, there is a large variety of experts. However, there is no absolute definition of the term 'expert', rather it is a positional term. Whether an actor was asked for an interview for this book depended on his or her potential knowledge or experience of the implementation of gender mainstreaming in the Commission. This does not suggest that these are experts per se or 'experts from sociological mercy' (Meuser/ Nagel 2002: 73). They are merely experts for the particular research question of this study.

For this book, people were asked to contribute as experts when they were in a direct way responsible for the implementation of gender mainstreaming in their daily work. One reason why actors were approached for an interview was their participation in the formulation and monitoring of the implementation of gender mainstreaming through their work in Committees within the Commission or in the European Parliament or in the European Women's Lobby. Other reasons why employees were approached to serve as experts were when they had strategy formulation or advising functions was part of their job or when they were responsible for monitoring, auditing or evaluating general policies within the Commission, and, last but not least, when they were involved with training and personnel management.

It is important that not only those in the higher management positions were addressed as experts but also and especially those on the second and third level. It is usually at those levels that decisions are prepared and implemented and hence presumably the most detailed knowledge on the internal structure and events is available here (Meuser/ Nagel 2002: 74).

Sampling

There are two fundamentally different sampling strategies: pre-determination of the sampling and the determination of the sampling structure during the course of research. The selection of the sampling method should depend on the aim of the research, i.e. whether the research is trying to chiefly verify or falsify existing theory or to develop new theory. Pre-determination of the sampling means that a field is structured into different social groups before the empirical survey or enquiry. This method is particularly useful for the differentiation, verification and further analysis of the assumed similarities and differences between certain groups. However, it is less useful for developing a theory since this approach limits the scope for the development and change of a theory (Flick 1998: 81).

The German psychologist Uwe Flick (1998) describes a third way to combine the pre-determination and theoretical sampling methods: thematical coding (Flick 1998: 206-211). This approach was followed in this book. Thematical coding is based on Strauss (1991) and was particularly developed for comparative studies where different groups are defined which are linked to the research question from the outset. It is assumed that the different groups which are sampled have different perspectives on a particular issue. The different groups are thus pre-determined and are not developed according to the interpretation at that particular moment as is the case with Strauss' approach (Flick 1998: 206-211). Theoretical sampling is done within the groups to select specific cases.

In this book, in the beginning of the research process, the field was structured into different social groups regarding DGs, hierarchical position and function. During the course of research, the theoretical sampling within these different groups resulted in the realisation that these groups did not show any significant difference. Therefore, the sampling structure was determined by means of theoretical sampling.

The theoretical sampling process fits well to the recursive theory model of structuration theory developed by Giddens (1984) and the process variants of Neoinstitutionalist theory of DiMaggio (1988) and Zucker (1991) which form the basis of the theoretical framework of this study.

The basic principle of theoretical sampling consists in the selection of cases or groups of cases according to concrete content criteria according to their relevance instead of their representation. The sample is chosen according to the (expected) value of new perspectives for the developing theory, based on the state of the art of theory. The central question for the selection of data is 'Which groups or sub-groups do I next take into account for the data aggregation? For what reason?' The possibilities of multiple comparisons are endless, therefore groups must be chosen according to theoretical criteria (Glaser/ Strauss 1975: 47). Because of the numerous possibilities for the inclusion of more people, groups and cases etc., there the necessity of defining criteria arises, that is, of narrowing down the potentially endless possibilities by defining selection criteria. These criteria will be grounded in theory, where the theory developed from empirical analysis, is the benchmark. The criteria are: how promising is the next case, and how relevant it might be with regard to the developing theory?

A second, similar question is, when should the researcher stop including new cases? Glaser and Strauss develop the criteria of 'theoretical saturation' (Glaser/ Strauss 1975: 61). Saturation means that no additional data can be found through which the researcher could further develop the properties and significance of the category (Flick 1998: 82-3). Saturation, however, can be an ambiguous concept in the research process. Research is usually dependent on external factors such as funding and it is thus not usually possible to seek complete saturation without constraints. Another critical point is that some researchers might never find their work saturated.

With regard to the research question, a variety of strategies was used to select potential interview partners. The implementation of gender mainstreaming is relatively new within the Commission and thus two DGs, DG Employment and Social Affairs and DG Personnel and Administration were examined. There were two reasons for this: Firstly, both of these DGs have Equal Opportunities Units. The one which is attached to DG Employment and Social Affairs coordinates gender mainstreaming on the policy side, and although the policy side of Member States is not at the centre of interest here, the Equal Opportunities Unit provides important know-how for the implementation of gender mainstreaming within DG Employment and Social Affairs. DG Employment and Social Affairs was one of the first DGs to become involved with gender mainstreaming as a result of the introduction of gender mainstreaming into the Structural Funds in 1994. These funds are, in fact, partially administered by DG Employment and Social Affairs.

The Equal Opportunities Unit in DG Personnel and Administration coordinates the implementation of gender mainstreaming within the Commission. Due to the Commission's internal mobility scheme, according to which all civil servants should change unit after five years at the most, various people who used to work in the Equal Opportunities Units are now responsible for its implementation in other units and thus gender mainstreaming expertise is being spread throughout the DGs. Additionally, the primary concern of both DGs is with employment in the widest sense: DG Personnel and Administration with regard to the internal work organisation, DG Employment and Social Affairs with regard to employment policies and work organisation in Member States. Hence by tradition they have been most reflective of the issues of equal opportunities and gender mainstreaming. The reason behind the selection of two DGs (rather than a larger number) was mainly practical; the aim of the study was not to examine the largest possible breadth of actors but rather, to make an in-depth study of particular contexts.

29 expert interviews were conducted, of which 25 were with employees from the Commission – 13 from DG Employment and Social Affairs and 12 from DG Personnel and Administration. Eight of the 25 interviewees were men and seventeen were women. 19 of the 25 interviewees belonged to the grade 'A' (administrators and managers). From the 19 'A' interviewees, six were working in management, 13 were administrators, three interviewees were assistants and another three were secretaries. Two Members of the European Parliament were interviewed and two employees from the European Women's Lobby, all four interviewees were women. The interviews lasted between half an hour and one and a half hours each.

The Commission employees interviewed came from different hierarchical levels and grades. Ten were involved directly with gender mainstreaming, 15 were selected because their job description included work organisation or strategic management in the widest sense. Those interviewed were mostly civil servants but Detached National Experts[4] were also included. The interviews took place in Summer 2000 and Winter 2001/2002. All interviewees were ensured of anonymity and thus only their general status group[5] (management, administrator, assistant, secretary) is mentioned. However, most interviewees are administrators and managers, since they were most directly concerned with the implementation of gender mainstreaming. The distribution of interviewees from the European Commission is also illustrated in table 1 according to gender, hierarchical level, whether they are part of the gender mainstreaming advocacy-network and for which DG they work.

Those working within the lowest grade within the Commission, 'D' grades who do mostly manual work were not included in this book. A pre-test with six different 'D' grades showed that they were not familiar with the concept of gender mainstreaming or indeed with other policies of the Commission. Furthermore, they did not participate in the customary induction or training courses of the Commission and thus this limited knowledge is not surprising.

---

4   Detached National Experts are employees from national civil services who are seconded to work at the Commission for several years.
5   For a description of the differences between the grades, refer to chapter 7.

Table 1: Breakdown of the Interviews conducted within the Commission

	Women	Men	Total
Total	17	8	25
DG: Employment and Social Affairs	8	5	13
DG: Personnel and Administration	9	3	12
Part of the Gender Mainstreaming Advocacy-Network	8	2	10
Hierarchical level:			
A – Manager/ess	3	3	6
A - Administrator	8	5	12
B - Assistant	3	0	3
C - Secretary	3	0	3

Source: Own illustration

Empirical Design

Thus, it is important at the outset of the study to convince Commission officials that the suggested research will be carried out in an ethical manner according to the guidelines laid down by the British and German sociological association[6], by, for example, reassuring them that the results of the interview would de made fully anonymous. This goes hand in hand with carefully respecting something that was said 'off the record' i.e. when the speaker did not want a piece of information or a comment to be quoted. The interviewees were asked if they agreed to the interview being taped. They were also told that they could request to have the tape recorder stopped at any point, that they could have me delete passages, and that they could refuse to answer individual questions. No one took advantage of the offer to have the tape recorder stopped or to have individual passages deleted. However, some actors refused to answer individual questions and volunteered 'off the record' information after the end of the interview. Such information has not been used in this study. The interviewees were assured that the information would be anonymous, i.e. their names, nationality and DG are not stated in the text. Two people did not want their interviews recorded. During these interviews I took extensive notes which I typed up immediately afterwards.

---

6   For the complete ethical standards in Sociology, refer to the ethical standards of the German Sociological Association (Deutsche Gesellschaft für Soziologie) (1992) and its British counterpart the British Sociological Association (1994).

Interview Questions

The purpose of the interviews was to capture the conceptions, meanings and attitudes of the employees towards gender mainstreaming. The interviews contained questions on the following five broad topics: The professional background of the actors, the understanding of gender mainstreaming by actors, the possible commitment to gender mainstreaming and the perceived institutionalisation of gender mainstreaming. Finally the actors were asked what they saw as barriers to the implementation of gender mainstreaming.

The interview started with 'warm-up' questions on the professional background of the actors i.e. how long they had been working for the Commission and in which areas they had worked on.

The second issue focused on the interviewees' understanding of gender mainstreaming and their opinion on gender mainstreaming, i.e. what the actors associated with gender mainstreaming and how they would design gender mainstreaming. The interviewees were also asked what they regarded as success criteria for gender mainstreaming. Since the implementation of gender mainstreaming is viewed as a process in this book, it was particularly important to assess how the interviewees viewed this process. The interviewees were queried what changes they perceived with regard to gender mainstreaming and on which occasion they first took account of gender mainstreaming. They were also questioned what they thought of the implementation of gender mainstreaming in the European Commission. In addition, I requested them to elaborate on their understanding of innovations, to provide examples of successful and unsuccessful innovations within the Commission and to what extent they thought gender mainstreaming was an innovation. The last question of my second set of questions was on the most important role models of the European Commission and the DGs they were working in[7].

The third set of questions circled around the possible commitment of the actors to gender mainstreaming. The interviewees were queried whether or to what extent they were involved with gender mainstreaming and whether gender mainstreaming was part of their administrative routines.

The fourth interview topic was about the perception of actors to what extent gender mainstreaming can be seen as institutionalised within the Commission. I enquired to what extent there existed a common understanding on gender mainstreaming between different actors and between different DGs and whether the interviewees cooperated with other DGs or organisations on gender mainstreaming.

---

7   As will be explained towards the end of this chapter, questions on the differences between DG Employment and Social Affairs and DG Personnel and Administration were stressed more in the beginning of the research process.

The fifth set of interview questions was about possible barriers the interviewees saw with regard to the implementation of gender mainstreaming. They were asked to what extent they themselves encountered problems with the implementation of gender mainstreaming. They were also queried how they felt about sanctions with regard to gender mainstreaming.

Interpretation of Results

There are two fundamental questions with regard to the interpretation of results: firstly the methodology of interpretation and secondly, the validation of data.

The interpretation of results was made according to the qualitative content analysis developed by the German psychologist Philipp Mayring (2000). This method aims to preserve the advantages of qualitative content analysis as developed within communication studies and to transfer and further develop them into qualitative-interpretative interpretation steps of analysis (Mayring 2000: 3).

Inductive category development means that the development of categories is made transparent, which is not yet the norm. The central idea of qualitative text analysis is that categories are developed as closely as possible to the original text.

For this book, the inductive elements of Mayring's approach were followed. The categories for the selection of text passages were determined according to the set of research questions, i.e. how gender mainstreaming is implemented in the European Commission. This was done by following the interview texts closely, with the categories from the theoretical framework in mind. In the beginning of the research process, the differences between DG Employment and Social Affairs and DG Personnel and Administration played an important role. The research categories partly circled around the role models of the DGs, the relation of each DG to the other DGs and to the rest of the Commission and the working culture within the DG. After the subsumption of these categories and their revision using the interview material, the differences between actors of the different DGs with regard to gender mainstreaming were insignificant. Therefore, the questions on particularities of both DGs were reduced and the following categories were examined: the understanding and construction of gender mainstreaming, interests and resources of actors, rules of gender mainstreaming, resources of gender mainstreaming, barriers to the implementation of gender mainstreaming, gender mainstreaming as an institution, the institutionalisation of gender mainstreaming and gender mainstreaming as an innovation.

2   Definition and Evolution of Gender Mainstreaming

2.1   Introduction

The aim of this chapter is to define the key term of this study 'gender main-streaming'. The term 'gender mainstreaming' will be defined and embedded within academic debates. Within the context of the whole book, this chapter will look at the definition and evolution of gender mainstreaming in the European Commission. The legal framework on equal opportunities and gender mainstreaming will be illustrated. Furthermore, the definition of gender mainstreaming of the European Commission will be elaborated, as will its operationalisation within the Commission from an organisational point of view. And different critiques of gender mainstreaming will be illustrated and evaluated. Chapter 7 will examine to what extent this official definition is understood and taken into account by actors within the European Commission.

Ortmann et al. (2000) define the term 'evolution' as unintended change, while intended change is referred to as organisational change. They elaborate:

Naturally there are connections: evolution also works via reorganisation, whose factual consequence are by the way never totally intended. However, evolution also proceeds from a change which was unintended from the outset and via a selection. Evolution, as we use the expression, does not implicate a further development, however this might be defined (Ortmann et al. 2000: 333)[8].

Looking at the way in which gender mainstreaming was implemented in the European Commission, we could expect that the change constituted an 'intended change' rather than an 'evolution' in the above definition by Ortmann: The Commission signed the Platform for Action in 1995 (UN 1995), which envisaged the implementation of gender mainstreaming by all signatories; it implemented gender mainstreaming via the Commission Communication (Council of the European Union 1996) and the Treaty of Amsterdam (Council of the European Union 1997a).

However, I shall argue in chapter 3 that the introduction of gender main-streaming constituted an element of decoupling (Meyer/ Rowan 1991[1977]), i.e. that the European Commission pretends to implement gender main-streaming in order to be consistent with the norms of the UN. The internal implementation of gender mainstreaming is far from being institutionalised.

---

8   Translation by the author.

Therefore, the structural elements of gender mainstreaming are decoupled from the daily routines and activities of the organisation. The development of gender mainstreaming in the European Commission can thus be described as 'evolution' rather than as 'organisational change' in the definition by Ortmann et al. (2000).

Following Sonia Mazey (1998), I shall argue in this book that gender mainstreaming has been established as a new policy frame. Based on Snow et al. (1986) and Verloo (1999) I shall argue that the four frame alignment processes outlined by Snow et al. (1986) were put into place chiefly as a result of the Commission communication 'Incorporating equal opportunities for women and men into all community policies and activities' (European Commission 1996) and the subsequent 'Third Action Programme on Equal Opportunities' (European Commission 1997a).There were however other factors as well, i.e., other general developments in European gender policies. The four frame alignment processes are frame bridging, frame amplification, frame extension and frame transformation and will be elaborated later in this chapter. Part of these frame alignment processes are 'policy frames' i.e. a way of selecting, organising, interpreting and making sense of a complex reality to provide guideposts for understanding and analysing, persuading and acting (Rein/ Schön 1993). However, the proposition that gender mainstreaming has been established as a new policy frame is not sufficient in itself. The implementation depends in practice on the 'fit' between the policy frame and the dominant frames of elites. My hypothesis is that by framing gender mainstreaming within New Public Management approaches and as a normative concept of the United Nations, there is created a high degree of 'fit' between the gender mainstreaming frame and the dominant frame within the European Commission.

2.2 Definition of Gender Mainstreaming

The conception and origins of gender mainstreaming will briefly be introduced in this section. Special emphasis will be put on making transparent the underlying assumptions of the gender mainstreaming concept such as the embeddedness of social gender in organisations, the implications of gender mainstreaming on power structures within organisation, and the role of structural inequality. The consequences as to who is involved with gender mainstreaming will also be examined in this section. Particularly important for the content of this book is the relationship of gender mainstreaming to other equal opportunities concepts and the scope of gender mainstreaming, which will be discussed in the second part of the section.

Gender mainstreaming implies a commitment to incorporate gender into all areas of public policy, rather than considering women's issues as a discrete policy problem (Mazey 2001: 2). It is a strategy that aims to abolish, in a sustainable manner, the existing inequalities between men and women in society. In contrast to equal treatment and affirmative action, gender mainstreaming targets both genders and particularly the relationship between both genders and ignores the one sided orientation of women as the single topic of change (Jung/ Küpper 2001: 9). Gender mainstreaming is a proactive strategy, which endeavours to change the structures conducive to or enabling discrimination.

Gender mainstreaming is the preliminary result of a learning process of several decades of different women's policies (Callenius 2002: 65). The term 'mainstreaming' first entered the international development debates in 1984 when the United Nations Development Fund for Women (UNIFEM) was restructured. UNIFEM was given the task to specifically support women, to achieve equality for women and to enable women to access mainstream agenda-setting on development issues (Braunmühl 2002: 17).

Gender mainstreaming was first introduced on the global level outside of the development discussions at the World Conference of Women in Beijing in 1995 where it was part of the Final Platform for Action in Section 189 and in the following sections[9] (UN 1995). The term 'gender mainstreaming' is not used explicitly in the Platform for Action, rather the concept is described as follows:

Governments and other actors should promote an active and visible policy of mainstreaming a gender perspective in all policies and programmes so that before decisions are taken, an analysis is made of the effects on women and men, respectively (UN 1995).

The fact that the term 'gender mainstreaming' is not used explicitly in the Platform for Action might have had several reasons: The term gender mainstreaming only became prominent after the Beijing Conference and hence the signatories might have wanted to avoid a term till then largely obscure. Alternatively, or indeed in addition to the above, the signatories might have dreaded using a term like gender mainstreaming with far reaching consequences to all levels of the United Nations. Another possibility is that some signatories might have preferred paraphrasing and describing the concept 'gender mainstreaming' to make the contents clear rather than using a specific term which might be interpreted in different ways.

Gender mainstreaming is a concept which aims at both the organisations and the policies pursued by these organisations. One of the basic assumptions of gender mainstreaming is that 'social gender' is deeply embedded in the organisation and that it determines social interaction at all levels (Bretherton

---

9   See chapter 6 for a detailed listing of the other Sections in the Platform for Action, which
     refer to gender mainstreaming.

2001: 61). As mentioned in the above official definition of the European Commission, all political concepts and measures are examined with regard to their gender specific impacts.

The gender mainstreaming approach assumes that the origin of gender inequality is not the individual understanding between men and women but rather, gender hierarchy in society. Power does not only exist between people but also in the interpretations and definitions of reality. Thus it becomes obvious that the state is not only responsible for the elimination of gender inequality, but that, in part, it actually causes the inequality (Verloo 1999). Following Verloo, it becomes obvious that the gender mainstreaming approach attempts to consider the potentially different impacts on both genders in the planning, implementation, monitoring and evaluation of policies. One of the possibly unintended contingent effects of gender mainstreaming is that it is necessary to analyse domination structures in organisations and make them transparent.

Since gender mainstreaming is defined in a way that all policies should be screened with regard to their consequences on both genders, it implies that equal opportunities officers are no longer the only people responsible for equality, for they cannot be familiar with all policies in an organisation. Rather, all organisational units are formally responsible. According to Monika Goldmann, the

function of the women's equality officer changes considerably. She becomes a gender equality manageress, who has a presenting, supporting and consulting function. Furthermore she can no longer be seen as the single responsible person for the success of the different processes[10] (Goldmann 2001: 6).

Alison Woodward found that some feminists feel threatened by just this, since it leads away from special women's offices and the concentration of 'power', and gender analyses become widely distributed (Woodward 1999a: 133). According to the report of the expert committee on the situation of universities of a federated state in Germany (North-Rhine Westphalia; Expertenrat 2001), equal opportunities officers ought to be seen as 'change agents', as important actors in the innovation process. Following the expert committee cited above, the inclusion of the competencies and experiences of equal opportunities officers appears to be an important prerequisite to avoid possible conflicts between gender mainstreaming vs. equal opportunities. Beveridge et al. go further in their suggestion on who should be implicated in the gender mainstreaming process. They develop a 'participatory-democratic model' (Beveridge et al. 2000: 390), i.e. they want to encourage affected groups to participate in the drafting of mainstreaming policies.

---

10 Translation by the author.

The relationship of Gender Mainstreaming to other Equal
Opportunities Concepts and the Scope of Gender Mainstreaming

Academic debates on gender mainstreaming exist on two different levels, first of all on the relationship of gender mainstreaming to other equal opportunities policies, and secondly with regard to the scope and efficiency of the concept. The aim of this section is to present a state of the art of the most important articles published on gender mainstreaming. Firstly, the categorisation of equal opportunities policies into equal treatment, positive action and gender mainstreaming by Teresa Rees will be presented. Secondly, the scope of the gender mainstreaming concept will be elaborated and thirdly the efficiency and rationality of gender mainstreaming will be discussed. Fourthly, a critical stance will be illustrated to indicate to what extent gender mainstreaming can be seen as a goal in itself.

One of the first academic accounts of the implementation of equal opportunities policies in education, training, and labour market policies by the European Commission, was written by the British social scientist Teresa Rees (1998). She offers a fundamental categorisation for different equal opportunities models by distinguishing between three models of equal opportunities which are all evident in EU policy making: equal treatment, positive action and gender mainstreaming. This categorisation, which is often cited by scholars researching equal opportunities in the EU (e.g. Mazey 2001, Woodward 2003), will be briefly summarised and some critical points will be raised after the illustration.

According to Rees (1998) the *equal treatment approach* is based on a liberal principle of equal rights and treatment before the law. Gender equality is defined as giving women and men de jure equal rights. In policy implementation, this approach leads to the introduction of anti-discrimination legislation and equal opportunities policies. In EU policy making, this approach can be traced back to the equality provision in Article 119 in the Treaty of Rome (1957) and the adoption of the first equality directives in the 1970s and 1980s. Rees refers to this approach as 'tinkering' since it is essentially about 'tidying up' the legislation and procedures for equal treatment (Rees 1998: 42).

Following Rees, the *positive action or positive discrimination* approaches of equal opportunities are rooted in a focus upon inequalities of outcome and seek to address these through a 'deficit model', i.e. by focusing on the characteristics of the under-performing group and making good their alleged 'deficiencies' (Bernstein 1971). Positive action and positive discrimination are important tools in achieving greater equality in organisations and constitute important aims for of the women's movements (Schmidt 1998).

However, Rees contends that there are two problems with the positive action approach. Firstly the underlying norm for most policy-making is male.

Rees depicts this by saying that the objective of positive action programmes is to 'enable women to march to the male stride' (Rees 1998: 189). She states that since women's legs are on average shorter than men's, it is much harder for them to walk comfortably to the male stride when it is taken as the norm (Rees 1998: 185). Secondly, as Squires argues, theoretical discussions and policies about gender injustice lead the discussion 'away from analyses of structural systems of oppression to a debate of reallocation of resources or privileges to individuals, i.e. a narrowly distributive conception of justice' (Squires 1994:1). This second strategy is referred to by Rees as 'tailoring', since it allows for add-on, supplementary measures to take account of women's special position.

Rees regards gender mainstreaming as the third strategy and potentially the most far reaching and is therefore referred to as 'transforming'. It is based on the recognition of gender differences between men and women with regard to the different division of domestic labour and socio-economic differences. Gender mainstreaming means an equal visibility and participation of both sexes in public and private life. Rees states that:

Mainstreaming entails a paradigm shift in thinking towards the development of policy and practice. It requires being able to see the ways in which current practice is gendered in its construction, despite appearing to be gender neutral. (...) Much of the taken-for-granted inequality needs to be questioned, such as the imbalance between the regularity with which resources are allocated to providing car parks for new factories but not workplace nurseries. Statistics can provide a starting point to understanding how disadvantage is structured. The analysis of discourse (...) can also reveal androcentric biases in the social construction of concepts such as skill (Rees 1998: 194).

Rees particularly stresses the transformative capacity of gender mainstreaming to move beyond the tinkering and tailoring of equal treatment and positive action approaches (Rees 1998: 34-48).

The categorisation of gender mainstreaming as the third strategy is not merely an analytical distinction but also a political weighing by Rees on the qualitative differences between positive action and gender mainstreaming. However, the above categorisations are very generalised. For example, the positive action or positive discrimination approaches of equal opportunities are not always based on 'deficit models' and do not adhere to an alleged male norm for policy-making: partly they too aim to redress structural discriminations for women (Schmidt 1998). Since the European Commission stresses that gender mainstreaming should be seen as a dual strategy, the distinctions, especially between the second and third strategies, remain largely on an analytical level.

The second level of debate on gender mainstreaming focuses on the scope of the concept. Indeed, this is also linked to the first debate, i.e. where the boundaries of the concepts are, and to what extent there are qualitative differences between gender mainstreaming as opposed to equal opportunities. The debate goes further and also assesses the potential efficiency of the concept.

The Dutch political scientist and chair of the Council of Europe Group of Specialists on Gender Mainstreaming[11] Mieke Verloo is sceptical about the expectations raised by gender mainstreaming, i.e. that this strategy could successfully address structural inequalities (Verloo 1999). Such expectations were expressed by e.g. the Council of Europe (1998) and Rees (1998). Verloo argues that firstly, the structural problems are much varied between the different Member States and even within Member States and thus the strategies will have to be varied, too. Secondly, Verloo doubts whether the problems of the different structural inequalities are similar enough to adopt similar strategies. She suggests that we need more knowledge about the different kinds of structural inequalities, before we can develop strategies on how to deal with them (Verloo 1999: 9-10).

The US-American sociologist Alison Woodward (1999a) sees mainstreaming as a 'rational' approach in terms of being aimed at better reaching a goal, i.e., in terms of efficiency. Yet, she regards it as

irrational in terms of its potentially subversive and transformative effects. It challenges the idea that a policy can be 'gender neutral' and aims to reveal that the norm behind much policy is in fact the 'Man' (Woodward 1999a: 133).

Following Woodward, gender mainstreaming offers a 'rational' strategy to make policy more responsive to women and thereby more democratic, and, which thereby 'might have transformative aims and effects' (Woodward 1999a: 137). Woodward proposes the hypothesis that the greater and more deeply entrenched are the resistance and the masculine rationality in a public administrative setting, the more likely it is that any initiative to mainstream will stand as an extremely simple instrument, incapable of inducing fundamental changes. However, Woodward warns that:

For feminist women, mainstreaming is also seen as controversial and even dangerous because it steps away from specifically women's policy machineries and spreads the concentration of 'power' and gender expertise (Woodward 1999a: 133).

Woodward also sees the danger of abusing the mainstreaming policy as an excuse to reduce specifically directed programmes for women (for a discussion on this, see the section on problems with the implementation of gender mainstreaming).

---

11 The Council of Europe should not be confused with the Council of Ministers or the European Council. The Council of Europe was founded in 1949 and aims to strengthen the unity of the European continent and to protect the dignity of the citizens of Europe. The Council of Europe has 49 members including Russia and Turkey. The Council of Ministers and the European Council represent the interests of the member states of the EU.

The US-American educated political scientists Jacqui True and Michael Mintrom regard gender mainstreaming not as a goal in itself:

[...gender mainstreaming is] not merely a liberal policy to include women. Rather, it is a more radical strategy for achieving gender equality that involves traditional state efforts to address gender imbalances by developing specific policies for women (e.g. reproductive health or employment equity policies) (The brackets were added in the original; True/ Mintrom 2001: 33).

Looking at gender mainstreaming on a global level, True and Mintrom state that the purpose of mainstreaming is to alter the existing social and political order that leads to gendered outcomes (True/ Mintrom 2001). Such outcomes include structural inequalities between men and women. For example, True and Mintrom contend that in Russia and some other Eastern European states, the life expectancy of men is 20 years less than that of women (True/ Mintrom 2001: 33)[12].

Based on the existing literature and empirical studies on gender main-streaming, it seems that the following five points are of the utmost importance for the successful implementation of gender mainstreaming:

- Level of understanding in terms of gender policy issues i.e. to what extent the actors have understood gender mainstreaming (Woodward 2003)
- Commitment to gender mainstreaming, i.e. an all-encompassing commit-ment to changing gender relations (Woodward 2003)
- The environmental context of resistance to gender initiatives: this analyses the extent to which there are vested interests that might be opposed to the transformation of gender relations (Braunmühl 2002)
- The anchoring of responsibility for the implementation of gender main-streaming (Schmidt 2001a)
- Some form of participatory element of gender mainstreaming (Bretherton 2001).

Precisely how gender mainstreaming is to be achieved is dependant on normative views on organisational efficiency, equality and justice. This book provides an in-depth study of the implementation of gender mainstreaming within the European Commission. Gender mainstreaming is a relatively new policy approach, and there are few existing procedural experiences to indi-cate how existing policies will affect gender relations in the future.

---

12 Unfortunately, the authors do not state which Eastern European countries they refer to. Data from the United Nations suggest that the difference of men's and women's life expectancy at birth in the EU is 6 years on average; in Lithuania 9; Slovenia; Estonia and Latvia 8; in the Czech Republic, Hungary, Rumania and Poland 7; in Slovakia 6; in Bulgaria and Turkey 5; in Cyprus and Malta 4 years (United Nations 2000). According to the CIA, in Russia men's life expectancy at birth is on average 12 years lower than women's (CIA 2002).

2.3 Semantic Approach to the Term 'Gender Mainstreaming'

All terms, in which a whole process is semiotically summarised, elude definition; definable is only that which has no history (Nietzsche 1980 [1910]: 13)[13].

In sociological usage, *gender* is differentiated from sex. Scott traces the sex/ gender distinction back to the 1960s when feminists borrowed the term from endocrinologists and psychoanalysts, mainly John Money and Robert Stoller (Scott 1999: 22). While sex refers to the biological distinction between male, female or hermaphrodite, gender is used for culturally-imposed behavioural and temperamental traits deemed socially appropriate to the sexes. These traits are learnt via a complex and continuing process of socialisation[14].

The noun *'mainstream'* is used to describe the majority or 'normal' strand of opinion. Within women's movements, the term 'mainstream' is traditionally regarded as negative since its meaning was to be at the level of the dominant patriarchal policy. The term 'mainstreaming' was originally used in the English language to describe the process by which mentally or physically challenged children were sent to 'mainstream' schools, i.e. those for the alleged 'normal' kids. It is worth pointing out that the term 'mainstreaming' is not limited to disabled groups or women. Indeed, within the EU, ethnic minorities, gay and lesbian groups, and the elderly are also calling for a more inclusive strategy of equality and they use the term 'mainstreaming' to illustrate their demands for the inclusion of ethnic, sexual orientation, and old age minority concerns. Another example of the implementation of a mainstreaming policy is the EU environmental policy, which requires all EU legislative proposals be accompanied by an environmental audit and that they be compatible with the commitment to environmentally sustainable economic development (Mazey 2001: 9).

If the meaning of the two terms is transposed to the concept of gender mainstreaming, it can be surmised that from a semantic point of view, gender mainstreaming means the inclusion of all questions relating to gender in the mainstream of policy-making, as opposed to a special area.

In the academic literature on gender mainstreaming, three main causes for misunderstandings and confusions on the term gender mainstreaming can be found. Firstly, because the term 'gender mainstreaming' is an artificial construct, secondly because the term is seen as inherently illogical and thirdly

---

13 The German original of the above citation is: 'Alle Begriffe, in denen sich ein ganzer Prozeß semiotisch zusammenfaßt, entziehen sich der Definition; definierbar ist nur das, was keine Geschichte hat' (Nietzsche 1980 [1910]: 13).

14 The debates about the distinction between sex and gender plays an important role within gender studies, see e.g. Oakley 1972; Lorber 1994; Honneger and Arni 1999; Scott 1999; Wetterer 2002.

because the term moves away from women's issues. All these reasons will be elaborated in turn, while the general critiques of the concept of gender mainstreaming, which move beyond the linguistics, will be assessed at the end of the chapter.

The first of the most important reasons for the confusion about gender mainstreaming arises from the fact that from the official languages of the European Union[15], the term exists only in English and Swedish as a combination of hitherto existing terms[16]. All other languages use the English term or a mixture of their own language and English (e.g. in French: 'mainstreaming du genre'), which might confuse people and lead to a defensive reaction against the concept since it is regarded as foreign because of the foreign name. However, in some Member States this might also have the opposite effect, i.e. that the concept is regarded as very modern because of the newly constructed English term. This will be elaborated later in this chapter.

Within the European Commission though, this does not present a problem, since employees are used to juggling different languages and switching back and forth between them. Only one interviewee from within the Commission who had a linguistic background criticised the awkward name of the concept (see chapter 7)[17].

Secondly, there is an inherent logical problem regarding the term gender mainstreaming. On the one hand, gender mainstreaming is distinguished from positive action and equal opportunities policies in the definition of the European Commission, while on the other hand, positive action is part of gender mainstreaming in the definition of the European Commission (European Commission 1996). The distinction between the two is thus difficult, and they are often confused.

Another logical problem with the term gender mainstreaming is pointed out by Alison Woodward. She contends that 'to mainstream' is a creation of a new verb, which cannot be found in a standard English language dictionary. Woodward's (2003) comments on the term gender mainstreaming are as follows:

Even more problematically in terms of concepts is the fact that the job of gender mainstreaming according to some of its main proponents, aims to revolutionarily transform standard practice to reflect gender balance rather than inequality – in other words, the

---

15 The official languages of the European Union are English, French, German, Spanish, Italian, Portuguese, Swedish, Finnish, Dutch, Danish and Greek.

16 In Sweden, the newly constructed term *Jämtegrering* is used for gender mainstreaming, which combines elements of the Swedish words for gender equality (*jämställdhet*) and for integration (*integrering*) (Verloo 2000: 11).

17 The language confusion over terms of gender equality resulted in the publication of a glossary for interpreters on terms related to gender mainstreaming or equal opportunities (European Commission 1998b).

'mainstream' or status quo would be very different post-mainstreaming (Woodward 2003: 13).

At first sight this would seem to be a paradox i.e. the status quo is different in a world which is 'post-mainstreamed'. This suggests that there can never be an end-state with regard to gender mainstreaming, since the post-mainstreaming state will always be different to the mainstream. This emphasises the importance of examining the process of gender main-streaming recursively. It is essential to study the process of gender mainstreaming and to see how the structure and behaviour of different actors influence each other. This enables us to examine to what extent the status quo or the 'mainstream' changes due to gender mainstreaming. Giddens' theory of structuration (1984) enables us to examine the recursiveness between action and structure, and will be elaborated in chapter 3.

Thirdly, the concept of gender mainstreaming has travelled from the realms of feminist theory to policy application and has been highly contested as a concept. With regard to the first critique that the term 'gender mainstreaming' moves away from women's issues, True and Mintrom contend that gender mainstreaming "...on the one hand, suggests a shift away from a focus on 'women's issues,'" and on the other that it politicises traditional male and female roles (The quotation marks were added in the original text; True/ Mintrom 2001: 31). Indeed, both parts of the argument are important and will be further elaborated in the section on the framing of gender mainstreaming later in this chapter.

2.4 Legal Framework for Equal Opportunities and Positive Action in the European Union

2.4.1 The development of EU Women's Policies and the Significance of Article 119 in the Treaties of Rome

The development of women's policies of the European Community has followed closely the changes in the social dimension of the Union. The basis of all future women's policies was laid in the negotiations over the Treaties of Rome which were signed in 1957, and which entered into force in 1958. Since it was obvious that there would be intensified economic competition between Member States, the need developed for the union to have an inde-pendent social policy to take care of the necessity for social cohesion as defined in the Treaty of Rome[18]. Social policy was, however, developed only in connection with the labour market, with the result that the EU did not have any competence in areas such as domestic violence and social benefits.

Fundamental differences regarding the way social systems were understood led to conflict between the German and French governments. In France, social contributions were more closely integrated into the pay system and the government argued that indirect labour costs ought to be harmonised with the Community. The German government, on the other hand, argued that the indirect labour costs are just one factor among many which determine competitiveness. Other factors consist of taxes, productivity, work relations, and location. The International Labour Organisation (ILO) in Geneva published a statement on this and supported the German position (Ostner/ Lewis 1998: 199). As a result, Article 119 was drafted stipulating that 'men and women should receive equal pay for equal work' (Treaty of Rome 1957, Article 119). The exact wording of the Article will be elaborated later in this chapter).

France was under pressure from the employee associations, which were traditionally responsible for social security and family support, and she insisted that Article 119 was included in the Treaties of Rome (Ostner/ Lewis 1998: 199)[19]. France's insistence, however, for the introduction of Article 119 into the Treaties of Rome was really motivated by a concern about her competitiveness rather than a desire to be involved in the struggle for equal opportunities and social equality. Despite this, Article 119 is still the legal basis for European women's policies (Ostner/ Lewis 1998: 198-9, Bergmann 1999: 41); and because the introduction of improved social security in France was the result of the fight by French workers for equal pay during and after the war, Article 119 can be seen as an indirect effect of these fights.

2.4.1.1 The Effects of Article 119 in the Treaties of Rome

According to Warner (1984), Article 119 was ignored by all Member States throughout the 1960s. However, four related developments coincided towards

---

18 Article 2 of the Treaty states that 'The Community shall have as its task, by establishing a common market and an economic and monetary union and by implementing the common policies or activities referred to in Articles 3 and 3a, to promote throughout the Community a harmonious and balanced development of economic activities, sustainable and non-inflationary growth respecting the environment, a high degree of convergence of economic performance, a high level of employment and of social protection, the raising of the standard of living and quality of life, and economic and social cohesion and solidarity among Member States' (Treaty of Rome 1957).
19 During the negotiations about the Treaty of Rome, France was the only negotiating country to have equal opportunities laws. Different equal opportunities laws were passed in France between 1946 and 1950 (Hoskyns 1996: 55).

the end of this period and the beginning of the 1970s to bring Article 119 onto the EU policy agenda.

The first event was the resistance of female workers in an armaments factory in the Belgian town of Herstal, who used Article 119 in their strike for equal pay, which took place between February and May 1966. This was the first time that the implementation of Article 119 was demanded publicly. In this factory, virtually all women were categorised within the lowest pay groups. A breakthrough was achieved only as a result of the intervention of the Minister of Labour. Management capitulated and the demands of the workers were largely satisfied (Hoskyns 1996: 65-70).

The second important event for the implementation of Article 119 was the involvement of the Belgian lawyer Eliane Vogel-Polsky, who, with the Defrenne case, fought in court for a strict interpretation of Article 119 from 1971-1977. Vogel-Polsky was inspired by the strike of the Herstal workers and wanted to use Article 119 in court. However, she was not supported by the trade unions since they did not want to threaten their national collective bargaining powers by strengthening European level powers (Hoskyns 1996: 69). Vogel-Polsky used the discrimination against stewardesses by the state-owned airline Sabena to create a precedence case for Article 119. In the case Defrenne vs. the Belgian state, Gabrielle Defrenne, a stewardess, went to court against Sabena because she had had to leave the landsite personnel of the airline without receiving a pension relating to that of her male colleagues. The European Court of Justice decided in Defrenne II[20] that Sabena discriminated against Defrenne and required the airline to make compensation payments for the lost income.

The third development, which is closely related to the first two, is the growth of women's movements throughout Western Europe and in many other parts of the world. As Hoskyns (1996) and Schmidt (2000) have shown, these women's movements created considerable pressure for the improvement of women's rights in the workplace, in both national and in European legislation.

Fourthly, during the 1970s EU leaders, anxious to increase the popular legitimacy of the EU, turned their attention to EU social policy, which was seen as a field through which they could increase the legitimacy of European integration (Meehan 1990; Mazey 1995).

---

20 The law suits on Defrenne were taken to the European Court of Justice on three different accounts. Defrenne I referred to the unequal treatment in the area of social security. Defrenne II is about pay discrimination, and Defrenne III is about the financial effects the difference in pensionable age has on women and men (Ostner/ Lewis 1998: 233, footnote 19).

2.4.1.2 Types of EU Legislation

There are seven different forms of legislation in the European Union: Regulations, Directives, Decisions, Commission Recommendations, Commission Communications, Council Opinions, and Council Resolutions.

A *Regulation* is binding in its entirety and directly applicable to Member States, i.e. no national law is needed to make it binding. It comes into effect once it is published in the official journal. So far, no regulation has been passed with regard to equal opportunities. A *Directive* is binding upon the Member State, to which it is addressed, but leaves it to the national authorities to choose the form and method of implementation. It also has to be published in the Official Journal, but its publication is not a condition for its coming into effect. A *Decision* is binding in its entirety upon those to whom it is addressed, which can be Member States, enterprises or individuals. It is rather an instrument of the administrative implementation of EC law; and it can be published, but this is not a condition for its entering into force. *Commission Recommendations* and *Commission Communications* and *Council Opinions* and *Council Resolutions* have no binding force but indicate policy directions. They do not need to be published in the Official Journal (Verband der Europäischen Beamten 2001: 121).

2.4.1.3 First Wave Directives from 1975 until 1992

From 1975 onwards ten directives were developed based on Article 119[21]. The first six were based upon a narrow concern of social policy as being primarily interested in economic affairs (Cunningham 1992, Schunter-Kleemann 1992: 33)[22]. The 1975 Equal Pay Directive introduced the principle of equal pay between women and men 'for work of equal value'. This was followed by four Equal Treatment Directives: The 1976 Equal Treatment Directive established the right to equal treatment of women and men with regard to employment, vocational training, promotion, and working conditions. The 1978 Equal Treatment Directive provided for equal treatment with regard to statutory social security schemes, while the two 1986 Directives concerned equal treatment with regard to occupational social security and equal treatment with regard to agriculture and self-employment. The 1992 Directive introduced some basic principles relating to maternity leave.

---

21 All Directives are summarised in the annexe.
22 Cunningham (1992) put forward this argument with regard to the first five Directives, the sixth Directive was decided after her article was published.

2.4.1.4 Second Wave Directives from 1992 until 2002

The following three new Directives and a modification of an existing Directive offer a more general interpretation of social policy and include indirect effects of discrimination. The 1996 Directive introduced the principle of parental leave, which did not exist in all Member States until that date. The 1997 Directive was concerned with the burden of proof in sex discrimination, and the other 1997 Directive regulated part-time work. In 2002 a Directive was decided which amended the 1975 Equal Pay Directive[23].

The application of all Directives, however, has highlighted their limitations. Changes in gender gaps relating to the employment rate, the unemployment rate and wages, remain minimal (Schmidt 2003a). A major problem, mostly related to the first six Directives, is that they are limited to a close interpretation of social policy, related to employment policies. Conditions which enable a fair division of labour in the household, an important prerequisite for the implementation of equal opportunities policies, are limited to national legislation (Ostner/ Lewis 1998: 218).

Secondly, there are normative differences between the gender regimes in different Member States: for example, whether men are seen as the providers for the family (male breadwinner model), or whether women are seen as having primary responsibility for the education of children and the care of other family members in need for care (female caregiver model) (Pfau-Effinger 1996). The German political scientist Brigitte Young differentiates between gender regimes and gender orders. She defines gender regimes as 'institutionalised gender practices and forms which are structures rooted in societal practices as a netting of norms, regulations and principles.' Gender orders are the 'personification of a series of these institutionalised practices which together constitute a 'macro-politics of gender'[24] (Young 1998: 177).

Another problem associated with the Equal Pay Directive is the absence of a proper concept of 'equal pay' and 'equal treatment'. In EU legislation equal treatment means that persons who are to be treated equally need to be 'situated in a similar manner'. This can lead to problems regarding special protection laws for pregnant women, since there is no comparable situation for men (Mazey 1995: 599; Ostner/ Lewis 1998: 216).

Finally, since Directives are not directly applicable, there is a considerable gap in the ways the Directives are implemented into national legislation of each country, as well as problems of non-implementation and non-compliance. Fourthly, despite the equal treatment legislation, indirect discrimination still persists. In these cases it is the use of criteria other than gender that formally impedes access, for example, by the introduction of height restrictions (Mazey 1995: 599).

---

23 For a detailed study on the implementation of the Directives, see Liebert (2002).
24 Translation by the author.

2.4.1.5 Recommendations, Resolutions and Declarations on Equal Opportunities of Women and Men

Some follow-up legislation by the EU has been regulated in 'soft law', i.e., Council Resolutions and Declarations and Commission Regulations. However, there is an even wider gap in the extent to which soft law is implemented than there is with 'hard law'. The difference between the two is that the former consists of legally non-binding norms, whereas the latter is legally binding.

The most important recommendations, declarations and resolutions are summarised in table 2. The decision with the most far-reaching consequences with regard to gender mainstreaming is the 1996 Commission Communication on 'Incorporating equal opportunities for women and men into all Community policies and activities' (European Commission 1996), which will be examined in detail later in this chapter.

Another important legal act was the Commission's decision to commit itself formally to gender balance in all expert groups and committees set up by the Commission. The decision, which extends to both new and existing groups and committees, sets a target of at least 40% for each sex in each group or committee in the medium term (European Commission 2000). The Commission binds itself formally to review the results of this commitment in three years' time and to take whatever action deemed necessary in the light of that review.

The 1994 Council Resolution on gender mainstreaming in the Structural Funds enables it to press for sanctions in applications for funding where equal opportunities are not established. The Council resolution states that

The Council of the European Union (...) 6. Invites the Member States:
(a) to contribute towards ensuring that due account is taken of promoting the principle of equal opportunities for men and women on the labour market in measures co-financed by the European Structural Funds, in particular the European Social Fund (Council of the European Union 1994).

Despite the soft wording, 'The Council of the European Union [...] invites the Member States [...]' towards ensuring the implementation of equal opportunities, this passage has, in the past, been interpreted by European officials who monitor the projects, as well as by national officials who are responsible for the selection of projects, to mean that only those projects which have adequately implemented gender mainstreaming (interview 20, male administrator) should be co-financed by the Union.

Table 2: Selected Recommendations, Communications, Declarations and
Resolutions on Equal Opportunities of Women and Men and
Gender Mainstreaming

1981	Commission Decision 82/43/EEC of 9 December 1981 relating to the setting up of an advisory committee on equal opportunities for women and men (European Commission 1982)
1982	Council Resolution of 12 July 1982 on the promotion of equal opportunities for women (Council of the European Union 1982)
1984	Council Recommendation of 13 December 1984 on the promotion of positive action for women (Council of the European Union 1984)
1986	Second Council Resolution of 24 July 1986 on the promotion of equal opportunities for women (Council of the European Union 1986a)
1990	Council Resolution of 29 May 1990 on the protection of the dignity of women and men at work (Council of the European Union 1990)
1991	Commission Recommendation of 27 November 1991 on the protection of the dignity of women and men at work, including the code of practice to combat sexual harassment (European Commission 1992)
1991	Council Declaration of 19 December 1991 on the implementation of the Commission Recommendation on the protection of the dignity of women and men at work (Council of the European Union 1992a)
1994	Council Resolution of 22 June 1994 on the promotion of equal opportunities for men and women through action by the European Structural Funds (Council of the European Union 1994)
1995	Council Resolution of 27 March 1995 on the balanced participation of men and women in decision-making (Council of the European Union 1995a)
1995	Commission Decision of 19 July 1995 amending Decision 82/43/EEC relating to the setting up of an advisory committee on equal opportunities for women and men (European Commission 1995a)
1995	Resolution of the Council and the representatives of the Governments of the Member States, meeting within the Council of 5 October 1995 on the image of women and men portrayed in advertising and the media (Council of the European Union 1995b)
1996	Commission Communication from the Commission of 21 February 1996 'Incorporating equal opportunities for women and men into all Community policies and activities' (European Commission 1996)
1997	Council Resolution of 4 December 1997 concerning the report on the state of women's health in the European Community (Council of the European Union 1997a)

Source: Own illustration

2.4.1.6 Action Programmes and Employment Guidelines for Member States

In addition to the legislation, the European Union started a number of Community programmes to support equal opportunities within the Union. Most importantly, five *Medium Term Community Action Programmes for Men and Women* were decided. These aimed at introducing the equal opportunities dimension into all policies, projects and measures implemented at community, national, regional and local level.

Between 1991 and 1999 the Union funded a special employment programme for women which was called Employment-NOW (New Opportunities for Women). The specific aim of Employment-NOW was to:

- reduce unemployment amongst women
- improve the position of those already in the workforce
- develop innovative strategies in response to changes in the organisation of work and job requirements, with a view to reconciling employment and family life.

In December 1997, on a proposal from the Commission, the Council adopted guidelines for employment, the main aims of which include strengthening equal opportunities policies. The guidelines are to be reflected in practical measures and included in national action plans drawn up by the Member States (Council Resolution of 15 December 1997).

2.4.1.7 Positive Action Programmes within the European Commission

Three different 'Positive Action Programmes' have been put in place within the Commission. These should not be confused with the above mentioned Medium Term Action Programmes, which target the implementation of gender mainstreaming and equal opportunities in the Member States.

The aim of the 'First Positive Action Programme (1988-1990)' was to increase the number of female civil servants in the under-represented grades, in responsible positions and in technical and scientific functions. Another task was to improve the promotion chances of women and to further their career opportunities. The implementation of the programme took place mainly in recruitment and training, and in measures to improve the social infrastructure as well as awareness measures. The principle, 'when there is equal qualification and/ or equal merit, priority should be given to women', was applied. However, priority for women was not applied automatically. The official evaluation of this programme was mixed since structural inequalities persisted despite an augmentation of women in middle management positions (European Commission 1997a).

The 'Second Positive Action Programme (1992-1996)' had the same objectives as the first, though reconciliation measures were given greater stress in this programme. An important change to the First Positive Action Programme is that targets are fixed for the whole of the institution for each grade and each year, especially as regards the targeting of new recruits. The Second Positive Action Programme has another new feature, which is to follow a decentralised approach by means of equal opportunities plans for each DG. Each plan consists of an analysis of the DG concerned and identifies areas where actions are most needed. Thus each DG has the power to implement measures which are best adapted to its specific situation. Notably, DG Administration, in collaboration with COPEC, created the Equal Opportunities Unit to monitor and evaluate the Second Positive Action Programme as well as the ensuing programmes.

The 'Third Action Programme for Equal Opportunities for Women and Men' (1997-2000, extended until 2001) specifically envisages a 'move from the "positive action" approach to the "mainstreaming approach", with all that this implies in terms of a profound change in mentality' (European Commission 1997: 1). This 'move' should not be seen as exclusive; it is stressed that gender mainstreaming would mean both positive action and gender mainstreaming. Since a number of important frame alignments took place in the 'Third Action Programme' it will be further examined in the section on frame alignment processes later in this chapter.

The new provisions on equal opportunities in the Treaty of Amsterdam and the 'Third Action Programme' led to the revision of the Staff Regulations. After a revision carried out in 1998, the European civil servants' Staff Regulations stipulate in Article 1 B) that 'officials have a right to equality of treatment without reference, direct or indirect, to race, political, philosophical or religious convictions, to sex or sexual orientation, without prejudice to the relevant statutory dispositions' (European Commission 2002a). In paragraph 2, it is stated that measures can be undertaken in order to 'facilitate a professional activity by the under-represented sex or to prevent or compensate the disadvantages in the professional career.' It is important to note here that the Commission as a supranational institution is neither bound by EU legislation nor by Belgian legislation but only by their own Staff Regulations. However, the staff regulation at least have to reflect the spirit of the European Treaties. The Court of Justice of the European Communities has a special chamber for law suits brought by Commission officials.

2.5 The Definition of Gender Mainstreaming within the European Commission

This book is a study on the implementation of gender mainstreaming in the European Commission. Therefore no original definition of gender mainstreaming will be developed, rather, the definition of gender mainstreaming by the Commission and its implementation, will be studied. The definition developed earlier in this chapter is based on the Commission's definition and thus the extent to which the Commission has implemented the concept will be examined in the conclusion of this book.

My thesis is that the fact that various Member States implemented gender mainstreaming despite an absent legal obligation can be seen as an example of coercive isomorphism as explained by DiMaggio and Powell (1991b: 67).

Surprisingly, there is not one authoritative definition on gender mainstreaming within the EU. Gender mainstreaming is defined and described slightly differently in the Treaty of Amsterdam and the various Communications, Recommendations, Resolutions and Declarations by the European Institutions which mention it.

One, often cited, definition of the Commission's approach to gender mainstreaming in EU legislation, and which is mentioned in many texts by scholars and politicians, can be found in the Commission Communication: 'Incorporating equal opportunities for women and men into all Community policies and activities' (European Commission 1996):

This [gender mainstreaming] involves not only not restricting efforts to promote equality in the implementation of specific measures to help women, but mobilising all general policies and measures specifically for the purpose of achieving equality by actively and openly taking into account, at the planning stage, their possible effects on the respective situation of men and women (gender perspective). This means systematically examining measures and policies and taking into account their possible effects when defining and implementing them (The brackets are added in the original text; European Commission 1996: 1).

This Communication is the most comprehensive definition of gender mainstreaming by the Commission.

In this Communication and in many other publications, the Commission stresses that gender mainstreaming is understood as incorporating a dual approach, namely, that it consists of both gender mainstreaming and positive action (European Commission 1996, European Commission 2000). Gender mainstreaming in the definition of the Commission does not finish with positive action, nor simply with equal opportunities but rather strengthens this approach and complements it. Following the inception of gender mainstreaming, the Commission failed to stress that it understood gender mainstreaming to be a dual track strategy, which led to fierce protests from women's groups, especially from the European Women's Lobby (Interview female officer EWL 22) (refer to chapter 5). The Commission asserted in 2000 that '[…] in the light of continuing inequalities it will be indispensable in the future to implement specific positive action policies parallel to gender mainstreaming' (European Commission 2000: 3). The Commission calls the dual track approach of gender mainstreaming the 'Commission approach' (European Commission 2000). However, as mentioned before, a Commission

Communication is not legally binding but constitutes soft law, which has a normative character.

The legal base for gender mainstreaming can be found in Articles 2 and 3 of the Treaty of Amsterdam, which was signed in 1997 and came into force in 1999:

The Community shall have as its task, by establishing a common market and an economic and monetary union and by implementing common policies or activities referred to in Articles 3 and 3a, to promote throughout the Community a harmonious, balanced and sustainable development of economic activities, a high level of employment and of social protection, equality between men and women, sustainable and non-inflationary growth, a high degree of competitiveness and convergence of economic performance, a high level of protection and improvement of the quality of the environment, the raising of the standard of living and quality of life, and economic and social cohesion and solidarity among Member States (Treaty of Amsterdam 1997, Article 2).

Article 3 of the Treaty of Amsterdam defines the area for which gender mainstreaming is relevant:

In all the activities referred to in this Article, the Community shall aim to eliminate inequalities, and to promote equality, between men and women (Treaty of Amsterdam 1997, Article 3.2).

The activities referred to in this Article are all those areas which fall under the authority of the European Union, i.e., all those areas that are defined in the first pillar of the Maastricht Treaty (Maastricht Treaty 1992)[25]. The Amsterdam Treaty does not specifically use the term 'gender mainstreaming' as an aim of the Union; however, the passage stating that 'the Community shall aim to eliminate inequalities, and to promote equality, between men and women' has been interpreted as a description of gender mainstreaming. Indeed, when asked why the term gender mainstreaming is not included in the Treaty, one actor in the Commission responded:

There have been enough misunderstandings with regard to gender mainstreaming. We preferred to have a description rather than just spell out the term (Interview manageress 4).

As will be shown in chapter 7, the largest women's organisation in the EU, the European Women's Lobby, was also sceptical about the introduction of gender mainstreaming in the European Treaties; thus, the inclusion of the description of gender mainstreaming appears to be a strategic choice of both Commission and the European Women's Lobby.

Article 13 (ex Article 6a) of the Treaty of Amsterdam states the following:

Without prejudice to the other provisions of this Treaty and within the limits of the powers conferred by it upon the Community, the Council, acting unanimously on a proposal from the Commission and after consulting the European Parliament, may take appropriate action

---

25   For a listing of all the activities of the European Union referred to, see the annexe.

to combat discrimination based on sex, racial or ethnic origin, religion or belief, disability, age or sexual orientation (Treaty of Amsterdam 1997, Article 13).

However, this 'can' provision with regard to discrimination based on sex does not equate to an enforceable fundamental law against discrimination, as it was demanded by women's groups (Sanjuán 1998: 2).

Article 141.4 (ex-Article 119 from the Treaty of Rome (European Economic Community 1957)) of the Treaty of Amsterdam (1997) specifically allows positive action in the field of employment and vocational activities in favour of the under-represented sex, i.e., not necessarily women.

With a view to ensuring full equality in practice between men and women in working life, the principle of equal treatment shall not prevent any Member State from maintaining or adopting measures providing for specific advantages in order to make it easier for the under-represented sex to pursue a vocational activity or to prevent or compensate for disadvantages in professional careers (Treaty of Amsterdam, 1997, Article 141.4).

The passage on expressly allowing specific measures for the disadvantaged was included in the Treaty of Amsterdam (signed in 1997). The initial Treaty of Rome (signed in 1957) in Article 119[26] only stated that:

Each Member State shall during the first stage ensure and subsequently maintain the application of the principle that men and women should receive equal pay for equal work. For the purpose of this Article, 'pay' means the ordinary basic or minimum wage or salary and any other consideration, whether in cash or in kind, which the worker receives, directly or indirectly, in respect of his employment from his employer.
Equal pay without discrimination based on sex means:
a) that pay for the same work at piece rates shall be calculated on the basis of the same unit of measurement;
b) that pay for work at time rates shall be the same for the same job (Treaty of Rome (1957), Article 119).

These provisions, which are at least partly attributable to the concerted lobbying of the European Women's Lobby and the Nordic Member States during the 1996 Intergovernmental Conference (see chapter 5), significantly strengthen the Treaty basis for EC sex equality policies. They also extend the scope for anti-discrimination laws on the European level to sources of dis-crimination that lie beyond the workplace, which is an important change to previous policies. The modifications in the Amsterdam Treaty, regarding national measures on positive actions for the under-represented sex, is particularly important. As Mazey puts it,

In short, it [the endorsement of gender mainstreaming in the Amsterdam Treaty] challenges the liberal (and widely accepted) legal definition of equality as equal treatment, which posits that public policies should be gender neutral (The round brackets are included in the original citation) (Mazey 2001: 35).

---

26   The initial Article 119 was renumbered in the Treaty of Maastricht (signed in 1992) and constitutes Article 141.1 and 141.2 in the Treaty of Amsterdam (signed in 1997).

Despite the fact that Treaty provisions are not directly effective, they provide 'legal authority and political cover' (Pollack/ Hafner-Burton 2000: 13) for gender mainstreaming. In all Member States of the European Union, elements of gender mainstreaming are implemented at national, regional and local level, partly because of the alleged legal obligation of gender mainstreaming in the Treaty of Amsterdam[27]. However, since gender mainstreaming has not yet been transposed into a Directive, Regulation or Decision, it is merely a normative specification, which is not legally enforceable[28]. The fact that various Member States implemented gender mainstreaming despite a missing legal obligation can be seen as an example of coercive isomorphism as explained by DiMaggio and Powell (1991b: 67). The coercive isomorphism in the Member States results from informal pressures exerted from the Commission, upon which they are dependent, and also by cultural expectations in various Member States – a success of the velvet triangle of various women's movements, femocrats and academics (Woodward 2001b, see chapter 5).

Furthermore, the Charter on Fundamental Rights of the European Union states that

Equality between men and women must be ensured in all areas, including employment, work and pay. The principle of equality shall not prevent the maintenance or adoption of measures providing for specific advantages in favour of the under-represented sex (Charter of Fundamental Rights, Article 23: Equality between men and women).

Even though the Charter is not yet incorporated into the Treaties establishing the European Union, and is thus non-binding, it further strengthens the institutional basis for gender mainstreaming[29]. In addition, if any action or measure by a European institution counteracts the spirit of the Charter, the European Parliament has the obligation to communicate this to the Council of Ministers.

---

27 Sweden has specific laws on gender mainstreaming which have been in force since 1994, i.e., long before the Treaty of Amsterdam.

28 A different situation exists, however, for the ten accession countries which joined the European Union in 2004. During the accession negotiations, the implementation of gender mainstreaming formed part of the negotiations. The candidate countries are expected to join the *aquis communautaire* of the European Union as defined in the Treaties as primary law.

29 The Charter was proclaimed at the European Council in Nice on 7 December 2000, by the presidents of the Council, the European Parliament and the Commission. At the insistence of the UK government, the Charter was not incorporated into the Treaty (Mazey 2001: 36). The draft treaty of the European Convention states that the Charter becomes an integral part of the Treaties (European Convention 2003: 10).

2.6 Operationalisation of Gender Mainstreaming in the European Commission from an organisational Approach

In order to examine the operationalisation of gender mainstreaming within the European Commission, I developed a model based on the definitions and interpretations of gender mainstreaming of Commission documents. There are two different kinds of criteria to measure organisations: internal and external yardsticks, by which an assessment of the implementation of a concept within organisations is made. Other, more radical interpretations and constructions of gender mainstreaming (as, for example, Bretherton 2001) are not taken into account in this model, since it does not make sense to examine the implementation of a concept which the European Commission does not aim to achieve.

Every demand for structural change within organisations requires that actors rethink their routines and possibly modify them. As with any other form of organisational change, gender mainstreaming meets barriers and resistances within conventional structures and their actors. One of the fundamental questions is whether politics, in this case the gender main-streaming target, must be modified to fit into the existing structures or whether the structures are re-negotiated in order to implement the policy, i.e., gender mainstreaming. Which of the alternatives takes place is mainly a question of power (Meuser 1989: 118).

My thesis is that the more powerful the position of one of the two groups of actors, i.e., either the gender mainstreaming coordination unit, or the indi-vidual organisational units which implement gender mainstreaming, and the greater the power available to it to define its own position as legally given, the more this particular group will be able to influence the negotiating process in a particular way. Officials responsible for gender mainstreaming who are in a legally strong position may be confronted with an avoidance power of the implementing group in the lower ranks. For an examination of the implementation of gender mainstreaming within the European Commission, it is thus important to take into account the hierarchical position of the interviewed actors.

In order to implement the target, which is to mobilise all general policies and measures for the purpose of achieving equality, it is necessary to include all units in the implementation to oversee the implementation of gender mainstreaming: a central authority could not have the necessary expertise in all the areas the Commission is dealing with.

2.6.1 Phases of Gender Mainstreaming

For the successful implementation of gender mainstreaming, the process by which it is carried out is very important. In the following part, I have built up a model based on a figure developed by the Equal Opportunities Commission (1997) to show the 'process character' of gender mainstreaming. The key elements of gender mainstreaming will be shown in the different work flows in figure 1 and will be explained further in the text which follows. The description of the different phases of gender mainstreaming serves mainly for the analytical distinction of different gender mainstreaming components like gender analysis, gender impact assessment, gender training, gender segregated statistics and monitoring and evaluation, which form part of the phases and which will be described below.

Figure 1: Key Elements of Gender Mainstreaming

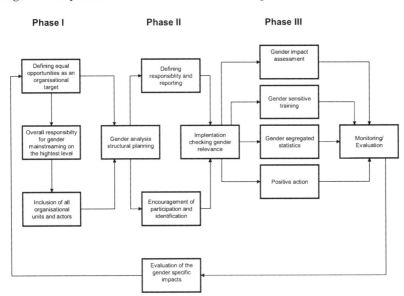

Source: Further development of Equal Opportunities Commission (1997) and Schmidt (2000)

53

2.6.1.1 Phase I: Creation of Important Preconditions for the Implementation of Gender Mainstreaming

Definition of Equal Opportunities as an Organisational Aim

The single most important condition for the introduction of gender mainstreaming in organisations consists in defining equal opportunities as an organisational goal. While, in the approaches so far, the responsibility for equal opportunities has been laid on the equal opportunities officers, gender mainstreaming puts the onus of the work on the whole organisation, i.e. all organisational units need to analyse the impact of their work specialisation on both genders.

Responsibility of Gender Mainstreaming at the highest Level

Gender mainstreaming is a concept which is often implemented in a top-down fashion, i.e., from the higher hierarchical levels into the organisation as a whole. However, gender mainstreaming is not a top-down concept qua definition, as is often falsely stated (see for example Belwe 2002: 2). Neither the cited definitions of the UN Platform for Action of the Beijing Women's Conference (1995), nor the definition of the European Commission states that gender mainstreaming is necessarily a top-down approach. Indeed, Beveridge et al. develop a 'participatory-democratic model' of gender mainstreaming (Beveridge et al. 2000: 390), that is, they want to encourage affected groups to participate in drafting mainstreaming policies. The development of participatory elements of gender mainstreaming is in line with normative demands of women's movements that affected groups ought to participate in the formulation of policies that affect them.

However, the *de facto* implementation of gender mainstreaming within the Commission clearly exhibits a top-down approach. This is most obvious in the symbolic foundation of the Commission Group on Gender Mainstreaming, which will be elaborated in chapter 7. Research on the implementation of policies shows that that top-down processes can only be implemented in a meaningful manner if many organisational actors participate in the design and implementation of the concepts, as opposed to new concepts being merely ordered from the top (Meuser 1989). The implementation of the top-down principle assumes a clear hierarchical implementation structure, which in reality, exists rather seldom. With the implementation of gender mainstreaming, different factors like power relationships, conflicting interests and norms must be included – factors which determine the relationship of the policy formulation and policy implementation levels (Meuser 1989: 17). This point is, therefore, closely tied to the next, namely, the inclusion of as many actors as possible into the gender mainstreaming process.

Inclusion of all Actors for more Gender Equality

One consequence of gender mainstreaming is that women are no longer solely responsible for equal opportunities. The Commission specifies in the cited definition of gender mainstreaming that 'equal opportunities can only be achieved by women and men' (European Commission 1996). Gender mainstreaming demands an analysis and a redesign of women's and men's roles and their interactions. The inclusion of family structures within the gender mainstreaming target is an important novelty for the European Commission towards the realisation of equal opportunities. Before the adoption of the Gender Mainstreaming Communication (European Commission 1996), the EU did not define the situation of women outside the labour markets as a policy area for the EU. This is reflected in the orientation of the Treaties of Rome on the Common Market (which were signed in 1957 and became effective in 1958), which concentrated on the labour market and freedom of movement. The Court of Justice of the European Communities stuck closely to this point of view and kept out of any questions of the domestic sphere. Ostner and Lewis concluded that in the perception of the Court the domestic division of labour between the genders was a free choice and should be left to the individuals concerned or to national legislation. They were not touched by the supranational legislation of the European Union (Ostner/ Lewis 1998: 214).

2.6.1.2 Phase II Gender Analysis/ Structural Planning

The Commission suggests its employees ask two questions in order to establish gender relevance and to enable gender analysis and structural planning:

– Does the proposal concern one or more target groups? Will it affect the daily life of part(s) of the population?
– Are there differences between women and men in this policy field (with regard to rights, resources, participation, values and norms related to gender) (European Commission 1997a: 4)?

These questions are fundamentally important for any gender balance. However, it is unclear to what extent they are actually taken into account by the employees.

Defining Responsibilities and Reporting

In the second phase of gender mainstreaming it is particularly important to implement the different aims and structures of gender mainstreaming in the individual organisational units. The responsibility for gender mainstreaming must be defined in all areas and every organisational unit should create a coordinator for gender mainstreaming. This is important in order to be able to solve area specific questions about gender mainstreaming, occurring within different areas. The co-ordinators are, at the same time, responsible for the reporting of gender mainstreaming, which is important for its later evaluation.

Within the Commission, the Group of Commissioners develops broad policy guidelines on gender mainstreaming. The Gender Equality Unit and the Inter-service Group co-ordinate gender mainstreaming implementation between the different services. Each DG nominates a gender mainstreaming co-ordinator, who drafts an annual report which then forms part of an annual internal Gender Equality Report published within the Commission by DG Administration and Personnel[30].

Encouragement of Participation and Identification

The responsible persons within each unit must be convinced of the relevance of equal opportunities as an organisational target. Gender mainstreaming can only be implemented in the next phase if the hierarchy can be motivated to aim for gender mainstreaming as an organisational target.

2.6.1.3 Phase III: The Implementation of Gender Mainstreaming

Since the process is very important for the successful implementation of gender mainstreaming, the most important instruments of gender mainstreaming are described in this section of the chapter. An important step in the gender mainstreaming process is to establish whether gender is relevant in a particular area. For example, analysis of the gender specific differences serves as a foundation for a gender impact assessment, which will be elaborated in this section.

Gender Impact Assessment

The previous equal opportunities policies often allow for intervention when there is a concrete problem regarding inequalities between the genders. The equal opportunities officers work out solutions to this concrete problem. Short-term solutions, especially, can be meaningful and effective. Gender mainstreaming however starts with all planning and decision-making processes and also with those which are not necessarily seen traditionally as gender discriminating. All policies should be checked with regard to their gender specific impacts. The Commission defines Gender Impact assessment as follows:

---

30   Refer to the organisation chart of the Commission Services in the annexe.

Gender impact assessment means to compare and assess, according to gender relevant criteria, the current situation and trend with the expected development resulting from the introduction of the proposed policy (European Commission 1997a: 4).

The Commission lists the following criteria for gender impact assessment:

- participation (sex-composition of the target/ population group(s), representation of women and men in decision-making positions
- resources (distribution of crucial resources such as time, space, information and money, political and economic power, education and training, job and professional career, new technologies, health care services, housing, means of transport, leisure)
- norms and values which influence gender roles, division of labour by gender, the attitudes and behaviour of women and men respectively, and inequalities in the value attached to men and women or to masculine and feminine characteristics
- rights pertaining to direct or indirect sex-discrimination, human rights (including freedom from sexual violence and degradation), and access to justice, in the legal, political or socio-economic environment (European Commission 1997a: 5).

According to the Gender Impact Assessment Guide of the European Commission, each employee is supposed to check the following:

How can European policies contribute to the elimination of existing inequalities and promote equality between women and men (in compliance with Articles 2 and 3 of the Treaty of Amsterdam); in participation rates, in the distribution of resources, benefits, tasks and responsibilities in private and public life, in the value and attention accorded to male and female, to masculine and feminine characteristics, behaviour and priorities (European Commission 1997a: 5)?

The second point is particularly interesting. The employees are asked to pro-actively search for ways to implement the targets of the Treaty of Amsterdam. However, it is important to note the status of the Gender Impact Assessment Guide. It is not an official Commission document decided by the College of Commissioners, the highest authority within the Commission, but, rather, was adopted by the Inter-Service Mainstreaming Group on Gender Equality, which carries much less authority within the Commission services.

The Commission exemplifies gender impact assessment with regard to employment desegregation[31]. Employment desegregation policies have traditionally been aimed at widening the occupational choices for women. These efforts need to be complemented by positive action aimed at promoting the participation of men in 'female' professions (which corresponds to

---

31 This example has no direct link to the implementation of gender mainstreaming within the Commission but is still illustrated here for clarification of the concept of gender impact assessment.

participation of the above Commission's criteria for gender impact assessment). The current gendered division of labour restricts the number of potential candidates for a vacancy. The 'glass ceiling'[32] remains a barrier to female access to high-level posts (which corresponds to *norms and values* of the Commission's criteria). With the current demographic trend towards an ageing population, and increased work force participation by women, employment opportunities in the care sector are likely to rise. Incentive (which corresponds to *rights* of the Commission's criteria) to promote male participation in the care sector could help in meeting an increasing demand for labour in this sector. This could offer new job opportunities for unskilled and semi-skilled men, while at the same time promoting a more equal pattern of work distribution between women and men. Positive action in favour of men in relation to childcare, has been initiated in Norway. The idea is that new male role models will impact positively on the gender socialisation of boys and girls. It might also contribute to modifying existing norms and values regarding 'men's' and 'women's' work. The problem of low pay in the alleged 'female professions' (which corresponds to *resources* of the Commission's criteria) is an additional barrier to the recruitment of men to these occupations. A more equal representation of men in these professions would, however, be likely to impact positively on wage levels (European Commission 1997a: 5). As will be shown in chapter 7, the different job grades within the Commission present a clear dominance of women in lower paid secretarial categories and of men in the higher categories and in technical areas.

Gender Training

The aim of gender training is, principally, to teach competencies to actors with regard to gender issues. Gender training aims to promote gender sensitivities. Discussing the social construction of gender and gender differences, it might lead to an improvement in the understanding of women and men in organisations. It is particularly important to teach the top levels of hierarchy that gender mainstreaming can only be implemented in a convincing way if the managers and manageresses themselves have reflected on their personal role behaviour, and if they are outspoken about it. This is due to the fact that employees assess the credibility and competence of management staff mainly in the area of their personal behaviour (Geppert 2001: 29). In the 'Women in Development' programme of the United Nations, gender training has been successfully implemented since the 1980s (Razavi/ Miller 1994: 23). The Commission organised gender training in various DGs, among them DG

---

32   The term 'glass ceiling' refers to the fact that women encounter many hidden barriers to become part of top hierarchies, like for example the 'old boys network' and sexual harassment.

Personnel and Administration and DG Employment and Social Affairs. The gender training was aimed at directors and Heads of Units. The success of these training schemes will be studied in chapter 7.

Gender segregated Statistics

Gender segregated statistics enable us to aggregate detailed information about gender specific differences in both the public and the private spheres. The Commission explained the necessity for gender segregated statistics in the following manner:

...it is necessary and important to base the policy of equality between women and men on a sound statistical analysis of the situation of women and men in the various areas of life and the changes taking place in society (European Commission 1996: 3).

The inclusion of gender segregated data into European statistics is however a long term process.

Positive Action Programmes

The positive action approach of the Commission is defined in the Council Recommendation 'Promotion on positive action for women':

To adopt a positive action policy designed to eliminate existing inequalities affecting women in working life and to promote a better balance between the sexes in employment, comprising appropriate general and specific measures [...] in order
(a) to eliminate or counteract the prejudicial effects on women in employment or seeking employment which arise from existing attitudes, behaviour and structures based on the idea of a traditional division of roles in society between men and women;
(b) to encourage the participation of women in various occupations in those sectors of working life where they are at present under-represented, particularly in the sectors of the future, and at higher levels of responsibility in order to achieve better use of human resources (Council of the European Union 1984).

Positive action is thus aimed at rectifying existing inequalities by specifically supporting women in order to promote a better balance of the sexes in employment. However, the positive action policies consist mostly of reactive intervention, whereas gender mainstreaming, seeking to achieve structural changes at all levels of the organisation, consists of pro-active interventions on top of positive action measures. Positive action programmes can consist of training programmes especially for women, for example in the area of new media or technical vocations where, hitherto, women have been underrepresented. The difference and connection between positive action and gender mainstreaming is summarised in figure 2:

Figure 2: The dual track Approach of the Commission to Gender Mainstreaming

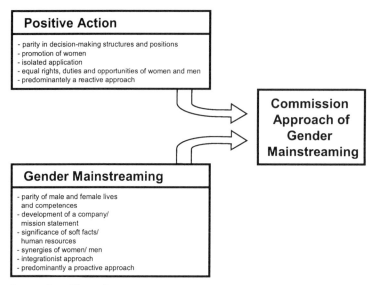

Positive Action

- parity in decision-making structures and positions
- promotion of women
- isolated application
- equal rights, duties and opportunities of women and men
- predominantely a reactive approach

Commission Approach of Gender Mainstreaming

Gender Mainstreaming

- parity of male and female lives
  and competences
- development of a company/
  mission statement
- significance of soft facts/
  human resources
- synergies of women/ men
- integrationist approach
- predominantly a proactive approach

Source: Own illustration

As we can see from figure 2, one of the fundamental differences between gender mainstreaming and positive action is that positive action consists mainly in a reactive approach, while gender mainstreaming is predominately a proactive approach. As has already been emphasised, this difference depends very much on the interpretation and implementation of each concept within the organisations.

The starting point for an equal opportunities policy is a specific disadvantage resulting from gender inequality. A specific policy for that problem is then developed through equality machinery. Equal opportunities policies can act faster than those designed for mainstreaming, but are usually limited to specific policy areas. The starting point for gender mainstreaming is a policy which already exists. The policy process is then reorganised so that the actors normally involved in the policy take a gender perspective into account with the aim that gender equality as a goal is reached. Gender mainstreaming is a fundamental strategy – it may take some time before it is implemented, but it has a potential for a sustainable change[33].

---

33 The differences between the two concepts will be further discussed in the section on critiques of gender mainstreaming later in this chapter.

The most important difference between gender mainstreaming and equal opportunities is that equal opportunities is often post hoc, i.e., equal opportunities measures have only indirect and circumscribed effects. As Rees summarises, 'the essence of mainstreaming is that EO [equal opportunities] thinking is integrated into the policy development process from the beginning' (Rees 1998: 194).

Jewson (1995) developed five models for the articulation of equal opportunities on employment policies and practice:

— *serendipity*, which is an ad hoc approach on equal opportunities
— *dissociation*, which means that formal equal opportunities policies exist but are not systematically implemented
— *accommodation*, i.e., equal opportunities practice is consolidated around a formal policy but lacks strategic thinking and a systematic follow-through
— *integration*, which is a comprehensive pro-active equal opportunities practice which focuses on a detailed and ongoing formal policy
— *assimilation*, i.e., the absorption of equal opportunities policy and its implementation into routines

Jewson et al.'s assimilation concept comes closest to gender mainstreaming and has many similarities to managing diversity. The authors point out in the assimilation model how the emphasis shifts from groups and distributive justice to individuals and their self-realisation, which is a clear depoliticisation and individualisation of equal opportunities policies. Hitherto used equal opportunities and positive action relate to justice based on the concept of women as a group. However, as Rees points out, Jewson et al.'s assimilation model carries the inherent danger that by 'becoming everything they become nothing' (Rees 1998: 195). Meanwhile the 'special' safeguards of EO [equal opportunities], such as equality officers, units and so on, may be dismantled in the name of mainstreaming' (Rees 1998: 195).

Monitoring/Evaluation

Dina Sensi (1997) who has carried out an extensive study on monitoring and gender mainstreaming on the order of the Commission, summarised three different evaluation scenarios which she found in different organisations. The first is a lack of evaluation. The most important opinion of decision-makers in these organisations is, according to her, that 'gender mainstreaming is not in itself considered as being a change which needs to be planned and administered' (Sensi 1997: 10)[34]. The second scenario is that there is a follow-up or a technocratic evaluation. This could mean that a questionnaire

---

34 Translation by the author.

is sent to the other services of the administration. The responses consist more in descriptions of actions than an evaluation. According to Sensi

[…] it [the technocratic evaluation] is a posterior follow-up whose function is essentially to close a balance sheet. The balance in itself has an informative and justifying function' (Sensi 1997: 11)[35]

The third scenario is a proactive follow-up approach and evaluation. There is continuous monitoring from the co-ordinating position.

The function of the follow-up and the evaluation is essentially formative in this scenario, i.e., the results of the evaluation are directly useful to mainstreaming itself (Sensi 1997: 11)[36].

The third scenario promises to be the most effective.

According to Sensi, three phases need to be implemented for effective monitoring:

1. Execution of a monitoring and evaluation plan from the organisational unit, which has the main responsibility for gender mainstreaming.
2. Process observation of gender mainstreaming, i.e., the implementation of the different targets and the schedule of the gender mainstreaming instruments should be continuously monitored.
3. Evaluation of the gender mainstreaming process. The evaluation needs to take place in all organisational units and the results should be interchangeable.

The evaluation ought to be recursively connected with the future gender mainstreaming plan, therefore the whole gender mainstreaming process is illustrated as a circular system[37]. The evaluation system within the Commission will be examined according to the three scenarios and the indicators for effective monitoring developed by Sensi. The circular system of the evaluation processes fits particularly well with the recursive processes that ought to be examined as a result of the theoretical framework of this study.

---

35 Translation by the author.
36 Translation by the author.
37 For a detailed examination of monitoring and evaluation of gender mainstreaming see Sensi (1997).

2.7 Frame Alignment Processes with regard to Gender Mainstreaming

This section will examine whether the construction of gender mainstreaming within the European Commission can be seen as a policy innovation. This is one of the two main research questions of this book. The definition of policy innovation will be based on Mieke Verloo (1999). Verloo, the chair of *the Group of Experts on Mainstreaming of the Council of Europe,* examines the potential of gender mainstreaming as a policy innovation, which she defines as a process of creating new policy frames based on Snow et al. The importance of taking into account the process character of an innovation will be elaborated later on in chapter 4.

Frames, a term coined by Goffman (1974), refer to schemata used by individuals to organise, perceive, and make sense of their experiences in the world. These frames may or may not reflect reality and are constantly evolving as events and existing personal attitudes interact. Snow et al. (1986) distinguish four frame alignment processes. *Frame alignments* are defined after Snow et al. as the 'linkage of individual and SMO [Small Movement Organisation] analytical orientations, such that some set of individual interests, values and beliefs and SMO activities, goals, and ideology are congruent and complementary' (Snow et al. 1986: 464). *Frame alignment processes* simply illustrate that several such frame alignments took place.

Frame bridging means linking existing unconnected frames to a particular issue. Snow et al. define frame bridging as follows:

(...) frame bridging involves the linkage of an SMO [Small Movement Organisation] with what McCarthy (1986) has referred to as unmobilised sentiment pools or public opinion preference clusters (Snow et al. 1986: 467).

Frame amplification clarifies and invigorates a frame that bears on a particular issue, problem or set of events.

Frame extension expands the boundaries of a movement's primary framework to include broader interests. *Frame transformation* refers to the redefinition of activities, events and biographies (Snow et al. 1986: 467-476)

that are already meaningful from the point of view of some primary framework, so that they are now seen by the participants as something completely different (Verloo 1999: 3).

Snow et al. initially identified the four frame alignment processes when examining religious movements, the peace movement and several neighbourhood movements (Snow et al. 1986).

As mentioned above, the frame alignment processes were initially developed with regard to social movement organisations. Nevertheless, the transfer of the concept to an administration would appear to be unproblematic since administrations can also aim to achieve frame alignments. The aim of frame alignments by social movement organisations is to mobilise existing or new activities. Clearly this is not the case with the Commission where the aim would be to increase the legitimacy of the Commission. The analysis of frame alignment processes can thus shed light as to what extent and with what aims organisation might try to construct new frames. Indeed, Rein and Schön have applied the concept of framing to public policy. They argue that policymakers are guided in their work by what the authors call a 'policy frame' which is defined as 'a way of selecting, organising, interpreting and making sense of a complex reality to provide guideposts for knowing, analysing, persuading, and acting' (Rein/ Schön 1993: 146).

The Group of Experts on Mainstreaming of the Council of Europe, which is chaired by Verloo, demonstrated that various instances of frame extension took place in the Council of Europe with regard to gender mainstreaming:

Mainstreaming is linked to other goals that are of central importance to the Council of Europe, such as democracy and human rights. The introduction of gender does not victimise women or blame men. The framing is rather that the problem is gender hierarchy, not women (Council of Europe 1998: 6).

As outlined with regard to the frame extension, the Council of Europe stresses the failure of existing strategies, which prepares the way for the presentation of gender mainstreaming as a new strategy.

In the following passage, the frame alignment processes within the European Commission will be examined mainly with regard to the framing of gender mainstreaming.

Frame bridging is the most general and most basic of the four frame alignment processes. Frame bridging in the European Union first took place when Article 119, which stipulated equal pay for equal work, was included in the Treaty of Rome in 1957. Frame bridging is instantiated here because the new paradigm of equal pay, which was one of the few articles concerned with 'social legislation', was included in the Treaty of Rome.

The consequent drafting of ten Directives, which are primarily concerned with Equal Opportunities between 1975 and 2002, is a further frame bridging in the process of implementing the equal pay paradigm in the European Economic Community (as the European Union was called until the Treaty of Maastricht, which was signed in 1992 and entered into force in 1993). Various authors have linked the drafting of the Directives to the increasingly stronger women's movements in the Member States (Schunter-Kleemann 1992, Hoskyns 1996, Schmidt 2000). The foundation and funding of the European Women's Lobby in 1990 with the strong support of the European Commission constituted another frame bridging since the Commission extended its responsibilities by interpreting equal opportunities to include the so called "private sphere" (refer to chapter 5). This was important since, until this point, the equal opportunities policies of the Commission had been based on a very narrow definition of equal opportunities in the sphere of economic development. Lastly, the publication of the journal 'Women's Information' by the Women's Information Unit within the Commission constituted an important frame bridging since its target groups were femocrats, female academics, and activists from women's movements.

Snow et al. distinguish between two different types of *frame amplification*: value amplification and belief amplification. Value amplification means that values can be construed as modes of conduct or states of existence that are thought to be worthy of protection. Belief amplification refers to the aim of some movements to attain or promote beliefs as ideational elements (Snow et al. 1986: 469-470). In the case of the Commission, only the former form of frame amplification plays a role. Value amplification is important on two different accounts: Firstly, gender mainstreaming is closely linked to values such as equality and secondly, gender mainstreaming is associated with the United Nations. Each point will be examined in turn. Traditionally equal opportunities policies have been closely linked to gender equality. As outlined in the section on the critique on gender mainstreaming, many actors have been critical of gender mainstreaming partly for fear that it might not link up with the ideals of women's movements such as gender equality. However, the 1996 Commission communication specifically links up with values such as gender equality (European Commission 1996). In the introduction of the Communication, the relevance of gender equality is described in the following way:

Equality between men and women is now indisputably recognised as a basic principle of democracy and respect to humankind. (...) The challenge facing the European Union is to build this new partnership between women and men, taking into account the historic and cultural diversity of Member States, and drawing on this to develop a European approach to equality which is both pluralistic and humanistic and which constitutes the basis for action both in the Community and in the rest of the world (European Commission 1996: 1).

Later on in the Communication, the need for gender mainstreaming to face this challenge is explained and thus gender mainstreaming is clearly linked to equality, which in its European dimension is both pluralistic and humanistic.

The Commission also describes in the Communication how important it perceives its own role to be in the negotiations of the UN World Conference of Women in Beijing in 1995 with regard to gender mainstreaming.

The Union's commitment to this objective [a new partnership between women and men] is a logical extension of the active role it played at the recent United Nations conference held in Beijing, in particular its involvement in formulating the final declaration and the action platform.

For this purpose, it is necessary to promote equality between women and men in all activities and policies at all levels. This is the principle of 'mainstreaming', a policy adopted by the Community, and attention was drawn to its crucial importance at the Beijing conference (European Commission 1996: 1).

Frame extension means that an organisation (in the original examination by Snow et al. this referred to a social movement organisation) attempts to enlarge its adherent pool by portraying its activities as 'attending to or being congruent with' the values or interests of potential adherents (Snow et al. 1986: 472). I shall examine the 1996 Commission Communication to show that a lot of frame alignments took place in this Communication. Firstly, by establishing the above- cited 'new partnership between men and women', the Commission includes men in the game. In equal opportunities policies men played only a secondary role and indeed this was one criticism of equal opportunities policies up to that point: they favoured women and disadvantaged men, in other words, they practised unequal treatment. Secondly the Commission extended the primary boundary of equal opportunities to gender mainstreaming to include values such as economic reasons:

Furthermore, European societies would thus provide a forward-looking solution to the demographic and family changes with which they are confronted and which, given the ageing population, transform women's employment into a definite advantage for the economy which should be put to the best possible use with a view to ensuring optimum use of human resources (European Commission 1996: 2).

Women's movements that traditionally advocated women's policies did not primarily argue with economic advantages; thus, the focus on these economic advantages can be seen as an example of frame extension. More actors are tempted to be convinced in favour of gender mainstreaming, i.e., in favour of extending the target group of equal opportunities from those interested in justice to those interested in economic advantages.

Thirdly, the mere usage of the term 'gender' in the general definition of the cited 1996 Commission Communication, rather than simply using 'men and women' links up with the academic discourse and the discourse of women's movements (European Commission 1996: 1). The above-cited definition states that 'their possible effects on the respective situations of men and women (gender perspective)' are actively and openly taken into account at the planning stage (European Commission 1996: 1).

Frame transformation takes place particularly with regard to cultural issues, which are specified in what follows, and defines that all community policies ought to be mainstreamed. Equal opportunities policies and gender mainstreaming are two of the few policies where the Commission comments on changing cultures. Within European politics, it is normally taboo to mention the mere fact of the possibility of cultural change towards a certain aim: European leaders repeatedly stress the importance of cultural diversity within the Union as one of the distinguishing features of Europe, especially vis-à-vis the United States of America (Héritier 1999). Any aimed cultural change would be seen to give up part of this cultural diversity and to become a homogenous mass. The next paragraph emphasises that the historic and cultural diversity of the Member States needs to be preserved. In the follow-ing two passages, the envisaged cultural change is elaborated further:

The promotion of equality must not be confused with the simple objective of balancing the statistics: it is a question of balancing long-lasting changes in parental roles, family structures, institutional practices, the organisation of work and time, etc., and does not merely concern women, their personal development and independence, but also concerns men and the whole of society, in which it can encourage progress and be a token of democracy and pluralism (European Commission 1996: 3).

Another passage explains the necessity of cultural changes further:

Such a change requires not only progress in the field of legislation but also nothing short of a cultural transformation of individual behaviour as much as of attitudes and collective practices, and determined political action based on the broadest possible mobilisation (European Commission 1996: 1).

The earlier as well as the following passage, makes it clear that gender main-streaming encompasses both genders, and all Community programmes.

This does not mean simply making Community programmes or resources more accessible to women, but rather the simultaneous mobilisation of legal instruments, financial resources and the Community's analytical and organisational capacities in order to introduce in all areas the desire to build balanced relationships between women and men (European Commission 1996: 3).

The frame transformation took place firstly because the Commission sees the necessity of a cultural transformation, including the domestic division of labour. Secondly, the Commission established gender mainstreaming as a horizontal strategy that includes all Community programmes.

The contents of the 1996 Communication were transposed into the 'Third Action Programme' of the Commission. Even though the name suggests that this transfer has not taken place for it is called 'Third Action Programme on Equal Opportunities for Women and Men' and does not mention gender mainstreaming in the title, a number of important frame transformations did occur. Like the 1996 Communication of the Commission, the 'Third Action Programme' also links equal opportunities to fundamental values: 'Equal opportunities for women and men is now recognised as a basic principle of democracy and respect for humankind' (European Commission 1997a: 3). The Third Action Programme envisages a 'profound change in mentality' (European Commission 1997a: 1). It also aims to develop a gender-sensitive work culture, which is defined as a 'work culture which takes account of female and male values, of differences in attitudes, in priorities, in working methods, as well as of gender specific needs' (European Commission 1997a: 7). The aim to change the work culture would mean a fundamental organisa-tional change. Unfortunately, the 'Third Action Programme' does not specify how female and male values can be distinguished and what the differences between the attitudes, priorities and working methods are.

The 'Third Action Programme' acknowledged that the gender mainstreaming approach requires an increased effort of sensitisation and awareness raising of staff. In addition, there need to be adjustments in the organisation of work and in the operation of personnel policies to improve its compatibility with family responsibilities. It also requires an equal share of responsibilities, and increased involvement of women in decision making, as well as their professional development throughout their working life. Chapter 7 will examine to what extent the Action Programme was actually put into practice.

Up to the year 2002, the 1996 Commission Communication remains the most detailed account on gender mainstreaming. The principle of gender mainstreaming is cited in various Commission documents and in European legislation passed since 1996 and 1997. In these texts, however, gender mainstreaming is not further developed.

Summarising the frame alignment processes that took place with regard to gender mainstreaming, frame bridging refers to the inclusion of the equal pay paradigm in the Treaty of Rome (European Economic Community 1957) and the subsequent drafting of ten Directives concerning equal treatment and equal opportunities. In addition, the Commission included the private sphere into its concept of equal opportunities, broadening its previous narrow interpretation, which was only concerned with equal opportunities linked to economic developments. Frame amplification refers to the fact that the Commission Communication on gender mainstreaming (European Commission 1996) links up with the academic discourse on gender. Frame extension took place because firstly the Commission defined an equal responsibility for the realisation of equal opportunities and gender mainstreaming for both men and women and secondly that the Commission extends the rationale for equal opportunities to include economic reasons. Finally, frame transformation took place because the Commission envisaged a cultural change by introducing gender mainstreaming (European Commission 1996: 3).

2.8 Critiques of Gender Mainstreaming

There are a variety of critiques of the gender mainstreaming concept of which there appear to be three main, different streams.

- a theoretical critique about gender mainstreaming as reconfirming the duality of genders
- a normative critique that feminists should not strive for the mainstream

- a critique regarding the framing of gender mainstreaming, i.e., that it is either the same as the hitherto-existing equal opportunities or positive action policies, or that the idea for gender mainstreaming has existed since the second wave of women's movements in the 1970s
- a critique on the implementation of gender mainstreaming, that either it is seen as too complicated for practical implementation, that it gets rid of other equal opportunities policies or positive action and that gender mainstreaming is just promoted by various gender experts to create jobs for themselves.

I shall illustrate these critiques and assess them in turn.

2.8.1 Fundamental Critique: Gender Mainstreaming is perceived to reify the Duality of Genders

As was briefly discussed with regard to the term 'gender', there is a criticism that the term gender reifies the duality of genders and this critique is logically extended to gender mainstreaming.

Gudrun-Axeli Knapp discusses guidelines for equal opportunities policies, which can also be discussed with regard to gender mainstreaming. With her article she aims to assess the uses of theoretical approaches to the issue of women's and gender research, for practical purposes. Her ideas will be summarised briefly in what follows. Knapp (1997: 78-82) develops three leading principles or guidelines for equal opportunities policies: Equality, difference and deconstruction. These three headings name three perspectives which are in a recursive process with each other. On its own each heading would lead to a specific and well-known dilemma. These are elaborated below. *Equality* refers to the legal level. It means equal treatment and equal opportunities for men and women in the sense that direct and indirect discrimination of people with regard to their gender is prohibited. Equality as the sole orientation can lead to the dilemma that equal treatment of unequals does not decrease inequality, but rather increases it. Instead, the structural inequalities need to be taken into consideration.

Difference is based on the structural inequality of both genders which exists in all societies. Difference is based on gender relation as a social structural relationship, which determines men and women and makes them different and unequal. *Difference* as a sole orientation of equal opportunities policies is not only associated with the danger of the continuation of gender specific attributions and the reactivation of stereotypes. The orientation on difference and only on difference, reproduces the binary thinking and classification cluster. Even when difference refers to a valorisation of the female, this will not enable a change in the view that the adherence to gender is a highly significant fact, which is one of the premises as to why gender hierarchical structures persist.

Deconstruction refers mostly to the discursive level. It is a corrective and critical potential in order to make male-female categories visible and delegitimate them. The dilemma of deconstruction consists in the fact that since deconstruction radically questions the categorisations into binary thinking, it is also questioning any general account on gender specific situations. Deconstruction is thus insignificant for the implementation of equal opportunities since the main concern of equal opportunities cannot be solved or even addressed within the frames of deconstruction (Knapp 1997: 78-82; Wetterer 2002: 33-4).

Gender mainstreaming is clearly based on the difference paradigm (Rees 1998). Equal opportunities and thus the equality paradigm are seen as a basis and complimentary necessity to gender mainstreaming. However, the deconstructivist account is not discussed with regard to the practical implications for equal opportunities and gender mainstreaming. This is not so surprising given that Knapp herself admits that such accounts are insignificant for the implementation of equal opportunities (Knapp 1997). At the end of the analysis, gender mainstreaming does reify the duality of genders in the way that it makes both genders visible with the aim of overcoming gender differences.

Another central argument criticising gender mainstreaming is that it is often framed within New Public Management (NPM) theories, which aim to implement management theories into public administrations. The basic difference between NPM and public administration approaches is that the NPM approaches often focus on the achievement of targets and benchmarks rather than on compliance with rules. Indeed, like NPM, gender mainstreaming focuses on the achievement of organisational aims, as has been shown in the previous section. This is one of the reasons why the language and expertise of gender mainstreaming officers can be totally different to that of equal opportunities officers and why gender mainstreaming is linked to special training.

This argument is brought forward by Wetterer, who writes that:

Well one can see GM [gender mainstreaming] & MD [managing diversity] virtually as a huge job-creation programme for female gender experts. And what makes the whole thing perfect is that both strategies function in their implementation as a huge further education measure which demonstrates repeatedly to the users of gender competence how important this competence is and for what areas it will be indispensable (Wetterer 2002: 32)[38].

Wetterer herself contextualises this contention that it is quite normal for a new profession to argue for the special importance of a particular field and to argue for the necessity of expertise in this field (Wetterer 2002: 32).

---

38   Translation by the author.

The training of gender expertise is very resource intensive. Some feminist organisations criticise gender training and indeed gender mainstreaming in general because, by using the term gender instead of using the terms women and men, women are again becoming invisible. Deconstructivists, however, argue the opposite way, that by making gender more visible, both genders will become more important and thus it is impossible to overcome the division of gender.

According to Ritti and Gouldner's empirical evidence on the effects of coercive isomorphism (1979) (refer to chapter 3), the employment of equal opportunities, albeit for 'ceremonial' purposes, might still change the organisation. If organisations are willing to pay for gender expertise, the long term benefits of making both genders more visible might result in more equal opportunities for both sexes and this could, indeed, result in the development that allows gender to become less important in the long term.

2.8.2 Normative Critique on the Concept of Gender Mainstreaming

The German philosopher and pedagogue Christina Thürmer-Rohr wonders whether feminism should not be regarded as a school of thought which is per se against the current. According to her, the 'mainstream' is 'desperate not harmless watercourses'[39], i.e., she is warning that feminists ought to be careful of the dangers of becoming part of the mainstream and possibly adapting to the mainstream. Indeed, this leads to the question to what extent gender mainstreaming which was mainly evolved at the UN level can be regarded as an inherently "feminist" concept and if so what this would entail.

2.8.3 Framing of Gender Mainstreaming: Gender Mainstreaming is perceived to be the same as Equal Opportunities

Gender mainstreaming is often criticised as being just the same as equal opportunities and also because the new strategies are presented in a language which sounds more 'modern and much more professional' (Wetterer 2002: 26)[40]. As has been shown before in this chapter, in the dual track approach of the Commission, equal opportunities are part of gender mainstreaming. The difference between equal opportunities/ affirmative action and gender mainstreaming very much depends on context. In Germany for example, the equal opportunities officers in North-Rhine Westphalia have on a local level long had competencies both in all policy development and with regard to the

---

39 Translation by the author. Christina Thürmer-Rohr during a conference of the Heinrich Böll Foundation in Berlin on 3.11.2000. Cited in Pinl (2002: 3).
40 Translation by the author.

budget; this constitutes far more powers than a clear cut division between equal opportunities and gender mainstreaming would suggest. The difference between them remains, however, in that the offices of those equal opportunities officers were often free-standing and without much power, whereas with gender mainstreaming they would be situated at the highest level of the organisation.

Also, as already discussed in an earlier section, Goldmann describes the fundamental change of the Equality officers: they are no longer the sole responsible party for equality, instead, all units become responsible for it, and the gender mainstreaming officials only co-ordinate the other units and become manageresses for the implementation of equal opportunities (Goldmann 1999).

2.8.4 Critique on the Implementation of Gender Mainstreaming

2.8.4.1 Gender Mainstreaming is perceived to get rid of other Equal Opportunities or Positive Action Strategies

In the past, gender mainstreaming was used for getting rid of unwanted structures. The most important example in this context is the attempt by some member of the EP to get rid of the Women's Committee. More specifically, the Budget Committee of the EP tried to close the Committee that was formerly called the 'Committee for the Rights of Women' with the argument that since the introduction of gender mainstreaming the special causes of women were to be dealt with in all committees. After strong protests by Members of the EP and the European Women's Lobby, the Committee for the Rights of Women was confirmed for another legislative period. It was however renamed as the 'Committee for Women's Rights and Equal Opportunities' in order to symbolise the idea that the Committee is concerned about equal opportunities for both sexes (Schmidt 2000: 206). However, the committee was only confirmed for half the legislative period, whereas all other committees were confirmed for the entire period. A Member of the European Parliament, Lissy Gröner describes this conflict as follows:

We realised it right away in the last legislative period in the Committee [Committee for the Rights of Women]. There was a big discussion from the budget people, as to whether there is a need for a Committee for the Rights of Women. Since the principle of mainstreaming is now enshrined in the treaties and since it is being dealt with everywhere, one member of each Committee could be ordered to keep mainstreaming in mind and that's that. And we would save on one Committee and save those expensive meetings. However, we prevailed and the Committee now has the order to implement mainstreaming (Interview with Lissy Gröner 2000).

The Commission itself acknowledged that funding and programmes which were formerly for women had been reallocated (European Commission

72

1998a: 11). In particular, the Commission was criticised from the EWL for having abolished the programme NOW in the name of gender mainstreaming and for the closure of the Women's Information Unit in the former DG X Information, Communication, Culture and Audiovisual (Interview female administrator 23)[41]. As was said before, the Commission has stated since 1998 that gender mainstreaming is to be understood as a dual track approach; gender mainstreaming is also clearly defined in that way in the UN Platform for Action. Thus, the argument that gender mainstreaming replaces positive action measures needs to be seen as a critique of the implementation of gender mainstreaming rather than a critique of the concept itself. Whether this critique is accurate for the implementation of gender mainstreaming in the Commission will be examined in the chapter 7.

2.8.4.2 Gender Mainstreaming is perceived as a 'tick and bash' Procedure

More cynical critiques of gender mainstreaming suggest that it might just become a 'ticking the boxes exercise' (Richardson 1996) or a 'tick and bash procedure that does not command serious attention if there are no sanctions to back it up, or if the *Realpolitik* means it can be safely ignored' (Rees 1998: 192). As with the implementation of any new policy, there is a danger that the rhetoric outweighs the actual impacts the policy has. However, as Oliver argues (1991: 161), even if an organisation is not convinced of equal opportunities and only implements it to be 'socially fit', it might still be implemented effectively if there is pressure within or from the outside of the organisation. As has been shown in the policy model on gender mainstreaming, only parts of gender mainstreaming, i.e., gender statistics, gender impact assessment and gender budgeting, are ad hoc and would allow such a ticking approach. The other components, especially those of phases I and II, involve fundamental changes in the structure of the organisation and thus go far beyond the possibility of just ticking a box.

Chapter 7 will examine to what extent the above categories have been implemented in the European Commission.

2.9   Conclusion

The term 'gender mainstreaming' has caused considerable misunderstandings within the European Union. This is due in part to the fact that the term is an

---

41   With the Commission restructuring in August 1999, the entire DG X was dissolved and the services were integrated into the other DGs, The Women's Information Unit, however, was entirely dissolved.

artificial creation of two terms which only exist in the Swedish and English languages; the other official languages in the EU use the English term. Another reason for the misunderstandings is that the term gender mainstreaming is partly used as a twin track approach: partly, therefore, gender mainstreaming is one of the two elements of exactly this same twin track approach, but this is illogical.

The concept itself is relatively new. It was initially developed by the women's movements in the 1970s and was referred to as 'the importance of gender equality as a transversal task'. The European Commission lobbied for the introduction of gender mainstreaming during the World Conference of Women in Beijing in 1995 where it was formally established in the Platform for Action. The most important commitment for gender mainstreaming from the Commission is in the 1996 Communication on 'Incorporating equal opportunities for women and men into all Community policies and activities' and the 'Third Action Programme on Equal Opportunitites' (European Commission 1997a). This chapter has shown that gender mainstreaming was strategically framed by the European Commission to fashion 'shared understandings of the world' (McAdam et al. 1996) that legitimate the Commission. All four frame alignments which Snow et al. (1986) developed with regard to social movement organisations took place relating to gender mainstreaming, i.e. frame bridging, frame alignment, frame extension and frame transformation. Frame transformation is the most important part since it symbolises a paradigm shift from equal opportunities to gender mainstreaming. Since gender mainstreaming is framed in the European Union within New Public Management theories and within the normative frame of the United Nations, there is a large fit between the dominant frames of the EU and gender mainstreaming. However, the framing led to an alienation of women's movements and of some feminist academics of gender mainstreaming since gender mainstreaming is not framed as being primarily concerned with equality of women and rights, but the framing is partly of economic concerns.

3 Organisational Theories and Gender Mainstreaming

3.1 Introduction

This chapter develops a theoretical framework for analysing gender main-streaming. There is a danger within organisation studies that organisations are defined in a way that leaves no place for people. Organisation studies have many terms and theories to explain the functioning of organisations. This is generally done without taking into account the concrete reality of organisations, in which living individuals, men and women act (Vollmerg et al. 1995: 9). 'New' organisation theories such as neo-institutionalism try to resolve this dilemma by bringing society back into the theory and by studying the links between society, individuals and organisations. Structuration theory as a social theory studies the links between society and individuals from the outset. The combination of neo-institutionalism and structuration theory forms the basis for the empirical research of gender mainstreaming in this book.

I shall especially pursue Meyer and Rowan's (1991 [1977]) concept of decoupling and confidence, which means that organisations attempt to fulfil norms expected from them by the outside world, by decoupling elements of structure from activities. This model will be elaborated more in detail later on and applied to gender mainstreaming, i.e. I argue that gender mainstreaming was implemented in the Commission due to the norms bestowed upon it by the United Nations and the European Women's movements and that their actual activities on gender mainstreaming are decoupled from the structure. For examining the decoupling process further, it is important to adopt an exterior and interior view on the European Commission in order to examine its structure, activities and outside pressures.

Neo-institutionalism permits an exterior view on organisations by taking into account the connection between the organisation and society. Structuration theory can be used as an interior view since it studies processes within the organisation. Based on DiMaggio's (1998) differentiation of previous neo-institutionalist accounts, I study institutionalisation as a process which allows to bring agency and interest back into the research. This allows to reflect the power structures within the Commission and among actors who mobilise around gender mainstreaming. Neo-institutionalism allows us to examine how institutions develop as a result of isomorphic processes. Neo-institutionalism moves away from the previously dominating view that organisations take rational decisions despite being bounded by limited information and resources. Rather, neo-institutionalism argues that organisations take the decisions they take, because they believe them to be regarded as rational and that the main aim of the organisation is to increase social legitimacy by these decisions. Rationality, in the view of neo-institutionalists, is socially constructed.

Structuration theory facilitates one's examination of the recursive processes between structure and action. Giddens' (1984) concept of rules and resources will be used to examine the modification of actions and structures, which are necessary for the implementation of innovations. Structuration theory enables to examine the emergence of particular organisational structures and to examine internal power dynamics within organisations further.

The most important foundational theories for neo-institutionalism and structuration theory will briefly be summarised. The notion of 'rationality and 'rationalisation' are utmost important for neo-institutionalism. The foundations of these two terms in Weber's concept of *rationalisation* in a bureaucracy (Weber 1976 [1921]) and *bounded rationality* by Simon (1957) will thus be elaborated in greater detail. Cohen et al.'s concept of the *garbage can model* further questions rationality in organisations and illustrates organisations as 'organised anarchies' (Cohen et al. 1972). The garbage can model is also an important basis for structuration theory and micro politics since the garbage can model is the first systematic account in which actors are illustrated to attempt to define problems from their point of view and use existing solutions (Neuberger 1995: 190), which is an important basis for structuration theory.

Neo-institutionalism and structuration theory will be analysed in more detail in the second part of the chapter. As numerous comprehensive accounts have been written on the differences between various organisation theories (e.g. Hatch 1997; Kieser 2001; Hasse and Krücken 1999), only the most important foundations for the theories used and further developed in this book will be analysed.

3.2   Foundational Organisational Theories

3.2.1 Weber's Analysis of Rationalisation and Bureaucracy

The German academic lawyer Max Weber (1864-1920) has become a reference point for sociological theory up to the present day and his theory forms an important basis for neo-institutionalism. In what follows I shall provide a short introduction to Weber and will refer to his theories throughout the text, in particular with reference to neo-institutionalism.

Weber applied the term 'rationalisation' to Western industrialised countries in order to capture a process of 'disenchantment of the world'[42], in which action was increasingly reduced to the routine administration of a world dominated by large-scale organisations and the specialised division of labour, which found their ultimate expression in bureaucracy[43]. Weber saw this process as uniquely European in origin. In a comparative analysis of European and Oriental religions and social structures he showed how Western religion alone was able to break the power of magic and was thus able to exercise a decisive influence on the rationalisation of economic and social life, independent of economic interests. Weber's protestant ethic thesis (Weber 1976 [1934]) consists in an analysis of how Western capitalist society and its origins can be used to explain that the decentralised Western political culture and the legacy of Roman law created the conditions for the development of individual rights and rational administration which capitalism needed and further fostered as it grew (Weber 1976 [1934]: 358-374).

Weber locates the analysis of bureaucracy within a theory of power, domination and legitimacy. In Weber's theory, modern rational bureaucracy is most closely approximated by 'legal authority' which is dominated by the principle of 'sine ira ac studio'. In Weber's words:

However, the second element mentioned, calculated rules, is the most important one for modern bureaucracy. The peculiarity of modern culture, and specially of its technical and economic basis, demands this very "calculability" of results. When fully developed, bureaucracy also stands in a specific sense, under the principle of 'sine ira ac studio.' Bureaucracy develops more perfectly, the more it is 'dehumanised', the more completely it succeeds in eliminating from official business love, hatred and all purely personal, irrational and emotional elements which escape calculation (Weber 1979 [1921]: 975)[44].

---

42 The German original is 'Entzauberung der Welt' (Weber 1994 [1919]: 612). Disenchantment with the world refers to the fact that in the 16th and 17th century some people felt squeezed by rationalism. Schiller referred to this as 'stripping Nature of God' (die Entgötterung der Natur). In German language, Weber's reference to Entzauberung der Welt is a word game to Schiller's Entgötterung der Natur.

43 Weber's bureaucracy model has been much criticised. Some scholars are sceptical that the specialised, partly implicit expert knowledge of inferiors, the horizontal cooperation, open communication and the necessity for independent action actually lead to universal realisation and the efficiency of bureaucratic structures. E.g. Markus Reihlen argues that the term 'heterarchy' ought to be used instead of bureaucracy for modern day bureaucracies (Reihlen 1998). In heterarchy, political authority is neither centralised (as under conditions of hierarchy)

44 The German original is: 'Aber auch für die moderne Bürokratie hat das zweite Element, die "berechenbaren Regeln", die eigentlich beherrschende Bedeutung. Die Eigenart der modernen Kultur, speziell ihres technisch-ökonomischen Unterbaus aber, verlangt gerade diese "Berechenbarkeit" des Erfolges. Die Bürokratie in ihrer Vollentwicklung steht in einem speziellen Sinn auch unter dem Prinzip des "sine ira ac studio". Ihre spezifische, dem Kapitalismus willkommene Eigenschaft entwickelt sie umso vollkommener, je mehr sie sich ‚entmenschlicht', je vollkommener, heißt das hier, ihr die spezifische Eigenschaft, welche ihr als Tugend nachgerühmt wird: die Ausschaltung von Liebe, Haß und aller rein

According to Weber (1976 [1921]), a bureaucracy needs as a framework: the development of a money economy, legal codification, the free market and the expansion of the administration (Weber 1976 [1921]). Weber's ideal type of bureaucracy involves

- domination based upon written rules in a hierarchy of specialised offices and positions
- recruitment based on qualification
- offices that are impersonal and distinguished from incumbents. They also need to be segregated from private life and private property (Weber 1976 [1934]: 358-374).

Office holding is thus a 'vocation' based on expert training, offering an office, a salary with pension and tenure and a career structure where promotion is by seniority and/ or ability. Bureaucracy, in its ideal form, is seen as more efficient compared to all previous types of bureaucracy due to its speed, predictability, precision and dispassionate treatment of 'cases' without taking account of personal considerations (Weber 1979 [1921]: 221-2). The spread of bureaucracy illustrates the process of rationalisation in the modern world, with contradictory consequences. On the one hand, bureaucracy is 'formally rational' and 'efficient' like a machine, while on the other hand it threatens human freedom, and thus might become dehumanising. In this latter sense, the ultimate foundation of bureaucracy is irrational (Jary and Jary 1995: 55).

Weber's approach offers fundamental insights for sociological theory until the present day. However, his theory has been further developed to take into account contingencies of individual actors. Part of these contingencies can be explained with the concept of bounded rationality and the resulting garbage can model of organisational choice which will be illustrated in the following.

3.2.2 Individual Decision-Making: The Development of the Concept of Bounded Rationality and the Garbage Can Model of Organisational Choice

The concept of bounded rationality originated with the works of Herbert A. Simon (1957) and James G. March and Herbert A. Simon (1958), based on Chester I. Barnard (1938) on decision-making in organisations. Barnard, March, Simon and Cohen (see next section on Cohen) do not regard the functions of organisations as primarily consisting in the establishment of

---

persönlichen, überhaupt aller irrationalen, dem Kalkül sich entziehenden Empfindungselemente aus der Erledigung der Amtsgeschäfte, gelingt.' (Weber 1976 [1921]: 563).

order in a top-down fashion. Rather, they focus on the individual logic of actors in the organisational everyday routines their concept is based on bounded rationality.

Barnard (1886-1961) was not an academic but rather a professional manager, namely, President of the New Jersey telecommunications company Bell Telephone and the Rockefeller Foundation. In his book 'The Function of the Executive' he argues that organisations do not consist of human beings but rather of actions. Co-operative systems (i.e. organisations) are systems of consciously coordinated acts, whereby even if some organisational members come and go, the structured nature of the organisation allows it to continue to function in a reliable manner (Barnard 1938). When the organisation works independently of particular human beings, there could be problems if the agents cease to be motivated enough to work for the organisation. Barnard thus developed a system of inducement-contribution balance: The organisation makes inducements to potential members that should make membership of an organisation attractive and in return contributions will be made to the organisation. This is particularly important because the contract of labour only establishes general membership. Just how much work is actually done depends on how much the organisation is able to attract its members' 'contributions' through 'inducements.' It is important to note that Barnard did not limit the concept of inducements to material ones but rather stressed the non-material inducements which might now be called organisational culture aspects[45].

Simon (1916-2001) was educated as a political scientist but his work was based interdisciplinary in the field of Psychology, Philosophy and Economics. Simon develops Barnard's concepts further by reformulating a general problem of decision-making[46]. Whereas Barnard concentrates on the motivational aspects of acting in organisations, Simon also integrates cognitive aspects (Simon 1957). Simon's early work (Simon 1976 [1945]: 88-90) was important in that he claimed that habit must not be seen as a purely passive element in behaviour, but rather as a means by which attention is focused on some selected aspects of a situation to the exclusion of competing arguments which might influence choice into another direction (see also DiMaggio/ Powell 1991a: 19). Later in life, Simon published extensively with March (born in 1928). March and Simon perceive the ideas of *bounded rationality* and *satisficing*[47] as fundamental characteristics of a reformulation of a rational decision-making theory (March/ Simon 1958: 139-140).

---

45 For a detailed analysis of the culture approach compare Schein 1992; Berger 1993; Franzpötter 1997; Hofstede 1998.

46 In 1978, Simon received the Alfred Nobel Memorial Prize in Economic Sciences for his work on decision-making in organisations.

47 'The term "satisficing" is a new word creation by March and Simon (1958) and is a combination of the terms "satisfying" and "optimising".'

The theory of bounded rationality is behavioural because the decision-making processes are seen not as decision-making logic but rather as being a feature of human behaviour, in making decisions, whose empirical characteristics and reasons are to be examined. Simon put this as follows: 'decision-making processes hold the key to the understanding of organisational phenomena' (Simon 1976 [1945]: xi). Bounded rationality implies that decisions always correspond with the view of the decision-maker. The decision-maker perceives the situation from his or her organisational position and is not able to take into account all the important information due to incomplete knowledge, the difficulty in reliably predicting future events and the limited set of alternatives for action. In March and Simon's words:

What kinds of choice and other problem-solving activities are needed to discover an adequate range of alternatives and consequences for choice depends on the criterion applied to the choice. In particular, finding the optimal alternative is a radically different problem from finding a satisfactory alternative (March/ Simon 1958: 140).

The authors define an *optimal* solution as one in which there exists a set of criteria which permits the alternatives to be compared and claim that, by means of these criteria an alternative is preferred. A *satisfactory* solution exists if there is a set of criteria that describes minimally satisfactory alternatives and that the alternative in question meets all these criteria. According to March and Simon:

Most human decision-making, whether individual or organisational, is concerned with the discovery and selection of satisfactory alternatives; only in exceptional cases is it concerned with the discovery and selection of optimal alternatives (March/ Simon 1958: 140-1).

As a result, the actor will be satisfied with a sub-optimal solution to a given problem. For example March and Simon provide the example that when the exercise consists in searching for the sharpest needle in a haystack and it is known to the actor that the needles have different qualities, s/he might still opt for the first which is sharp enough to sew something rather than look for the sharpest. Simon and March describe this as follows:

Optimizing is replaced by satisficing- the requirement that satisfactory levels of the criterion variables be attained (March/ Simon 1958: 169).

The Garbage Can Model of Organisational Choice

Cohen, March and Olsen took another important step towards deconstructing the back-then-prevalent common rational models within organisation theory by developing the *garbage can model* of organisational choice, also referred to as *organised anarchy* (Cohen et al. 1972: 1). The garbage can model was developed with regard to *ambiguous behaviours*, i.e. explanations and interpretations of behaviours which might appear to contradict classical theory. It was greatly influenced by the realisation that extreme cases of aggregate uncertainty in decision-making environments would trigger behavioural responses which, at least from a distance, might appear *irrational* or not in compliance at any rate with the total rationality of the homo economicus. The garbage can model was originally formulated in the context of the operation of universities, a familiar form of organised anarchy.

It attempted to expand organisational decision theory into the field of organisational anarchy, which is characterised by *problematic preferences, unclear technology* and *fluid participation* (Cohen et al. 1972: 1-2). Problematic preferences mean that the organisation operates on the basis of a variety of inconsistent and ill-defined preferences. Unclear technology means that important processes of the organisation are not understood by its members. It survives because the members run it on the basis of trial-and-error procedures. Fluid participation is defined by Cohen et al. to mean that participants vary in the amount of time and effort they devote to different areas, thus commitment varies from one to another. Cohen et al. describe their model for organised anarchies as follows:

Decision opportunities are fundamentally ambiguous stimuli. (...) Although organisations can often be viewed conveniently as vehicles for solving well-defined problems or structures within which conflict is resolved through bargaining, they also provide sets of procedures through which participants arrive at an interpretation of what they are doing and what they have done in the process of doing it. From this point of view, an organisation is a collection of choices looking for problems, issues and feelings looking for decision situations in which they might be aired, solutions looking for issues to which they might be the answer, and decision makers looking for work. (...) To understand processes within organisation, one can view a choice opportunity as a garbage can into which various kinds of problems and solutions are dumped by participants as they are generated. The mix of garbage in a single can depends on the mix of cans available, on the labels attached to the alternative cans, and on the speed with which garbage is collected and removed from the scene (Cohen et al. 1972: 2).

The name given to the model might explain part of the initial attraction of scholars, it could, however, also be the cause of misunderstandings, due to the connotations of rubbish associated with the term 'garbage can'. It originates in the concept of a productive mixture of items within a container and not from the idea that such mixtures, and their outcomes, are rubbish.

The theoretical breakthrough of the garbage can model is that, contrary to traditional decision theory, it disconnects problems, solutions and decision-makers from each other. Specific decisions do not follow an orderly process from problem to solution, but are rather the outcome of several relatively independent streams of events within the organisation.

The interrelation and particularly the contingent relationship of four of those streams was identified in Cohen, March and Olsen's original conceptualisation:

- *Problems* are the result of performance gaps or the inability to predict the future. Thus, problems may originate inside or outside the organisation and require attention.
- *Solutions* are answers that are more or less actively looking for a question. In organisational problem solving it is often only possible to know the question when you have the answer.
- *Participants* are fluid, they come and go. Participation may vary depending on the other time demands of participants.
- *Choice opportunities* 'are occasions when organisations are expected to produce behaviour that can be called a decision' (Cohen et al. 1972: 3).

It is important to note that the behavioural approach cannot be seen as a comprehensive theory, but rather as a critique of classical rational-bureaucratic organisational approaches. The behavioural approaches were able to put into perspective the unrealistic assumptions of the rationality model by introducing the terms of bounded and local rationality, 'satisficing' instead of optimal goal attainment, problem orientation and process emphasis when a solution is searched for, interpersonal negotiation and agreement and the significance of organisational learning.

The garbage can model can be seen as an important predecessor for micropolitics and structuration theory: Actors define situations or problems according to their own interpretations in order to apply existing solutions in which they are interested, to have access to decision opportunities and to 'keep things going' without being concerned with overall goals (Neuberger 1995: 190). Indeed, actors might not be able to be concerned with the overall goals of the organisation due to bounded rationality.

Applying the garbage can model to the implementation of gender mainstreaming in the Commission, this would mean that the actors would interpret gender mainstreaming with regard to their own interests and possibly pick individual items from gender mainstreaming which might be particularly important for them.

3.3   Neo-Institutionalism

3.3.1 Institutionalism as the Foundation for Neo-Institutionalism

This section aims to provide a short overview of institutionalism as the pretext for neo-institutionalism. As neo-institutionalism has a distinctly sociological flavour (DiMaggio/ Powell 1991a: 11) and the sociological approach is the most important one in the course of the further study, only the sociological strand of institutionalism will be illustrated[48].

Institutionalism comprises all those approaches which examine institutions and assume that they are important in attaining understanding of social agency and processes within society. When sociologists assume that individual behaviour is not determined by social norms and routines only in exceptional situations, it is possible to contend that sociology is mainly concerned with the analysis of the development, function and mode of action of institutions (Jepperson 1991: 159). Institutions are defined at this point in a very general way as an organised, established, procedure (Jepperson 1991: 143). Furthermore, the term will be based on Jepperson's contention that institutions need to be self-reproducing, i.e. their persistence is not dependent on recurrent collective mobilisation (Jepperson 1991: 145). The term institution will be further differentiated later on in this chapter.

Social institutions, despite being a product of human interaction, are experienced by individuals as objective. Although subjectively formed, they become 'crystallised'. They are, in Durkheim's terms, 'social facts', i.e. phenomena perceived by the individual as being both 'external' (to the particular person) and 'coercive', i.e. backed by sanctions (Durkheim 1995 [1910]: 103-140).

The definition as to what constitutes institutions differs widely between scholars: Weber (1976 [1921]) was convinced that economic success depends on the institutional context. Although he did not explicitly use the concept of 'institution', his work is permeated with a concern for understanding the ways in which cultural rules (ranging form mores to legally defined constitutions) define social structures and govern social behaviour, including economic structures and behaviour. Scott sees the following connection between Weber and institutionalism:

For example, his justly famous typology of administrative systems – traditional, charismatic, and rational-legal – represents three types of authority systems differing primarily in the types of belief or cultural systems that legitimate the exercise of authority (Scott 1995: 11).

Weber's description of the historic emergence of bureaucracies as a result of centralised states of economic markets (Weber 1946 [1919]) had a lasting effect on sociology and lead to the assumption that rational formal structure is the most effective way to coordinate and control the complex relational networks involved in modern technical or work activities. The foundation of centralised states and the penetration of societies by political centres also contributed to the rise and spread of formal organisation (Meyer/ Rowan 1991 [1977]: 43).

---

48   For a broader overview, see Scott (1995). Scott categorised the different early forms of Institutionalism into economics, political science and sociology.

Berger and Luckmann (1966), whose work is an important basis for neo-institutionalist accounts, provide a more general account when they suggest that 'total institutionalisation is, archetypically, liturgy – the total absence of "action". All "problems" are common; all "solutions" socially constructed and reified; all expectations common and publicly hegemonic' (Berger/ Luckmann 1966: 80)

DiMaggio and Powell (1991a) and Hasse and Krücken (1999) differentiate between old and neo-institutionalism. The most important differences between old institutionalism and neo-institutionalism consist firstly in the locus of institutionalisation: old institutionalism examines an organisation as a whole, while neo-institutionalism examines a field or society (DiMaggio/ Powell 1991a: 13). Secondly, the key forms of cognition are values, norms and attitudes within old institutionalism, while in neo-institutionalism they consist in classifications, routines, scripts and schema (DiMaggio/ Powell 1991a: 13). One of the most important author of old institutionalism is Selznick (1949)[49], based on Weber. Some of the most important authors of neo-institutionalism are Meyer and Rowan (1991 [1977]); Zucker (1988, 1991), DiMaggio and Powell (1991b [1983]); Jepperson (1991); Oliver (1991) and Meyer and Scott (1992 [1983]).

The locus of institutionalisation in this book consists in the institutionalisation of gender mainstreaming especially in two particular Directorates General, i.e. parts of the European Commission as the entire organisation. Neo-institutionalism enables to study particular parts of the organisation and particularly the embeddedness of the organisation in society which is also an important aspect of this book. Furthermore, the key forms of cognition in this book consist mainly in routines and schema which is a further reason to focus on neo-institutionalism rather than institutionalisation.

In the next section, we examine neo-institutionalism and the definition of the terms 'institution' and 'institutionalisation' further.

3.3.2 Theoretical Strands within Neo-Institutionalism

The most important foundational texts and differentiations and specifications for sociological neo-institutionalism will be presented below, as organised by different authors. There is no 'coherent' school of neo-institutionalist thought as such (Kieser 2001: 347) and therefore it is important to study the corner-stones of this theory one by one. Since there are different kinds of

---

49 Selznick, whom neo-institutionalists and critics of neo-institutionalists describe in unity as one of the most important representative of old institutionalism sees sociological neo-institutionalism as a further development of his own research (Selznick 1996) and thus rejects the novelty of sociological neo-institutionalism as a new school or paradigm. However, both neo-institutionalists and their critics see a break in tradition between old and neo-institutionalism (compare Hasse/Krücken 1999: 67, footnote 48).

neo-institutionalisms, and the groupings employed by the above authors vary greatly as to what neo-institutionalism means, the overview of different neo-institutionalist theories here is intended to show how I distinguish between the different neo-institutionalist schools in the course of this book[50].

Hall and Taylor (1996) have made one of the most wide-ranging analyses of different neo-institutionalisms. These authors distinguish three different forms of neo-institutionalisms: 'historical institutionalism', 'rational choice institutionalism' and 'sociological institutionalism' (Hall/ Taylor 1996: 936-8). All three institutionalisms were developed as a reaction to the behavioural perspectives prevalent in the 1960s and 1970s and try to elucidate the institutions' role in the determination of social and political outcomes. All three forms of institutionalisms share the idea that institutions have effects on outcomes, but differ in the suggested ways in which institutions have an impact. However, there is also considerable overlap between the approaches.

According to Hall and Taylor (1996) *historical institutionalism* has two basic assumptions. First of all there is a notion of group theories of politics, i.e. that conflict among rival groups for scarce resources lies at the heart of politics. Secondly, structural functionalists argue that polity is seen as an overall system of interacting parts. The most important research interest of historical institutionalism consists in the question of how institutions affect the behaviour of individuals. Within the calculus approach, human behaviour is seen as instrumental and based on strategic calculations. Within the cultural approach, behaviour is bounded by an individual's world-view.

Rational choice institutionalism is defined by Hall and Taylor (1996) as a micro analytical approach derived from Neo-classical economic analysis, which focuses on the collective outcomes of individual choice. Rational choice institutionalism is criticised for cultural bias: how does one define 'rational' across time and space?

The *sociological neo-institutionalism* was developed by Meyer and Rowan (1991 [1977]), Zucker (1988 [1977]) and by DiMaggio and Powell (1991a, 1991b [1983]). According to Hall and Taylor (1996), one of the fundamental research questions within neo-institutionalism is the connection between organisations and society: thus it refers strongly to Weber. The importance of Weber for DiMaggio and Powell can be seen in the inclusion of the famous 'iron cage'[51] metaphor from Weber in the title of their essay 'The Iron Cage Revisited: Institutional Isomorphism and Collective Rationality in Organisational Fields' (DiMaggio/ Powell 1991b [1983]), (Hasse/ Krücken 1999: 67, footnote 48). The 'iron cage' carries an 'implicit portrayal of humans as powerless and inert in the face of inexorable social processes' (DiMaggio/ Powell 1991b [1983]), which raises questions about

---

50 For a comprehensive overview of the different neo-institutionalist theories refer to DiMaggio and Powell 1991a; Mayntz and Scharpf 1995; Scott 1995.
51 The German original is *'stahlhartes Gehäuse'*.

the possibility of change, as DiMaggio self-critically notes (DiMaggio 1988: 18, footnote 50). Weber saw the legitimacy in organisations and bureaucratic domination

[...] as the means of transforming social action into rationally organised action. Therefore, as an instrument of rationally organising authority relations, bureaucracy was and is a power instrument of the first order for one who controls the bureaucratic apparatus: Under otherwise equal conditions, rationally organised and directed action (Gesellschaftshandeln) is superior to the very kinds of collective behaviour (Massenhandeln) and also social action (Gemeinschaftshandeln) opposing it. Where administration has been completely bureaucratised the resulting system of domination is practically indestructible (Weber 1979 [1921]: 987).[52]

Hall and Taylor's classification on different kinds of neo-institionalisms is summarised in table 3 (Hall/ Taylor 1996)[53].

DiMaggio and Powell (1991a) differentiate between the 'new institutional economics', 'the positive theory of institutions' and 'neo-institutionalism in the sociological tradition'. The empirical part of this book will be based partly on neo-institutionalism in the sociological tradition as defined by DiMaggio and Powell (1991a) (which was briefly illustrated in Hall and Taylor's classification and which will be further elaborated) since this enables us to study the links between the European Commission and its embeddedness in society. Hall and Taylor's description (1996) of one of the main weaknesses of sociological neo-institutionalism, i.e. that power struggles within organisations can be underestimated, will be taken account of in this book by combining sociological neo-institutionalism with structuration theory in the second part of this chapter.

---

52 The quotation in the German original: 'Die Bürokratisierung ist das spezifische Mittel, "Gemeinschaftshandeln" in rational geordnetes Gesellschaftshandeln zu überführen. Als Instrument der "Vergesellschaftung" der Herrschaftsbeziehungen war und ist sie daher ein Machtmittel allerersten Ranges für den, der über den bürokratischen Apparat verfügt. Denn unter sonst gleichen Chancen ist planvoll geordnetes und geleitetes "Gesellschaftshandeln" jedem widerstrebenden "Massen-" oder auch "Gemeinschaftshandeln" überlegen. Wo die Bürokratisierung der Verwaltung einmal restlos durchgeführt ist, da ist eine praktisch so gut wie unzerbrechliche Form der Herrschaftsbeziehungen geschaffen' (Weber 1976 [1921]: 569-70).

53 Mayntz and Scharpf (1995a) founded an actor-centred institutionalism which is not included in Hall and Taylor's typology.

Table 3: Comparing different kinds of Neo-Institutionalism

	Rational Choice Institutionalism[54]	Sociological Institutionalism[55]	Historical Institutionalism[56]
Definitions	Institutions are defined as the formal or informal procedures, routines, norms and conventions embedded in the organisational structure of the polity or political economy: – strategies induced by a given institutional setting may ossify into world view – power, especially asymmetrical power, plays a prominent role – path dependency of institutions – institutions are not the only causal force in politics.	Institutional rules perform agenda control: Actors have fixed preferences and behave instrumentally to maximise the attainment of these preferences – politics is seen as a series of collective action of dilemmas which are sub-optimal outcomes due to the prisoners' dilemma – emphasis on strategic interaction in the determination of political outcomes – the origins of Institutions are explained by deduction to arrive at a stylised specification of the function that an institution performs.	The definition of 'institutions' is broader than that of political scientists'. It includes: – formal rules – procedures or norms – symbolic systems – cognitive scripts – moral templates – culture and institutions shade into each other – self images and identities of social actors are said to be constituted from the institutional forms provided by social life – organisations adapt a new practice not because of greater efficiency but in order to legitimate the organisation or the participants.
Strengths	Has the most commodious conceptions of the relationship between institutions and behaviour.	Precise concept for relating institutions and behaviour: – aims to explain the connection between organisations and society – generalisable – good for theory building.	– Develops an expansive conception of why a particular institution might be chosen. – good to explain the presence of many apparent inefficiencies in social and political institutions.
Weaknesses	– No view on how institutions affect behaviour – deficits to explain causal chain through which the institutions are affecting the behaviour they are meant to explain.	– Simplistic image of human behaviour – preferences of actors might be exogenous – origins are deduced from consequences – analyses do not take into account imbalanced power structures.	– Power struggles can be underestimated.

Source: Based on the 1996 article by Hall and Taylor

---

54 The most important authors of rational choice institutionalism mentioned in Hall and Taylor (1996) are Weingast and Marshall (1988) and Moe (1984).
55 The most important authors of sociological institutionalism according to Hall and Taylor (1996) are Meyer and Rowan (1977); Zucker (1988, 1991); DiMaggio and Powell (1991); Jepperson (1991); Oliver (1991, 1992); Meyer and Scott (1992).
56 The most important authors of historical institutionalism regarding to Hall and Taylor (1996) are Thelen and Steinmo (1992), Thelen (1999) and Ikenberry (1988).

Within sociological neo-institutionalism, organisations are not the "optimal production sites", but rather historic formations within societies, which can only be understood as part of society but not on the basis of their alleged efficiencies or their pretended aims. Barely and Tolbert (1997) emphasise that sociological neo-institutionalists tend to stress cultural influences on decision-making. In their words:

Institutions, therefore, represent constraints on the options that individuals and collectives are likely to exercise, albeit constraints that are open to modification over time (Barley/Tolbert 1997: 93-4).

Sociological neo-institutionalism calls into question the matter of course terms and concepts like organisation, organisational reality and conceptions of reality (Türk 1989: 44). Türk also points out that the category of institution can be used to differentiate formations within society. Institutions symbolise the most important structuring elements within society, by acting as mechanisms of reproduction, i.e. the production of dominant structures persisting within society. Institutions are seen as being beyond individuals, i.e. individuals cannot just ignore institutions (Türk 2000: 145-146). Institutional theories of organisations represent an important break with rational-actor models and a strategy for explaining instances of organisational change that are not driven by processes of interest mobilisation. According to DiMaggio

The distinguishing contribution of institutional theory rests in the identification of causal mechanisms leading to organisational change and stability on the basis of preconscious understandings that organisational actors share, independent of their interests (DiMaggio 1988: 3).

The importance of institutionalism in modern organisational theory in the USA should not be underestimated. Tolbert and Zucker (1996) and Kieser (2001: 347) assert that the institutionalist approaches are themselves becoming an 'institution' within US-American organisational research.

3.3.3 Different Theories within sociological Neo-Institutionalism

In the following subchapter, different neo-institutionalist theories of the sociological tradition will be examined which are especially important for the study of the implementation of gender mainstreaming in the European Commission. Particular focus will be put on Meyer and Rowan (1991 [1977]), Zucker (1988 [1977]; 1991) DiMaggio and Powell (1991a, 1991b), DiMaggio (1988), Jepperson (1991), Oliver (1991) and Scott and Meyer (1991) for the following reasons:
    Meyer and Rowan's (1991 [1977]) novel idea on neo-institutionalism consists in the fact that they regard general structures as reflecting the myths of their institutional environments rather than the requirements of their work

as was previously contended. With regard to this book, this point is important since it enables to raise the question as to why gender mainstreaming was introduced at the Commission.

Zucker's (1988 [1977]) important contribution to neo-institutionalism consists in understanding institutionalisation as a process rather than a state which DiMaggio later includes in his own neo-institutionalist writing as a further development of his own model (DiMaggio 1988). Zucker's perspective is fundamental for this book in that gender mainstreaming will be examined from exactly this process perspective. Her micro analytical perspective is also an important foundation to study the power struggles between actors within the European Commission on the implementation of gender mainstreaming.

DiMaggio and Powell (1991a and 1991b [1983]) develop different isomorphisms, which explain how particular institutions are influenced by outside pressures. As already mentioned, the further development of DiMaggio (1988) to bring back interest and agency is an important prerequisite for this book.

As was stated in the introduction to this chapter, Jepperson's (1991) definition of institution and institutionalisation will be adopted in this book.

Oliver (1991) develops different strategic responses to institutionalised processes organisations may enact which range from 'acquiescence' as the most passive strategy to 'manipulation' as the most active strategy. These different strategies will be examined with regard to the reaction of the Commission and actors' within the Commission to the implementation of gender mainstreaming.

All these theoretical approaches within sociological neo-institutionalism will be further examined in this book.

3.3.3.1 The Importance of Formal Structure

Meyer and Rowan contend that organisations develop formal structures in order to achieve legitimacy and not necessarily as a more efficient problem solving mechanism (Meyer/ Rowan 1991 [1977]). This statement implies that the needs for legitimacy and efficiency are not the same, which is a further development or even renunciation of Weber. Meyer and Rowan argue that:

[...] formal structures of many organisations in post-industrial society (Bell 1973) dramatically reflect the myths of their institutional environments instead of the demands of their work activities (Meyer/ Rowan 1991 [1977]: 41).

Institutional rules are distinguished from prevailing social behaviours. Institutions inevitably involve normative obligations but often enter into social life as facts which must be taken into account by actors. Institutionalisations involve the processes by which social processes, obligations, or actualities come to take on a rule-like status in social thought and action, i.e. they are entirely internalised by the actors (Meyer/ Rowan 1991 [1977]: 41). Meyer and Rowan describe the connection between institutional rules and organisational structures as follows:

Institutional rules may have effects on organisational structures and their implementation in actual technical work which are very different from the effects generated by the networks of social behaviour and relationships which compose and surround a given organisation (Meyer/ Rowan 1991 [1977]: 41).

According to their thesis, formal organisational structures express myths which are institutionalised in their environment. Meyer and Rowan differentiate two key properties of formal organisations:

- They are rationalised prescriptions that identify various social purposes as technical ones and specify in a defined way the appropriate means to pursue these technical purposes rationally.
- They are highly institutionalised and therefore beyond the discretion of any individual or organisation. They must thus be taken for granted as legitimate, except from evaluations of their work outcome (Meyer/ Rowan 1991 [1977]: 44).

Meyer and Rowan (1991 [1977]) provide the institutionalisation of technologies as an example for myth binding within organisations. Technical procedures or production, accounting etc. become taken-for-granted means to accomplish organisational ends.

With regard to the relationship of organisations to their environment, Meyer and Rowan contend that organisations are structured in their environments by phenomena and tend to become isomorphic with them, i.e. the organisations become increasingly similar to their environments. The authors explain environmental isomorphism with the fact that formal organisations become matched with their environments by technical exchange and interdependencies. According to Meyer and Rowan, organisations structurally reflect a socially constructed reality (Berger/ Luckmann 1966). They contend that 'a most important aspect of isomorphism with environmental institutions is the evolution of organisational language' (Meyer/ Rowan 1991 [1977]: 50). Indeed, with regard to gender mainstreaming in the Commission, the evolution of an organisational language has proved to be particularly prominent and will be examined in chapter 7.

As myths interpret and explain the actions of individuals in everyday life such as love and jealousy, the myths of the assembly line or the myths of doctors explain organisational activity, the latter authors argue. The institutions become more stable by these taken-for-granted institutional rules – for example hospitals will usually be funded each year regardless of whether they cured patients or not. Meyer and Rowan see the danger of these institutional myths in that apart from technical efficiency, 'organisations which innovate in important structural ways bear considerable costs in legitimacy' (Meyer/ Rowan 1991 [1977]: 52). The authors suggest four partial solutions to the inconsistency between ceremonial rules and efficiency:

- An organisation can resist ceremonial requirements, but this may lead to illegitimacy and the organisation may lack stability.
- An organisation can cut off external relations and thereby maintain rigid conformity to institutionalised prescriptions, but internal participants and external constituents may soon become disillusioned with their inability to manage inter-institutional exchanges.
- An organisation can cynically acknowledge that its structure is inconsistent with work requirements, but this may sabotage its legitimacy.
- An organisation can promise reform but this delegitimises the present state of organisation.

To overcome the disadvantages of these partial solutions, Meyer and Rowan suggest two interrelated devices: decoupling and confidence.

According to Meyer and Rowan, in an ideal world, organisations that are built around efficiency aim to maintain close alignments between structures and activities. However, in Meyer and Rowan's words:

Because attempts to control and coordinate activities in institutionalised organisations lead to conflicts and loss of legitimacy, elements of structure are decoupled from activities and from each other (Meyer/ Rowan 1991 [1977]: 57).

This argument is illustrated by four points:

- Activities are performed beyond the purview of managers, and the organisation actively encourages professionalism.
- Goals are made ambiguous and categorical ends are replaced by technical ends, i.e. hospitals treat, not cure patients.
- Integration is avoided, implementation of programmes is neglected and inspection and evaluation are ceremonialised
- Human relations are made very important – individuals are left to work out technical interdependencies informally. The ability to coordinate things in violation of the rules in highly valued (Meyer/ Rowan 1991 [1977]: 57-58).

The advantages from decoupling consist in the fact that the assumption that formal structures are working is

buffered from the inconsistencies and anomalies involved in technical activities. Also, because integration is avoided, disputes and conflicts are minimised and an organisation can mobilise support from a broader range of external constituents. Thus, decoupling enables organisations to maintain a standardised, legitimating formal structures while their activities vary in response to practical considerations (Meyer/ Rowan 1991 [1977]: 58).

Although decoupled organisations lack central coordination, they can still function well by given confidence and good faith. Due to the logic of *confidence* and the wish to keep technical activities running smoothly and to avoid public embarrassment, the participants commit themselves to making things work out backstage (Meyer/ Rowan 1991 [1977]: 59).

In this book, I argue that the implementation of gender mainstreaming within the Commission can be seen as an example of decoupling and confidence as described by Meyer and Rowan (1991 [1977]). To the outside world, the European Commission pretends to implement gender main-streaming in order to be consistent with the norms and scripts of the United Nations and by demands of European women's movements. However, the internal implementation of gender mainstreaming is far from being institutionalised as will be shown in chapter 7. Therefore, the structural elements of gender mainstreaming are decoupled from the daily routines and activities of the organisation in order to adhere to the standardised, legitimating formal structure and in order not to destroy confidence with the environment.

3.3.3.2 Microlevel Institutional Research

Lynne Zucker bases her definition of institution on that of Hughes, in that 'institution' means 'some sort of establishment of relative permanence of a distinctly social sort' (Hughes 1936: 180, cited in Zucker 1991: 83). Zucker's approach is sometimes referred to as complementary to DiMaggio and Powell, and Meyer and Rowan as it examines the following two points:

–   The significance of perception and regularities in the processing and transmission of data for the regulation of social action are studied. Thereby, the cognitive change within social sciences is taken into account and is further developed within sociological neo-institutionalism.
–   Furthermore, the importance of the active acquirement and circulation of social rules is examined.

However, the new feature in Zucker's work is that, in three distinct experiments, each focusing on a different aspect of persistence, she examines the effects of different degrees of institutionalisation in constructed realities on cultural persistence:

The transmission experiment measures uniformity from one generation to the next. Given the assumption that all cultural understandings are socially constructed, the problem is to explain why some cultural understandings are so permanent and universal while others are unique to person, place and time. Zucker argues that continuity produces objectification and exteriority, i.e. the history of transmission provides a basis for assuming that the meaning of the act is part of intersubjective common sense.

The maintenance experiment measures the degree of maintenance of culture. One major assumption is that transmission of acts high on the scale of institutionalisation is sufficient to the maintenance of these acts. Zucker, however, argues that the degree of institutionalisation substantially affects the role and impact of direct social control. For acts low on institutionalisation direct social control is necessary, while for acts high on institutionalisation only transmission is required.

The resistance to change experiment measures the degree of resistance to attempts to change. Acts high on institutionalisation will be resistant to attempts to change them through personal influence because they are seen as external factors.

Zucker contends that acts are not simply institutionalised or not institutionalised. The meaning of an act may be perceived as more or less objective and exterior, depending on the context and depending on the actor, e.g. acts which are dependent on a specific actor are low on institution-alisation. By contrast, acts which are performed by an actor with a specific role are high on institutionalisation (Zucker 1991: 83-86).

Zucker's experimental design is a variation of the design of that which was initially developed by Sherif in 1936 and further developed by Jacobs and Campbell in 1961 on the so called auto-kinetic effect (Zucker 1991: 88-89). The auto-kinetic effect is a visual illusion – a stationary pinpoint of light presented in a totally dark room appears to move, smoothly or erratically. Zucker compared simulated formal organisational situations with simple group and individual situations. The results are based on the institutionalisa-tion thesis: if an organisational setting was simulated, which was enhanced by the fact that the first subject (an accomplice instructed on how to react) to make judgements on the movement of the light was given a leading function, their judgements then were adopted by the other subjects more frequently than in non-organisational settings. The alleged extreme judgement was also transmitted from generation to generation with small modifications. In the formal organisational setting, the subjects were more certain of their judge-ments than the subjects in other settings. The differences in the stability of the judgements during repetitions made after one week, were less obvious. The third round of experiments produced more obvious results once again. The same subjects, who were asked to repeat the tests, were confronted by another person (accomplice), who claimed a very small movement of light. It could be shown that the resistance against adaptations of change varied with the simulated organisational degree of the first experiment: the higher the degree of formality of the organisational setting, the less the subjects changed their mind on their original judgement.

Zucker's microlevel institutional research is a response to the macro-level[57] research which often focuses on content rather than process.

> By contrast, the microlevel approach [...] focuses upon institutionalisation as a process rather than as a state; upon the cognitive processes involved in the creation and trans-mission of institutions; upon their maintenance and resistance to change; and upon the role of language and symbols in those processes (The stress was added in the original; Zucker 1991 [1977]: 112).

The microlevel research provides a framework for examining institutionalisation versus resource dependence. Zucker contends that measures of the degree of institutionalisation constructed solely at the macrolevel confound institutionalisation with resource dependence. As an example of this, she contends that firms adopt affirmative-action personnel structures to the extent that they are dependent on federal contracts for revenues. Without micro-measurement strategies, it is impossible to judge whether such adoptions reflect institutionalisation per se, i.e. exteriority and objectiveness rather than strategic responses to external constraints.

Zucker was criticised by Türk (2000) with regard to her interpretation of the experiment described above. He contends that with her experimental design, one cannot examine the degree to which institutionalised practices or information are passed on, stabilise themselves or those who are resistant to pressure for change. Rather, the experiment determines the power of the organisational setting with regard to individual judgements. There are no attempts to hand down, stabilise, or question the institutional organisational setting of the experiment. Thus, the results of her experiment can cause shock by the way in which people disregard their own powers of judgement when they act in a (simulated) organisational setting[58] (Türk 2000: 129). Türk's criticism seems justified with regard to the experiments Zucker carried out, i.e. that using her types of experiments it is hard to measure how the practices and routines of institutions are passed on.

However, her approach to the study of institutionalisation as a process rather than as a state, and the study of the micropolitical aspects, are important pointers which furthered sociological neo-institutionalism tremendously and which also form an important basis for this book.

---

57 Jepperson distinguishes between two meanings of macro, firstly to 'spatial extensiveness or large numbers' and secondly to 'a high order of organisation within a structure having multiple orders of organisation' (Jepperson 1991: 161). In other words, macro can refer to effects of a collective, as well as to 'global effects upon a locality' (Jepperson 1991: 161, footnote 55).

58 Türk cites the Milgram experiment and the Stanford prisoner experiment as other examples.

3.3.3.3 Institutional Isomorphism and Collective Rationality

Similar to Zucker, DiMaggio and Powell argue that the current processes of organisational foundation and organisational change are not primarily driven forward by an efficiency imperative, but rather in a search for isomorphism, or in other words, structural homogeneity. Generally in organisational analysis, authors analyse the variation of firms or organisations. DiMaggio and Powell, however, seek to explain homogeneity, not variation (DiMaggio/ Powell 1991b [1983]: 64). According to the authors, organisations are embedded in *organisational fields*, within which there is pressure for a harmonisation of organisational forms. Organisational fields are a group of organisations which constitute an obvious type of *institutional life*, e.g. key suppliers, resource and product consumers, regulatory agencies, and other organisations that produce similar services or products. In drawing attention to not only competing firms or networks but to the totality of actors, the approach comprehends the importance of both *connectedness* and *structural equivalence* (DiMaggio/ Powell 1991b: 65).

DiMaggio and Powell define emerging fields in the following manner:

Fields only exist to the extent that they are institutionally defined. The process of institutional definition, or 'structuration' consists of four parts: an increase in the extent of interaction among organisations in the field; the emergence of sharply defined interorganisational structures of domination and patterns of coalition, an increase in the information load with which organisation in a field must contend, and the development of a mutual awareness among participants in a set of organisations that they are involved in a common enterprise' (DiMaggio/ Powell 1991b: 65).

It is important to note that this passage links the actions of organisations to a larger social structure, i.e. the field and that actors are referred to as knowledgeable in that there is a mutual awareness among participants and that institutions constrain the very actions that produce these institutions ('emergence of ...structures of domination') (Barley/ Tolbert 1997: 95). Barley and Tolbert show the parallel to the later structuration theory of the early institutionalists in that they postulate that 'institutions inhibit an inherent duality: they both arise from and constrain social action' (Barley/ Tolbert 1997: 95).

DiMaggio and Powell (1991b) differentiate three mechanisms which bring about institutional change of organisations with regard to isomorphism: coercive isomorphism, mimetic isomorphism, normative isomorphism. It is important to note that these differentiations are primarily analytical, i.e. even though the different mechanisms can be traced back to different conditions, they can hardly be differentiated empirically (DiMaggio/ Powell 1991b: 67-68).

Coercive isomorphism stems from political influence and the problem of legitimacy. To paraphrase DiMaggio and Powell, coercive isomorphism results from both formal and informal pressures exerted on organisations by other organisations upon which they are dependent and by cultural expectations in the society in which the organisations function, e.g. organisations employ affirmative action officers to fend off allegations of discrimination. The fact that these changes are largely 'ceremonial' does not mean that they are inconsequential. Ritti and Gouldner (1979) have contended that staff become involved in advocacy for their functions and that this can alter power relationships within organisations in the long run.

Mimetic isomorphism results from standard responses to uncertainty. When organisational technologies are poorly understood (March/ Olsen 1976) – or when the environment creates symbolic uncertainty, organisations may model themselves on other organisations. The advantages of mimetic behaviour are considerable as a viable solution may be found with little expense. Organisations usually model themselves on similar organisations in their field, which they perceive to be more legitimate or successful.

Normative isomorphism is usually associated with professionalisation. According to Larson (1977) and Collins (1979), professionalisation is the collective struggle of members of an occupation to define the conditions and methods of their work, to control 'the production of producers' (Larson: 1977: 49-52) and to establish a cognitive base and legitimisation for their occupational autonomy. Two aspects of professionalisation are important sources of isomorphism:

– the locating of formal education and of legitimisation in a cognitive base produced by university specialists
– elaboration of professional networks that span organisations and thus new models diffuse rapidly.

Applying DiMaggio's and Powell's (1991b [1983]) concept of mimetic isomorphism to the research question, I hypothesise that the environment of the Commission, i.e. European women's movements and the United Nations, creates uncertainty for the Commission (see chapter 6). The European Commission therefore copies gender mainstreaming from the UN level in order to increase its legitimacy. Applying the concept of normative isomorphism to gender mainstreaming, I hypothesise that the development of gender mainstreaming is closely tied to networks such as the gender mainstreaming advocacy-network[59].

---

59 The term 'advocacy-network' is based on Keck and Sikkink's (1998) definition of the term (see chapter 7). I purposefully do not use the term 'feminist policy machinery' which was coined by Stetson and Mazur (1995) since the term 'machinery' has a negative connotation.

3.3.3.4 Bringing back Interest and Agency into sociological Neo-Institutionalism

In a further development of DiMaggio's and Powell's (1991b [1983]) earlier theoretical assumptions, DiMaggio discusses two justifications as to why the pursuit of interest-free models and explanations is both reasonable and required by two ubiquitous conditions of organisational life:

- Institutional approaches to organisations have emphasised *factors that make actors unlikely to recognise or to act on their interests*' [60]. In early works, norms were prominent in this respect (Selznick 1949), whereas in more recent work, taken-for-granted assumptions about organisational reality have replaced norms (Zucker, 1991).
- Institutional theory has focused on *circumstances that cause actors who do recognise and try to act on their interests to be unable to do so effectively*[61]. Most prominent in this respect are the limits of cognition and coordination, which make it difficult or impossible for actors to understand the relationship between means and ends.' Example for this are March and Cohen's 'organised anarchies', in which ambiguous goals, uncertain technologies and unstable participation render the consequences of the actions of top managers unpredictable (Cohen/ March, 1974).

DiMaggio lists five problems to which institutionalist theory is most appropriate:

1. Institutional theory can be used to explain those aspects of organisational reality that are so exteriorised that no actor is likely to question them (Zucker 1988 [1977]: 2), (e.g. age grading is accepted by participants in schools).
2. Institutional theory may be adequate to explain most organisational phenomena in specific types of fields, for example those in which the legitimacy of member organisations is largely based on traditional authority (such as churches).
3. Once an organisational form is likely to become institutionalised, institutional arguments suggest the benefit of new analytical questions (e.g. questions about the determinants of homogeneity or heterogeneity of organisational members), new hypotheses (e.g. that professionalism or some state structures induce organisational conformity), and new modelling strategies (e.g. the use of diffusion and threshold models) in reacting to organisational change.

---

60   The stress was added in the original.
61   The stress was added in the original.

4. Where research is attempting to explain long-term change or where change in the institutional order can be documented and measured or where the distribution of interests can be presumed to be stable.
5. Where the aim of the research is to explain 'variation among nation states or other units with distinct institutional structures and where interest distributions and aggregation mechanisms are similar or themselves result from institutional factors, purely institutional arguments may suffice.' (DiMaggio 1988: 7). As an example, DiMaggio provides the classic example of Crozier's (1964, cited in DiMaggio 1988: 7) argument about the ways in which French corporate bureaucracies reflect historically embedded dilemmas and administrative strategies of the French state which differ from bureaucracies in other political systems with similar interests (DiMaggio 1988: 5-7).

DiMaggio states that even though institutionalists generally try to explain phenomena that do not reflect the behaviour of rational actors driven by clearly perceived interests, there are two kinds of interests fundamental to institutional theory: predictability and survival. I shall elaborate on these two interests in turn.

Institutionalist theory is based on the assumption that actors have a preference for predictability and certainty. Individuals' preferences for routinised and predictable environments lead to a lot of behaviour that creates and sustains institutions, as Zucker showed with regard to the current organisational and economic infrastructure, allegedly, emerging as a result of a crisis of uncertainty due to immigration, geographic mobility, and the high rate of start-up firms and their bankruptcy in the late nineteenth century (Zucker 1986, cited in DiMaggio 1988: 8).

The interest in survival of organisations leads them to accede to the demands of other organisations on which they depend for resources and legitimacy.

DiMaggio criticises the initial formations of institutionalism in that 'they are limited in scope to the diffusion and reproduction of successfully institutionalised organisational forms and practices' (DiMaggio 1988: 12) and also that they do not explain why some innovations are not institutionalised or some are deinstitutionalised. DiMaggio therefore suggests making the concepts of agency and interest more prominent within institutionalism. First of all, it is important to differentiate between institutionalisation as an outcome and as a process. The former places organisational structures and practices beyond the reach of interests and politics. The latter is profoundly political and reflects the power of organised interests and the actors who mobilise around these interests. Institutionalisation requires institutional work to legitimate that particular form: for example, legitimating accounts that organisational entrepreneurs advance about labour markets or services. If these are not endorsed by an organisational system that segments labour markets and classifies new products and services as qualitatively different from old ones, newly institutionalised forms will remain unstable in their structure, public theories and programs. An institutionalising organisational form thus requires the help of subsidiary actors to render its public policy plausible. The claims of *institutional entrepreneurs* (organised actors with sufficient resources) are supported by existing or newly mobilised actors who expect to reap benefits from the institutionalisation project. If an institutionalisation project succeeds, subsidiary actors are themselves legitimated and institutionalised and might become *subsidiary institutions*. For example, modern medical schools in universities play an essential role in legitimating the public claims of doctors and hospitals, to expertise and to the provision of specialised services, respectively. However, they also derive legitimacy of their own and partial autonomy from the hospital system (DiMaggio 1988: 15).

In this book, the institutionalisation of gender mainstreaming will be examined as a process, which enables us to take into account the power of organised interests and those that mobilise around these interests. This will be further examined in chapter 7.

3.3.3.5 Microinstitutional Approach: Strategic Responses to Institutional Processes

Christine Oliver examines the 'different strategic responses that organisations enact as a result of the institutional pressures toward conformity that are exerted on them and also to develop a preliminary conceptual framework for predicting the occurrence of the alternative strategies' (Oliver 1991: 145). She develops a typology of five different strategic responses to institutionalised processes that organisations may enact and which vary in active agency in the organisation from passivity to increasingly active resistance: acquiescence, compromise, avoidance, defiance and manipulation, each resulting in three different tactics (see Table 4). Oliver emphasises that active strategies also belong to the behavioural repertory of organisation (Kieser 2001b: 349).

Table 4: Strategic Responses of Organisations to Institutional Processes

Strategies	Tactics	Examples	
Acquiesce	Habit	Following invisible, taken-for-granted norms	
	Imitate	Mimicking institutional models	**passive**
	Comply	Obeying rules and accepting norms	
Compro-mise	Balance	Balancing the expectations of multiple constituents	
	Pacify	Placating and accommodating institutional elements	
	Bargain	Negotiating with institutional stakeholders	
Avoid	Conceal	Disguising nonconformity	
	Buffer	Loosening institutional attachments	
	Escape	Changing goals, activities, or domains	
Defy	Dismiss	Ignoring explicit norms and values	
	Challenge	Contesting rules and requirements	
	Attack	Assaulting the sources of institutional pressure	
Manipu-late	Co-opt	Importing influential constituents	
	Influence	Shaping values and criteria	**active**
	Control	Dominating institutional constituents and processes	

Source: Oliver 1991: 152

The theoretical rationale underlying conformity or resistance to institutional rules and expectations is determined by the ability and willingness of organisations to change. The conditions under which organisations are prepared to conform are determined by organisational scepticism, political self-interest and organisational control (Oliver 1991: 159). They are also determined by the extent to which a rule or expectation is already institutionalised, or by the degree of legitimacy, which can be won through the adoption of institutionalised rules and expectations and the power of an organisation to enforce its political self-interest (Kieser 2001b: 349). Limitations in the ability of organisations to conform to institutional requirements include inadequate organisational resources or capacity to meet the requirements for conformity, conflicting institutional pressures that make unilateral conformity unachievable and a lack of recognition and awareness of institutional expectations.

Kieser provides an example for strategic actions. He says that some companies threaten to change the place of production (and might end up changing) when legislative acts are planned to be changed (or are actually changed) with regard to environmental protection or the use of genetic technology. External demands which are backed with 'rational' arguments are rejected as 'non-rational' together with other arguments of 'rationality'. Demands for more environmental protection which are backed by the promise of a higher quality of life are rejected with the argumentative 'chain' that higher costs lead to loss of international competitiveness, which leads to loss of jobs which, in turn, leads to a decline of the gross national product which results in a loss of general quality of life (Kieser 2001b: 349). The antecedents of strategic responses according to Oliver (1991) are summarised in the following table:

Table 5: Antecedents of strategic Responses

Institutional Factor	Research Question	Predictive Dimension
Cause	Why is the organisation being pressured to conform to institutional rules or expectations?	Legitimacy or social fitness Efficiency or economic fitness
Constituents	Who is exerting institutional pressures to the organisation?	Multiplicity of constituent demands Dependence on institutional constituents
Content	To what norms or requirements is the organisation being pressured to conform	Consistency with organisational goals Discretionary constraints imposed on the organisation
Control	How or by what means are the institutional pressures being exerted?	Legal coercion or enforcement Voluntary diffusion of norms
Context	What is the environmental context within which institutional pressures are being exerted?	Environmental uncertainty Environmental interconnectedness

Source: Oliver 1991: 160

Each institutional factor will be explained in turn below:

Cause as an institutional Factor of strategic Responses

Oliver suggests two hypotheses regarding institutional antecedents and expected strategic responses: Her first hypothesis states that 'the lower the degree of social legitimacy perceived to be attainable from conformity to institutional pressures, the greater the likelihood of organisational resistance to institutional pressures.'

In her second hypothesis Oliver states that 'the lower the degree of economic gain perceived to be attainable from conformity to institutional pressures, the greater the likelihood of organisational resistance to institutional pressures' (Oliver 1991: 161-2).

According to both hypotheses, it is important to examine the reasons for institutional pressures and these can be arranged into two categories: social and economic fitness. Pressures that make organisations more socially fit include pollution regulations, promoting the health of employees or promoting equal opportunities. Pressures for economic fitness include demands of corporate donors and government on social service agencies to be more 'professional' and efficient. According to the first hypothesis, when an organisation expects that conformity will increase social or economic fitness, the most likely response will be acquiescence. However, scepticism about one of the two factors tends to arise when the expected benefits of conformity differ widely between those imposing the institutional pressure and those upon whom it is imposed. For example, corporations may doubt the legitimating effects of being an equal opportunity employer, despite the government's assurances that such a status would be beneficial to the company. One result can be that organisations 'will attempt to compromise on the requirements for conformity, avoid the conditions that make conformity necessary, defy the institutional requirements to which they are advised to conform, or manipulate the criteria or conditions of conformity' (Oliver 1991: 161). Whether the organisation chooses acquiescence or more resistant strategies, depends on the degree to which the organisation values the intended objectives that institutional constituents are trying to achieve in pressuring the organisation to be more socially or economically accountable.

Constituents as an institutional Factor of strategic Responses

Regarding the constituents of strategic responses, Oliver hypothesises that 'the greater the degree of constituent multiplicity, the greater the likelihood of organisational resistance to institutional pressure' (hypothesis 3). Multiplicity is defined as the degree of multiple, conflicting constituent expectations exerted on an organisation. Facing multiple conflicting pressures from constituents, organisations are likely to attempt avoidance strategies. For example an oil company may attempt to cover up the consequences of an oil spill in order to avoid being held responsible for the costs of a cleanup that will be disliked by shareholders but is demanded by the public. Oliver's fourth hypothesis is that 'the lower the degree of external dependence on pressurising constituents, the greater the likelihood of organisational resistance to institutional pressures.' (Oliver 1991: 162).

Content as an institutional Factor of strategic Responses

Oliver's hypothesis regarding the content of strategic responses is as follows: 'The lower the degree of consistency of institutional norms or requirements with organisational goals, the greater the likelihood of organisational resistance to institutional pressures' (hypothesis 5) (Oliver 1991: 163). This means that organisations will be more willing to acquiesce to external pressures when these pressures or expectations are compatible with internal goals. As an example Oliver provides Powell's (Powell 1988: 129 cited in

102

Oliver 1991: 165) observation on how the demands of external constituents tended to conflict with the internal logic of academic publishers and public television stations with the result that both organisations chose to ignore outside influence.

Oliver summarises her sixth hypothesis; that 'the greater the degree of discretionary constraints imposed on the organisation by institutional pressures, the greater the likelihood of organisational resistance to institutional pressures' (Oliver 1991: 164).

Control as an Institutional Factor of strategic Responses

With regard to control, Oliver hypothesises the following: 'The lower the degree of legal coercion behind institutional norms and requirements, the greater the likelihood of organisational resistance to institutional pressures (hypothesis 7).' An example for hypothesis 7 is that when government mandate buttresses cultural expectations, organisations are made more aware of public interests and will be less likely to respond defiantly because the consequences of non-compliance are more severe. Hypothesis 8: 'The lower the degree of voluntary diffusion of institutional norms, values, or practices, the greater the likelihood of organisational resistance to institutional pressures' (Oliver 1991: 168). An example of hypothesis 8 is that the military's ability to oppose the use of women in the [US] army became increasingly difficult as pressures for equal employment opportunities became more broadly supported by the public and the state. Thus, 'limits on the diffusion of norms and values also define the scope conditions of institutional conformity' (Oliver 1991: 168).

Context as an institutional Factor of strategic Responses

The context is important for the following two reasons: Oliver's ninth hypothesis is 'the lower the level of uncertainty in the organisation's environment, the greater the likelihood of organisational resistance to institutional pressures. Uncertainty is connected with multiplicity insofar as multiple conflicting pressures tend to increase uncertainty. When the environment of an organisation is uncertain and unpredictable, an organisation will invest a lot of effort to reinstall certainty by re-establishing the illusion of control and stability in order to overcome organisational outcomes. Finally, her tenth hypothesis is 'the lower the degree of interconnectedness in the institutional environment, the greater the likelihood of organisational resistance to institutional pressures' (Oliver 1991: 170).

I shall examine Oliver's hypotheses further in chapter 7.

3.3.3.6 Defining Institutions, Institutionalisation and institutional Effects with regard to Gender Mainstreaming

Meyer and Rowan (1991 [1977]: 346) (who draw on Berger and Luckmann (1966)) contend that institutions are socially constructed templates for action, generated and maintained through ongoing interactions. With regard to gender mainstreaming it is important to examine the extent to which actors have created gender mainstreaming as an institution, i.e. whether the implementation of gender mainstreaming has led to 'generalised expectations' and 'interpretations of behaviour' or 'typifications of habitualised actions that constitute institutions [which] are always shared' (Berger/ Luckmann 1966: 72). According to Barley and Tolbert, the relations and actions that emerge from this process gradually acquire the status of taken-for-granted facts that, in turn, shape future interactions (Barley/ Tolbert 1997: 94).

The US-American sociologist Ronald Jepperson (1991) differentiates the terms 'institutions', 'institutional effects' and 'institutionalisation'. In his definition, an '*institution* represents a social order or pattern that has attained a certain state or property; *institutionalisation* denotes the process of such attainment' (the emphasises were added by the author. Jepperson 1991: 145), whereby *order* or *pattern* means standardised interaction sequences. In Jepperson's words:

When departures from the pattern are counteracted in a regulated fashion, by repetitively activated, socially constructed, controls – that is, by some set of rewards and sanctions – we refer to a pattern as institutionalised. Put another way: institutions are those social patterns that, when chronically reproduced, owe their survival to relatively self-activating social processes (Jepperson 1991: 145).

The notion of rewards and sanctions are important in this context. For example Parsons differentiates norms from institutions by saying that institutions are self-policing, while norms are not. According to Parsons, a norm is institutionalised, if it is rewarded and sanctioned (Parsons 1951: 20).

Jepperson stresses that institutions need to be self-reproducing, i.e. their persistence is not dependant on recurrent collective mobilisation. He stresses the importance of not confusing institutionalisation with stability and provides as an example Tocqueville's analysis of the Old Regime and the French Revolution in which the French state was described as highly institutionalised, which made it extremely vulnerable to environmental change (Jepperson 1991: 145). Jepperson further differentiates the term institution in four different ways:

–   Whether a practice is an institution is relative to particular contexts. As an example he quotes that voting is considered to be an institutionalised social pattern in the United States although not in Haiti. This is the case because voting in the United States is embedded in various reproducing systems and is not dependent on repeated political interventions.

- The relativity of the context is extended further by stating that primary levels of organisation can operate as institutions relative to secondary levels of organisation. For example, a computer's basic operating system could be regarded as an institution relative to its word processing program.
- In addition, whether an object is an institution is relative to a particular dimension of a relationship. For example, Yale University is more an institution in the direct community it is based in than in other communities but less so than in other non-academic contexts.
- Lastly, whether something is an institution is relative to its centrality. 'In systems, cores are institutions relative to peripheries. The regime of international politico-economic coordination is more an external, objective, constraint for Ghana than for the IMF' (Jepperson 1991: 147), i.e. it is possible that an association is more of an institution for a non-member than for a member.

Jepperson is one of the few neo-institutionalist authors to clearly define the terms institution, institutional effect and institutionalisation. Unfortunately other scholars relate to the terms differently and sometimes without making their definition explicit at all. This book will be based on Jepperson's definition of the three terms.

Applying Jepperson's model of institution to our research questions, gender mainstreaming can be considered as an institution if it represents a social order or pattern (i.e. standardised interaction sequences) that has attained a certain state or property (Jepperson 1991: 145).

With regard to the first of Jepperson's four elements of an institution, the fact whether gender mainstreaming can be considered as an institution is relative to particular contexts. For example in DG Employment and Social Affairs, gender mainstreaming could constitute an institution because it might be embedded in various reproducing systems and is not dependent on repeated political intervention, while this might not be the case in DG Competition.

With regard to Jepperson's second description of an institution, gender mainstreaming could be regarded as an institution relative to other equal opportunities concepts or – extending the relativity of the context yet further – with regard to other transversal policies (e.g. environmental policy, knowledge society).

Relating gender mainstreaming to Jepperson's third description of an institution, i.e. the relativity to a particular dimension of a relationship would mean gender mainstreaming constitutes an institution within the gender mainstreaming advocacy-network, while this is not the case for the whole of the European Commission.

Applying gender mainstreaming to the last of Jepperson's attributes of an institution, whether gender mainstreaming is an institution depends on its centrality. The norms and scripts of the United Nations, such as the requirement to implement gender mainstreaming might be more of an institution for the European Commission as an international organisation than for Member States.

All these four attributes of an institution will be elaborated in chapter 7. In this book, Jepperson's definition of the term institution will be followed since it is clearly distinguished from institutionalisation and institutional effects.

3.3.3.7 Critiques of sociological Neo-Institutionalism

There is a wide variety of critique on sociological neo-institutionalism which ranges from a denunciation of the differences between old and neo-institutionalism to the questioning of the basic premises of sociological neo-institutionalism which I shall describe in more detail in the following.

Türk (2000) criticises sociological neo-institutionalism in that it is not in itself a social theory and that scholars who base their work on sociological neo-institutionalism seldom express which social theory they adhere to. According to him, the question what institutions are does not make sense, as one cannot define institutions without a context but only within a social theory. Türk sees Meyer as an exception since Meyer bases his theory on a theory of 'rationalistic modernity' and also mentions his interest in Wallerstein's world system approach (Türk, 2000: 145)[62].

However, this critique needs to be relativised since Zucker (1988 [1977]: 727-728) and Meyer and Rowan (1991 [1977]) all base their accounts on the phenomenological account of Berger and Luckmann (1966) (refer to previous section).

Türk stresses the importance of the neo-institutionalists' concept of institutions in that the category of institution can also be used to differentiate formations within society. Institutions symbolise the most important structuring elements within society, by acting as mechanisms of reproduction, i.e. the production of persistence of dominant structures within society. Institutions are seen as reaching beyond individuals, i.e. individuals cannot just ignore them (Türk 2000: 145-146). Barley and Tolbert criticise neo-institutionalists' concept of institutions in that they have ignored the way in which institutions are created, altered and reproduced, in part because their models of institutionalisation as a process are underdeveloped (Barley/Tolbert 1997: 93).

---

62 Unfortunately Türk does not supply any example for this.

Most important for this study is Türk's critique of the definition of institutionalisation: If all habitualised conversation (like Maturana 1985), everything that has become a habit is seen as an institution (e.g. from greetings to the military industrial complex) the category of institution would be identical with the term 'social' (Türk 2000: 146). In addition, it would not only be impossible to distinguish between structures which arise from experiences of actors and those structures that do not originate in the experience of actors but also impossible to separate those structures that are enforced by society and which must be adhered to (Türk 2000: 146-7). This differentiation is very important to sociological neo-institutionalists, especially Meyer and Rowan (1991 [1977]); Zucker (1991) and DiMaggio and Powell (1991a). For all of them, something is institutionalised if it does not originate in the experience of the acting subject, but is taken-for-granted.

Kieser further criticises the term institutionalisation by stating that it is not argued coherently. For example Meyer and Rowan (1991 [1977]) refer to the possible reactions of organisations to a set of different strategies for action and introduce, somewhat implicitly, the dimensions 'reflected' and 'intentional' into the argument. Implicitly means that single actors or groups of actors and their interests are normally pushed out of the explanation by referring only to organisations, which

adopt institutionalised elements or which protect their activities from checks. If individuals are mentioned in the accounts of institutionalists, this is done in abstract expressions like organisational actors (Kieser 2001b: 347-8).

Although this criticism may once have been on the mark, there now exists a substantial number of accounts where the actors are brought into the analysis more vigorously than in early institutionalist theories. For example DiMaggio (1988) differentiates neo-institutionalism by taking account of exactly the fact that actors are not sufficiently acknowledged in neo-institutionalism.

After having introduced the most important works of sociological neo-institutionalism, I shall now introduce Giddens' concept of structuration. After that I shall elaborate how both theories will be used to examine gender mainstreaming.

3.4   Giddens' Concept of Structuration

Giddens Structuration theory will be used to examine the internal processes within the European Commission during the implementation of gender mainstreaming. Structuration theory enables us to examine the reproduction of structures and actions. Giddens' (1984) concept of rules and resources will be used to examine the modification of actions and structures, which are necessary for the implementation of innovations.

Structuration theory should be considered as a social theory that covers the entire field of social and human sciences and not 'only' as a sociological theory. The theory of structuration was developed in a critical dialogue with four main tendencies within sociology: action theory, functionalism, structuralism and Marxism. Giddens regards action theory as having remained in a subjectivist position, which means it fails to explain the social structures and the conditions for action. Similarly, with functionalist and structuralist positions: they do not adequately account for agency, i.e. Giddens' assumption is that individuals possess a will and contribute to changing these structures. Both theories thus remain in a position of determinism which overlooks the fact that social structures are constraining and enabling at the same time (Giddens 1984).

Giddens' point of departure is that social science must abandon the eternal and endless epistemological discussion as to how reality should be known. Rather, it should focus on the ontological questions of how to conceptualise reality. For Giddens, this means a conceptualisation of the human being, of human action and the reproduction and transformation of social life.

The main aim of social sciences according to structuration theory is to study social practices across space and time and the domain of social sciences is 'neither the experience of the individual actor nor the existence of any form of societal totality' (Giddens 1984: 2).

Another precondition for the success is the development and redefinition of concepts:

The attempt to formulate a coherent account of human agency and of structure demands, however, a very considerable conceptual effort (Giddens 1984: xxi).

The theory of structuration is according to Giddens (Giddens 1984: xxi) an elaborate reflection on a citation from Marx:

Men make their own history, but they do not make it as they please; they do not make it under self-selected circumstances, but under circumstances existing already, given and transmitted from the past. The tradition of all dead generations weighs like a nightmare on the brains of the living. And just as they seem to be occupied with revolutionising themselves and things, creating something that did not exist before, precisely in such epochs of revolutionary crisis they anxiously conjure up the spirits of the past to their service, borrowing from them names, battle slogans, and costumes in order to present this new scene in world history in time-honoured disguise and borrowed language (Marx: 1999 [1869]: 3).[63]

---

63   The German original is as follows: 'Die Menschen machen ihre eigene Geschichte, aber sie machen sie nicht aus freien Stücken, nicht unter selbstgewählten, sondern unter unmittelbar vorgefundenen, gegebenen und überlieferten Umständen. Die Tradition aller toten

Giddens comments on the first part on Marx' citation (i.e. that men (or rather human beings) make their own history) 'Well so they do. But what a diversity of problems of social analysis this apparently innocuous pronouncement turns out to disclose' (Giddens 1984: xxi)! Indeed, structuration theory attempts to explain the connection between the given and the self-selected circumstances.

Giddens' theory of structuration is closely linked to critical theory:

The formulation of critical theory is not an option; theories and findings in the social sciences are likely to have practical (and political) consequences regardless of whether or not the sociological observer or policy-maker decides that they can be 'applied' to a given practical issue (The stress was added by Anthony Giddens. Giddens 1984: xxxv).

And 'structuration theory is intrinsically incomplete if not linked to a conception of social science as critical theory' (Giddens 1984: 287). Giddens thus links structuration inextricably to critical theory, which is an important theoretical framing.

It is first of all important to summarise Giddens most important definitions and concepts, as he defines a number of terms differently from other scholars.

3.4.1 Giddens' Notion of Social Practice

Since, according to structuration theory, the main aim is to study social practices as noted above, the entire project in 'The Constitution of Society' consists of defining social practice. The concept is defined in a long theoretical tradition in which the concepts of agent, power, action, structure, system and time-space are redefined so that they come to constitute practice. Giddens' contribution lies in defining the concepts and how they relate to each other so that together they define social practice, and in that they contain both a producing and a reproducing aspect, i.e. both an agency dimension and a structure/ system dimension (Giddens 1984: 2, Kaspersen 2000: 33-4).

3.4.2 Giddens' Notion of an Agent, Agency and Action

The agent is the point of departure for Giddens' structuration theory. Giddens' concept of agency is based on two fundamental human qualities:

Geschlechter lastet wie ein Alp auf dem Gehirne der Lebenden. Und wenn sie eben damit beschäftigt scheinen, sich und die Dinge umzuwälzen, noch nicht Dagewesenes zu schaffen, gerade in solchen Epochen revolutionärer Krise beschwören sie ängstlich die Geister der Vergangenheit zu ihrem Dienste herauf, entlehnen ihnen Namen, Schlachtparole, Kostüm, um in dieser altehrwürdigen Verkleidung und mit dieser erborgten Sprache die neuen Weltgeschichtsszene aufzuführen'. (Marx 1969: 115).

Firstly capability and secondly knowledgeability. Capability means the facility that agents are able to act otherwise. As a result, action logically involves power in the sense of transformative capacity. Knowledgeability means knowing how to go on in a practical sense.

A conception of action...has to place at the centre the everyday fact that social actors are knowledgeable about the conditions of social reproduction in which their day-to-day activities are enmeshed (Giddens 1982: 29).

The agent is knowledgeable, with information about most of the action she or he undertakes. This wealth of knowledge is expressed primarily as *practical consciousness*. Giddens provides the example of our ability to speak a language despite having no knowledge of linguistic theory or formal rules of syntax. What is more, we do so without any conscious reflections about them (Giddens 1984: 8). Many of our day-to-day activities are very routinised as, for example, the ways we get up, take a shower etc. Giddens emphasises that we have considerable knowledge about these actions, but that this knowledge is rarely formulated discursively, i.e. explicitly. It is a tacit knowledge, which means that our understanding requires that we know how to act. A *discursive consciousness* on the other hand means that we explicitly express an activity, for example, how and why we ride a bicycle. A competent actor can nearly always explain discursively the intentions in acting, and the reasons for it. However, s/he cannot necessarily do so with regard to the motives (Giddens 1984:6). By stressing the agent's knowledgeability, Giddens emphasises that systems and structures do not act behind the back of the actor. The will of the actor is strengthened by the agent's discursive capacity. Giddens also stresses that there is no bar between discursive and practical consciousness; there are only the differences between what can be said and what is characteristically simply done. However, there is a gulf between the consciousness levels and the unconsciousness, which due to repressions 'inhibits discursive formulations' (refer to figure 3) (Giddens 1984: 49).

Giddens emphasises the recursive character in social life. Recursiveness is called the duality principle.

...the essential recursiveness of social life, as constituted in social practices: structure is both medium and outcome of social practices. Structure enters simultaneously into the constitution of the agent and social practices, and 'exists' in the generating moments of this constitution (Giddens 1979: 5).

Two important principles from structuration theory are summarised in this passage:

- Structures are at the same time medium and the result of social practice.
- Social actors reproduce, through their actions, the conditions that enable their action (Walgenbach 2001: 358).

Figure 3: The Difference between discursive Consciousness and the
Unconscious according to Giddens

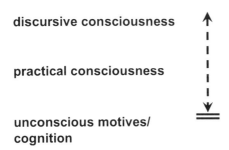

discursive consciousness

practical consciousness

**unconscious motives/
cognition**

Source: Based on Giddens 1984: 7

Giddens' notion of agency is fundamental for the understanding of structuration theory. He does not consider agency as a series of combined discrete acts. Rather, agency is a process oriented concept, it is without starting or endpoint, it is a process of structuration. It only gives meaning to speak of isolated acts at the very moment when the agent thinks back about a concrete event. Giddens' understanding of agency as a process is in contrast to most action theorists who see actions as unique, distinct elements, each having an underlying cause, purpose, intention, or motive. Instead of seeing intentionality as a concrete cause of a given action, Giddens states that intentionality should also be seen as a process (Giddens 1984: 5-16).

After having elaborated on Giddens notions of agent and agency, it is now important to look at his notion of action. According to Giddens:

'action' is not a combination of 'acts': 'acts' are constituted only by a discursive moment of attention to the durée of lived through experience (Giddens 1984: 3).

In Giddens' view, action cannot be discussed in separation from the body, its mediations with the surrounding world and the coherence of an acting self.

3.4.3 Giddens' Notion of Structure and Structuration

Giddens distinguishes between structure, system and structuration. *Structure* as a recursively organised sets of rules and resources is out of time and space, 'save in its instantiations and coordination as memory traces, and is marked by an 'absence of the subject'' (Quotation marks are added in the original. Giddens 1984: 25). A system consists 'of reproduced relations between actors or collectivities organised as regular social practices'. Structurations

111

'are conditions governing the continuity or transmutation of structures, and therefore the reproduction of social systems' (Giddens 1984: 25).

Giddens' notion on the recursiveness between domination, signification and legitimation is outlined in figure 4. As can be seen from the figure, the middle horizontal line (interpretative scheme, facility and norm) is the intermediary level (the medium) between interaction and structure. Organisation can be seen as the institutionalisation of reflectivity. Structure consists of the recursiveness between signification, domination and legitimation. Interaction consists of the recursive relationship between communication, power and sanction.

Figure 4: Recursiveness between Domination, Signification and Legitimation

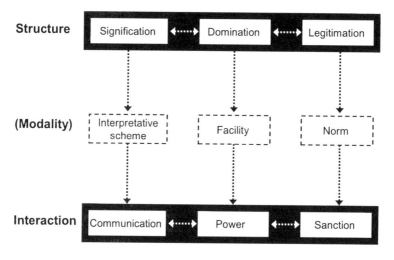

Source: Giddens 1984: 29

According to Giddens, *rules* relate on the one hand to the constitution of *meaning,* and on the other hand to the legitimation of modes of social conduct. Rules must be very broadly understood as the techniques and formulae that are used in the action, and they are deeply rooted in our tacit practical consciousness. Rules are procedures which are applied to the permanence and the reproduction of the social practices and they operate as formulaes that tell us 'how to go on' in social life (Giddens 1984: 22-3).

The concept of *resources* is closely linked to power as the medium by which the agent can exert transformative capacity. In Giddens words:

Resources are the media whereby transformative capacity is employed as power in the routine course of social interaction; but they are at the same time structural elements of

112

social systems as systems, reconstituted through their utilisation in social interaction (Giddens 1979: 92).

Giddens differentiates between allocative and authoritative resources. 'Allocative resources refer to capabilities – or, more accurately, to forms of transformative capacity – generating command over objects, goods or material phenomena' (Giddens 1984: 33). Authoritative resources refer to 'types of transformative capacity generating command over persons or actors' (Giddens 1984: 33). The difference between both types of resources is illustrated in the following table:

Table 6: Difference between allocative and authoritative Resources according to Giddens

Allocative Resources	Authoritative Resources
1 Material features of the environment (raw materials, material power sources)	1 Organisation of social time- space (temporal-spatial constitution of paths and regions)
2 Means of material production/ reproduction (instruments of production, technology)	2 Production/ reproduction of the body (organisation and relation of human beings in mutual association)
3 Produced goods (artefacts created by the interaction of 1 and 2)	3 Organisation of life chances (constitution of chances of self- development and self-expression)

Source: Based on Giddens 1984: 258

Ortmann (1995: 299, footnote 50) criticises Giddens in that the latter confuses the three distinctions on the definition of allocative and authoritative resources, i.e. material/ non-material, technical/ organisational and domination over nature or over persons

as if these distinctions coincide. However this is not at all the case, and for me the distinction allocative/authoritative is only meaningfully attached to the third distinction (Ortmann 1995: 299)[64].

However, in my reading of Giddens these three distinctions between allocative and authoritative resources do not contradict each other and the distinction is meant in a threefold way.

The *social system* in which structure is recursively implicated include the situated activities of human agents which are reproduced across time and space. The structuration of social systems are the conditions governing the continuity or structure and thus the reproduction of social systems. Important for the structuration concept is the duality of structure. The constitution of agents and structures are not two independent sets of phenomena or a dualism

---

64   Translation by the author.

but represent a duality. It is important to note that agency and structure are not opposed to each other.

3.4.4 Giddens' Notion of Institution

Generally speaking, Giddens defines those practices 'which have the greatest time-space extension within such totalities' as *institutions* (Giddens 1984: 17). He warns of substantivist concepts of economic, political and other institutions. Rather, Giddens defines the relationship between the three as follows:

Table 7: Differences between Types of Institutions

S-D-L	Symbolic orders/ modes of discourse
D (authoritative)-S-L	Political institutions
D (allocative)-SL	Economic institutions
L-D-S	Legal institutions

where S = signification, D = domination, L = legitimation

Source: Giddens 1984: 33

As can be seen from table 7, Giddens sees all three institutions determined by signification, domination and legitimation. However, the relevance of each attribute is different for the different types of institutions. Additionally, political institutions are determined by authoritative domination whereas economic institutions are determined by allocative domination.

3.4.5 Giddens' Notion of Organisations

Giddens defines organisations with respect to social movements in the following way:

Organisations and social movements are collectivities in which the reflexive regulation of the conditions of systems reproduction looms large in the continuity of day-to-day practices (Giddens 1984: 200).

The difference between organisations and social movements is that organisations characteristically operate within fixed locales, and positioning within them has the clarity of definition associated with roles (Giddens 1984: 200). Giddens also stated that:

Organisations and social movements are what Touraine calls 'decision-making units', utilising certain typical forms of resources (authoritative and allocative) within discursively mobilised forms of information flow (Giddens 1984: 203).

114

Giddens' definition of organisations is not, by far, as detailed as the definition by neo-institutionalists. As stated before, Giddens sees himself as a
social theorist, he is not seen as an organisational sociologist.

3.4.6 Empirical Foundation of Giddens' Theory of Structuration

Since Giddens sees structuration theory as a social theory, it is important for
the purpose of this study to see how he and others have transposed the theory
into empirical work.

Structuration theory entails two approaches to empirical research. They
consist of an *institutional analysis* and an analysis of *strategic conduct*
(Kaspersen 2000: 48). Institutional analysis is mainly concerned with the
structural properties that are the reproducing features of social systems. The
analysis of strategic conduct focuses on how the agent draws on the structural
properties (i.e. rules and resources) in the constitution of social relations
(Giddens 1984: 288). According to Giddens, each societal analysis should
contain both levels of analysis, that of the structure and that of the actor level,
and each analysis has to be rounded out by a concentration upon the duality
of structure. However, for practical empirical work, there needs to be a point
of departure. Giddens thus suggests a methodological *bracketing* (Giddens
1984: 288) of the two levels of analysis, e.g. that when one carries out an
analysis of strategic conduct, the institutional analysis must be placed in
brackets.

Giddens demonstrates an analysis of strategic conduct using Paul Willis'
'Learning to Labour' (Willis 1977), a study which, according to Giddens
conforms closely to the main empirical implications of structuration theory
(Giddens 1984: 289). Willis' study is a sociological and ethnographic
analysis of a group of working-class boys at the beginning of the 1970s.
Willis followed the group in their final year in a school located in a poor area
of Birmingham, and how they develop a counterculture that prepares them
for their role in the labour market.

The decisive part of Willis' work for Giddens is that he treats the boys as
actors who know a great deal, discursively and tacitly about their school
environment. In addition he shows how the rebellious attitudes of the boys
towards the authority system of the school have some unintended consequences for their future fate. When leaving school, the boys take up
unskilled, unrewarding jobs that again facilitate the reproduction of some
general features of capitalist-industrial labour. Constraint is thus shown to
operate through the active involvement of the agents, not seen as a force of
which they are passive recipients. Willis illustrates how the boys are able to
formulate their view of authority relations in school and how they react to
these.

Their discursive knowledge, however seldom results in any explicit formulation but rather results in a form of irony or sarcasm. On a practical level, the boys know the weakest points of the authority systems and how to get around them. On the level of both discursive and practical consciousness, Giddens stresses that even though one might think that the conformist children would be most knowledgeable about the social system of the school, Willis makes the point that on both levels of consciousness, the more unruly lads are more knowledgeable than the conformists. Giddens explains this as follows:

> Because they actively contest the authority relations of the school, they are adept at picking out where the bases of the teachers' claims to authority lie, and where their weakest points are as the wielders of discipline and as individual personalities. Opposition is expressed as a continuous nagging at what teachers expect and demand, usually stopping short of outright confrontation (Giddens 1984: 291).

Willis thus describes what Giddens calls the *dialectics of control,* which designates the two way character of the distributive aspect of power, i.e. how the less powerful manage resources in such a way as to exert control over the more powerful in established power relations (Giddens 1984: 16; 374). Although the boys are formally subordinated to several authorities, they still possess considerable power. They understand that the school can only discipline and expel so many members of the school and the boys have turned this situation to their own benefit, thereby developing power. Giddens adds that it is necessary to include an institutional analysis, something that Willis does not provide systematically. Giddens thus examines more closely the rules and resources that are connected to a broader understanding of the embeddedness of the boys' activities in time and space.

In the German language context, the economist Günter Ortmann transposed Giddens' structuration theory to organisation theory. In an article written by Günter Ortmann, Jörg Sydow and Arnold Windeler, the authors define an organisation 'as structuration, which has lost its naivety, its down-to-earthness and its innocence – reflexive structuration' (Ortmann et al. 2000: 315)[65]. The authors define reorganisation as intended organisational change in contrast to evolution which is a non-intended organisational change. With regard to reorganisation, change does not necessarily have to be realised as was initially intended. The authors have advanced Lévi Strauss' model of *bricolage,* 'a productive action, which works at an unfinished oeuvre with limited stocks of supply – like a box for handicrafts'[66] (Orthmann et al. 2000: 333). With this background, the *bricolage* can be seen in connection with path dependency (organisational tracks). Path dependency implies that the

---

65 Translation by the author. The German original is: Organisation als 'Strukturation, die ihre Naivität, ihre Naturwüchsigkeit, ihre Unschuld verloren hat – reflexive Strukturation.'
66 Translation by the author.

direction of processes depends both on its progression and on each small step, and is not determined from the outset.

3.4.7 Critique of Structuration Theory

One of the main criticisms of structuration theory is that it is an abstract process theory, which generated few empirical studies. However, this criticism seems unfair since Giddens, as outlined in the introduction of this chapter is not an organisation theorist; his aim is to describe a social theory. A small number of empirical studies using his perspectives have been published however, e.g. Ranson et al. (1980) and Riley (1983).

Furthermore, Giddens appeared reluctant to spell out his ideas as to how structuration theory ought to be applied in the context of empirical research, something for which he has often been criticised e.g. Gregson, 1989. Giddens gives the impression that the theory can and should be used in a rather pragmatic fashion, taking elements from it which are applicable to the research problem, whilst leaving the parts which are not relevant.

There is, of course, no obligation for anyone doing detailed empirical research, in a given localised setting, to take on board an array of abstract notions that would merely clutter up what could otherwise be described with economy and in ordinary language. The concepts of structuration theory, as with any competing theoretical perspective, should for many research purposes be regarded as sensitising devices, nothing more. That is to say, they may be useful for thinking about research problems and the interpretation of research results. But to suppose that being theoretically informed – which is the business of everyone working in the social sciences to be in some degree – means always operating with a welter of abstract concepts is as mischievous a doctrine as one which suggests that we can get along very well without ever using such concepts at all (Giddens 1984: 326-7).

Another feature which makes structuration theory difficult to put into empirical practice is that institutionalisation is a continuous process that can be studied only over time (Barley/ Tolbert 1997: 100) which is a difficult endeavour, given that most research projects have a very limited time schedule.

The most important criticism for the framework of this book has been voiced by Barley and Tolbert. They state that Giddens does not emphasise the degree to which institutions vary in their normative power and their effect on behaviour (Barley/ Tolbert 1997: 96). This appears to be precisely the weakest point of structuration theory, in that, by studying agency and structure, the importance of institutions cannot be sufficiently explained. In order to bring in the institutions, structuration theory and neo-institutionalism will be combined in this study.

3.5 Conclusion: Theoretical Framework for examining Gender Mainstreaming combining sociological Neo-Institutionalism and the Structuration Theory

The research question of this book is to what extent gender mainstreaming can be considered as an innovation and institution. The term 'institution' is defined according to Jepperson's definition (Jepperson 1991) that institutions represent a social order or pattern (i.e. standardised interaction sequences) that has attained a certain state or property. The term 'institutionalisation' will be defined to mean the attainment of such an order or pattern (Jepperson 1991).

My hypothesis is that the European Commission decoupled gender mainstreaming according to the concept of decoupling and confidence by Meyer and Rowan (1991 [1983]). This would mean that to the outside world, the European Commission maintains 'standardised legitimating formal structures' (Meyer and Rowan 1991 [1977]: 58) with regard to their commitment to gender mainstreaming in the Platform for Action in the UN World Conference of Women in Beijing in 1995, while the structures within the Commission are not adapted to gender mainstreaming. This hypothesis will be examined in chapter 7. In order to examine this hypothesis, it is important to look at the interior perspective within the organisation and the exterior perspective, i.e. taking account of the environment of the European Commission. The interior perspective will be examined by means of structuration theory, the exterior perspective will be examined by means of neo-institutionalism. The most relevant categories arising from both theories and indeed by combining both theories will be summarised in this section.

The preceding chapter has shown that sociological neo-institutionalism and structuration theory individually offer various complex explanatory models and patterns. However, for the study of gender mainstreaming, important gaps remain unresolved and the two theories will be combined in this study to supplement each other. It is thus important to examine the similarities and differences between the two theories.

First of all, the fundamental understanding of actors, organisation, institution and institutionalisation for the framework of this book will be elaborated based on neo-institutionalism and structuration theory. This book will examine to what extent the implementation of gender mainstreaming in the European Commission can be regarded as an innovation and/ or institution. The European Commission will be examined as an organisation which consists of different sub-organisations or Directorates General (DGs), of which two DGs will be examined in an examplatory way. The institutionalisation or structuration of gender mainstreaming will be studied with special emphasis on the actors within the organisation. It will be elaborated which rules and resources they possess and which strategic reactions they pursue relating to the implementation of gender mainstreaming.

After having introduced the most central works of neo-institutionalism in the sociological tradition[67] and structuration theory, I shall now summarise the importance of neo-institutionalism and structuration theory for my specific area of research of the previous sections.

3.5.1 Sociological Neo-Institutionalism as an appropriate theoretical Approach for the Study of Gender Mainstreaming

Sociological neo-institutionalism has been chosen as part of the theoretical framework for the study of gender mainstreaming in order to examine gender mainstreaming from an exterior position and to explore homogenisation or isomorphic processes with regard to gender mainstreaming.

The most important theoretical issues which arise from neo-institutionalism for this book are DiMaggio's approach to bring interests and agency back into the research (DiMaggio 1988) as well as Zucker's (1991), Jepperson's (1991) and DiMaggio's (1988) approach to study the process of institutionalisation and to take into account the relativity of institutionalisation processes (Jepperson 1991). Oliver's (1991) typology of strategic responses to institutionalised processes of organisations also plays an important role. These theoretical concepts will briefly be summarised in the following section.

DiMaggio's further development (DiMaggio 1988) of his and Powell's account (DiMaggio and Powell 1991b [1983]) to bring back interests and agency into sociological neo-institutionalism allows us to study the process of the possible institutionalisation of gender mainstreaming. It also enables us to study the power of organised interest lobbying and those lobbying around gender mainstreaming such as the Equal Opportunities Unit within the European Commission, the Committee for Equality between Women and Men of the European Parliament and European women's groups such as the European Women's Lobby.

Zucker's contention that acts are not simply institutionalised or not institutionalised (Zucker 1991: 83-86) is also an important prerequisite for the study of gender mainstreaming as an innovation. This means that institutionalisation cannot be examined in a dichotomised way, rather, that it is important to study the process of institutionalisation. In this context, it is relevant to take into account the relativity of an institution. Applying this contention to our research question, the meaning of gender mainstreaming may be perceived as more or less objective and exterior when Romano Prodi

---

67   The term 'neo-institutionalism in the sociological tradition' refers to the typfication of Hall and Taylor (1996).

heads a meeting with other Commissioners on gender mainstreaming, since Romano Prodi has the role of President of the Commission and thus this act is high on institutionalisation. However, if there is a perception that gender mainstreaming is very much dependent on some individuals in the individual units which do not have the power to modify rules and resources, then these acts count as low on institutionalisation.

However, it is also important to look at the potential contradiction between DiMaggio (1988) and Meyer and Rowan (1991 [1977]): According to Meyer and Rowan (1991 [1977]), an organisation which innovates in important structural ways may have considerable costs in legitimacy, while DiMaggio and Powell (1991b [1983]) on the other hand contend that coercive isomorphism results from both formal and informal pressure exerted on the organisation by other organisations upon which they are dependent and by cultural expectations in the society in which the organisations function. This, however, does not have to be contradictory: To increase legitimacy it is enough that the changes are largely ceremonial (Ritti/ Gouldner 1979; DiMaggio/ Powell (1991b [1983])) and thus there is no need for the substantial changes that, according to Meyer and Rowan (1991 [1977]), might threaten the legitimacy.

Formal pressure could come from the legal acts from the European Commission and the UN (see chapter 6 for a detailed analysis) and the inclusion of the concept of gender mainstreaming in the Treaty of Amsterdam. Informal pressure could include the fact that the European Commission is implementing gender mainstreaming because a lot of the other international organisations such as the United Nations and the World Bank are implementing it.[68]

Zucker (1987: 444) on the contrary, remarks that coercion has the effect of deinstitutionalising, since the coerced change is not taken for granted any longer. The sanctioning which is connected with coercion makes people aware that it would be possible to do things differently. Thus with regard to gender mainstreaming, there has to be an examination of the extent to which sanctions exist either due to formal or informal pressure.

Meyer and Rowan (1991 [1977]) see coerced isomorphism as the decisive starting point for the distribution of institutionalised rules. Hennersdorf (1998: 369, quoted in Krell 2001), in a comparative study, confirms this by concluding that success with regard to equal opportunities is largest in countries with special equal opportunities laws[69].

---

68 For a detailed study of the implementation of gender mainstreaming in the UNDP, the World Bank and the ILO see Razavi and Miller 1994.

69 The findings of this study are in contradiction to the Norwegian example, which has the fourth highest percentage of women's representation in the world. In the 4 September 2001 election for the *Stortinget,* women won 60 out of the total 165 seats which equals 36.4%. This is the case even though no special equal opportunities legislation for women MPs are in place (Inter-Parliamentary Union: 2003).

Applying DiMaggio's and Powell's (1991b [1983]) concept of mimetic isomorphism to the implementation of gender mainstreaming in the European Commission, I hypothesise that the environment of the Commission creates uncertainty for the Commission. The European Commission therefore copies gender mainstreaming from the UN level in order to increase its legitimacy. Applying the concept of normative isomorphism to gender mainstreaming, I hypothesise that the development of gender mainstreaming is closely tied to networks and professional organisations such as the gender mainstreaming advocacy-network. Both hypothesis will be examined further in the chapters 6 and 7.

Decoupling, as defined by Meyer and Rowan (1991 [1977]: 57), means that the actual activities are decoupled from their structure. In order to increase legitimacy, for example, enterprises may institutionalise equal opportunities as in the case of the creation of equal opportunities advisors. It would thus be important with regard to gender mainstreaming to examine whether this is happening and whether the people who are in the responsible positions in the Commission believe that the implementation of gender mainstreaming enhances the effectiveness and efficiency of the Commission.

Oliver (1991) develops different strategic responses to institutionalised processes organisations may enact which range from 'acquiescence' as the most passive strategy to 'manipulation' as the most active strategy. With regard to gender mainstreaming in the Commission it is important to examine how the Commission and the actors within the European Commission react to the implementation of gender mainstreaming and which strategies they pursue.

3.5.2 Structuration Theory as an appropriate theoretical Approach for the Study of Gender Mainstreaming Wolffensperger's Concept of engendered Structure

Structuration theory will be used in this book in order to examine the interior view within organisations. It will thus be examined in chapter 7 to what extent the outside presentation of the European Commission on gender mainstreaming is in line with changes with regard to gender mainstreaming within the European Commission. Resulting from this, it needs to be examined to what extent the requirements resulting from the 1996 Communication (European Commission 1996) are implemented in the European Commission. It also needs to be examined to what extent the gender mainstreaming aims are implemented within the Commission and to what extent they have become part of the normal routines of the actors within the Commission. According to structuration theory, structures consist of rules and resources, the modified rules and resources from the gender mainstreaming requirement thus need to be included in the everyday actions and routines of actors within the European Commission.

Wolffensperger stresses the potential of Giddens' work to overcome some of the dualisms in women's studies. Both voluntaristic theories, in which power and the constraining impact of structures of male domination are ignored, and also deterministic approaches, which neglect women's knowledgeability about their situation and their capacity to break rules and routines ought to be rectified and developed further, using Giddens model of structuration. In this manner, gender could be analysed in concrete situations and as domination by using the same conceptual framework. System constraints and agents' capabilities are seen as inseparably linked, and thus the pitfalls of determinism and voluntarism can be avoided (Wolffensperger 1991: 92).

Wolffensperger develops a model of engendered structure based on structuration theory, which will be described in more detail. Gender is at the heart of the model. The concept refers to domination, signification and legitimation as gender organising principles, as 'absences' structuring gender relations; and also to social practices in which these principles appear as *'présences'*, as rules and resources employed by agents. If a certain social system has a gendered character then it is important to analyse those properties of the gendered system properties that are organising social practices according to these properties of the gendered rules and resources. Gendered rules and resources would be conceived as media of twofold reproduction. Wolffensperger describes this as follows:

When employed in interaction, gender and social system are reproduced together; organised social differences between women and men are an integral part of social practices. It is only at the moment in which actors draw on gendered system properties that they reproduce the system involved as well as gender or gender relations. Thus, at the level of institutional analysis, gender rules and resources must be studied not only as media of system reproduction, but as media of gender reproduction as well (Wolffensperger 1991: 93).

Giddens' concept of structuration and Wolffensperger's adaptation can be summarised in the following graphical ways:

Figure 5 summarises the categories explained earlier in the chapter. Structure influences agency, which is the implementation of rules and resources. Resources are the media whereby transformative capacity is employed. Agency in turn reproduces face to face and time-space interaction, which produces practices and routines, i.e. institutions. The institutions reproduce structure, which make the structuration process 'complete'.

122

Figure 5: The Theory of Structuration according to Giddens (1984)

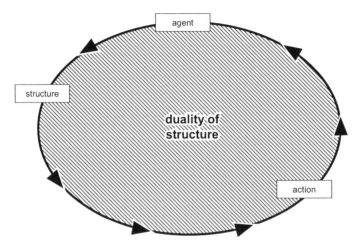

The structure is the medium and the outcome of the agent's action.

Source: Based on Kasperson 2000: 33

Figure 6: Wolffensperger's Adaptation of Giddens

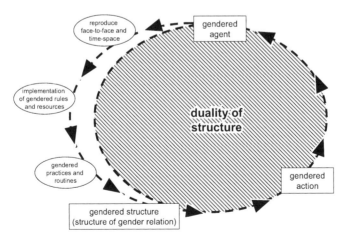

Source: Own Illustration

123

In Wolffensperger's application of Giddens' model, gender is included as a central category. As a result, the structure is *gendered* from the outset and it influences agency as to the implementation of *gendered rules* and resources. These reproduce *gendered practices* and routines which in turn reproduce the *gendered structure*.

3.5.3 Combining sociological Neo-Institutionalism and Structuration Theory

After having summarised the most central accounts of sociological neo-institutionalism and structuration theory for the course of this book, I shall now elaborate on how these two theories can be combined in a meaningful way.

Both structuration theory and institutionalism share the premise that action is largely organised by institutions. Both contend that institutions are created, maintained and changed through action.

Structuration theory, however, focuses on the dynamics by which institutions are reproduced and altered, a question that has rarely been studied by institutionalists, even though DiMaggio does attempt to introduce the process perspective into sociological neo-institutionalism. Unfortunately, structuration theory in contrast to neo-institutionalism, provides little guidance on empirical ways to study the processes by which everyday action revises or reproduces an institution. Indeed, within structuration theory it is possible to study by means of the concept of rules and resources why institutions are revised and reproduced, however, this concept does not explain why some particular institutions become institutions while others don't. Thus the combination between neo-institutionalism and structuration theory promises to be very fruitful for my research design.

Neo-institutionalists are interested in the study of homogenisation or isomorphism. With few exceptions (Zucker 1988 [1977], Jepperson 1991), neo-institutionalist scholars rarely study institutionalisation directly and only briefly question how particular organisational structures emerge, or why their diffusion is sometimes limited. To answer such questions, it is important to consider in structuration theory how actions affect the structuration process. Even though important parts of institutionalist theory are based on the claim that organisations are socially constructed (see for example Meyer/ Rowan 1991 [1977]), institutionalist scholars have not directly investigated the processes by which structures emerge from, or influence action (Barley/ Tolbert 1997: 96-113). In part, the neo-institutionalist model of isomorphism (DiMaggio/ Powell 1991a and 1991b [1983]) explains why some patterns are harmonised. It is not possible, however, to explain why these particular patterns are harmonised and not others.

Partly Meyer and Rowan's concept of decoupling and confidence provides guidance on this: They contend that organisations cannot coordinate their activities because of the inconsistencies through formal structure. A close connection of formal structures and activities would result in the fact that inefficiencies and inconsistencies become known in public. Therefore, the structural elements amongst themselves are decoupled, as well as from the activities of the organisation (Meyer/ Rowan 1991 [1977]).

Based on DiMaggio's differentiation of neo-institutionalism (DiMaggio 1988), institutionalisation will be studied as a process rather than an outcome. Examining the institutionalisation of gender mainstreaming as a process allows us to bring agency and interest into the research. This renders possible to capture the power structures reflected within the Commission and the actors who mobilise around gender mainstreaming.

The Commissioners' Group on Gender Equality acts as institutional entrepreneurs for gender mainstreaming. Institutional entrepreneurs are those actors who have sufficient resources to implement a new policy. The support of subsidiary actors is still limited: The Inter-Service Mainstreaming Group and Equal Opportunities Units can be considered as subsidiary actors, but their resources remain limited. Overall, not many actors could be mobilised yet for the gender mainstreaming project outside of those who are committed to gender mainstreaming qua function.

Below I operationalise the term *gender mainstreaming advocacy-network* in the context of the European Commission as the Commissioners' Group on Gender Equality, the Equal Opportunities Units and the Inter-Service Mainstreaming Group and the gender mainstreaming co-ordinators, i.e. all those who are professionally partly responsible for gender mainstreaming. According to Jepperson (1991), whether a practice is an institution, is relative to particular contexts. Therefore I argue that within the gender mainstreaming advocacy-network, gender mainstreaming has a high degree of institutionalisation, while in the Commission as a whole, this is not the case.

In order to learn more about these processes and in particular how action affects institutions, it is important to take Giddens' concept of structuration into account. In addition to offering more promising insights on the emergence of particular organisational structures, structuration theory also enables us to examine internal power dynamics further.

According to Barley and Tolbert (1997), there are four similarities between sociological neo-institutionalism and structuration theory. The first and most important assumption shared by both theories is that institutions and actions are inextricably linked, a process referred to by Giddens as structuration process. Secondly, both schools contend that institutionalisation, or as Giddens would say, structuration, is best understood as an ongoing dynamic process. Thirdly, variations are not simply treated as adaptations of technical and environmental changes. Lastly, both theories acknowledge that cultural constraints do not completely determine human action. Barley and Tolbert explain this further:

[...] institutions set bounds on rationality by restricting the opportunities and alternatives we perceive and, thereby, increase the probability of certain types of behaviour. However, just as perfect rationality is rare, so too is completely bounded rationality. Through choice and action, individuals and organisations can deliberately modify, and even eliminate, institutions[70] (Barley/ Tolbert 1997: 94).

As illustrated in figure 7, I shall combine sociological neo-institutionalism and structuration theory by using elements of structuration theory but at the same time taking into consideration neo-institutionalist theory in order to examine how institutions or practices and routines were created in the first place. The exact categories used to operationalise sociological neo-institutionalism and structuration theory for the study of gender mainstreaming and innovation will be explained in the next chapters. Figure 7 illustrates that the three different types of isomorphisms, i.e. coercive isomorphism, mimetic isomorphism and normative isomorphism arise from the environment of the organisation and society at large. The three isomorphisms influence the structuration and insitutionalisation processes.

---

70 The acquisition of suffrage by women in the United States, the dismantling of Apartheid in South Africa and the collapse of the Soviet Union are cited as examples of eliminations of institutions (Barley/Tolbert 1997: 94).

126

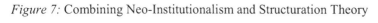

Figure 7: Combining Neo-Institutionalism and Structuration Theory

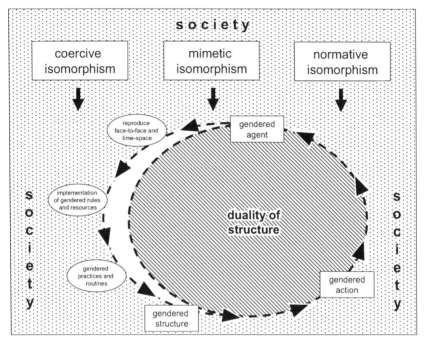

Source: Own Illustration

127

4 Organisational Innovation

4.1 Introduction

In everyday usage, the term innovation is used to describe artefacts, for example, a new technology or a new model of a car or a new process. Innovations can take different forms. Zaltman et al. regard innovation as 'any idea, practise, or material artefact' (Zaltman et al. 1973: 10).

In this study, in line with our combining structuration theory with neo-institutionalist theory, an interactive process perspective will be adopted to study innovation. Interactive process perspective studies the process of an innovation, i.e. taking individuals and actions into account and thereby showing important similarities to the structuration theory developed by Giddens, though it has been developed in parallel to structuration theory by Downs and Mohr (1976). In Mohr's view, the aim of process research is to explain 'the paring or other rearrangement of mutually autonomous objects [...] whose individual courses are determined independently of one another by forces external to the core of the theory' (Mohr 1982: 45-6, quoted in Slappendel 1996: 118). Slappendel sees three important aspects in empirical studies of the interactive process perspective which correspond to that in structuration theory in general: Firstly, that there is a widespread rejection of the rational economic model of decision-making and that instead, the non-rational aspects of organisational behaviour and the political context are perceived to be important. Secondly, the scholars will try to understand the dynamic nature of the innovation process and the changes that occur to the innovation during the process, i.e. that the innovation is not static but that it is transformed by it. Thirdly, the interactive process perspectives has methodological consequences in that the use of longitudinal case studies is dominant as well as a focus on induction.

4.2 Hauschild's Definition of Innovations

In order to examine an innovation within the organisation, it is important to examine how an innovation is perceived within the organisation, i.e. adopting the inward perspective. Hauschildt developed four different dimensions with regard to innovation, i.e. the content dimension, subjective dimension, process dimension and normative dimension that will be described in turn.

I) The content dimension asks what is new and differentiates between four different types of innovation. Firstly, the resource-induced innovation means that the needs have changed and that new resources are offered in order to fulfil the needs.

Rickards describes this process as follows:

Innovation is a process whereby new ideas are put into practice [...] Innovation as a creative, or open-systems process. To be more specific it is the process of matching the problems (needs) of systems with solutions which are new and relevant to those needs, and which can be supplied by the innovating organisation [...] (Rickards 1985: 28).

Secondly, the needs induced innovation means that new needs are developed, which are satisfied with unchanged means. Thirdly, a radical innovation means that new needs and new resources are offered to satisfy these purposes. Finally, incremental innovation means that needs and resources are unchanged. The innovative element consists either in the novel manner of the combination or in an essentially improved needs-resource relation. In Moore and Tushman's words:

Most generally, innovation can be seen as the synthesis of a market need with the means to achieve and produce a product to meet that need. Thus innovation requires coordination of research and development, marketing and production (Moore/Tushman 1982: 132).

II) The *subjective dimension* of the innovation asks, for whom the innovation is new. Hauschildt differentiates between five different perspectives: First, the individualistic perspective means that innovation refers to any individual which uses a new product or process in his or her work environment. Rogers describes this as follows:

An innovation is an idea, practice or object that is perceived as new by an individual or other unit of adoption. It matters little, so far as human behaviour is concerned, whether or not an idea is 'objectively' new as measured by the lapse of time since its first use or discovering. The perceived units of the idea for the individual determine his or her reaction to it. If the idea seems new to the individual, it is an innovation (Rogers 1962: 11).

Secondly, the micro economic perspective takes into consideration whether an idea is new to a particular firm. Witte describes this as follows:

A firm can see an innovation when it first uses a technical innovation, independent of whether other firms have used the innovation before them or not (Witte 1973: 3).

Thirdly, the sectoral economic approach means that the project or the process is introduced for the first time within a certain sector or a comparable group of firms.

Fourthly, the macro-economic perspective means that the innovation refers to the national area. This is supported by the facts that patents are traditionally granted on the national level, or, on the European level, since more recently[71]. Finally, the most far-reaching idea of innovation refers to the totality of humankind, i.e. that the innovation has not existed anywhere else before.

III) The processual dimension of innovation examines the boundaries of an innovation, i.e. where it starts and where it ends. According to Hauschildt, an innovation is more than simply an invention. The process can be differentiated into the following phases: idea (vague idea, that an innovation is possible within an object area), observation and discovery of a hitherto unknown substance, research (theoretical foundation and empirical verification of the discovery and observation), development (implementation of the observations in test plants), invention (i.e. deciding for a specific option), introduction of a new product and lastly, the continuous utilisation of the new product in series production.

IV) The normative dimension asks whether new is equal to successful. Some scholars suggest using the term innovation only for those products, which enable an improvement of a status quo. This refers to the target system of the user. The assumption of this system is that the user has a target system, that s/he can articulate her/his aims and that these targets can be understood by an outsider. The problem with this approach is that the interests of observers can vary considerably, i.e. nuclear energy, car and anti-baby pill can be assessed very differently by different actors with view to their normative function.

4.3 Applying the Concept of Innovation to Gender Mainstreaming

In this book, innovation will be defined along the four dimensions of Hauschildt because they contain a process dimension and they can best be adapted to the research question. However, Hauschildt's distinction between incremental and radical innovations, i.e. differentiating between these two kinds of innovations with regard to the combination between needs and resources will not be used as such. Rather, the distinction between the two concepts will be represented more as a continuum and not as a gulf between two polar opposites. Radical innovations will be defined to refer to substantial changes, and incremental innovation to less substantial, often gradual

---

71 The European Patents Office which is based in Munich, Germany was founded in 1973 and has 27 Member States (Austria, Greece, Belgium, Ireland, Switzerland, Italy, Cyprus, Liechtenstein, Germany, Luxembourg, Denmark, Monaco, Spain, Netherlands, Finland, Portugal, France, Sweden, United Kingdom, Turkey, Bulgaria, Romania, Slovenia, Estonia, Slovak Republic, Czech Republic and Hungary).

changes. While radical innovation represents an idea that is new, incremental innovation is less obvious. Incremental innovation is more closely related to the existing capabilities of the firm and/ or the existing knowledge and demand structures in the environment and might thus not be apparent on first sight without extensive knowledge on the specific organisation. Radical innovations imply a break, which tend to make the existing routines obsolete. As a result, the degree of technical and commercial uncertainty, the obstacles to organisational learning, and the commitment of organisational resources are far larger in the case of radical innovation than in the case of incremental innovation (Gjerding 1998: 6).

4.4 Conclusion

As we have seen in chapter 2, different scholars assess the type of innovation very differently. Verloo (1999) defines policy innovation as a process of creating new policy frames. She sees gender mainstreaming due to the framing of the Council of Europe as a fundamental innovation, which would involve high uncertainty for the organisation implementing it. Her definition of innovation is however only based on the policy aspect of an innovation and will not be further pursued here. Wetterer (2002) sees gender mainstreaming rather as a differentiation of existing equal opportunities policies.

In this book, gender mainstreaming will be examined with regard to Hauschildt's definition of innovations (Hauschildt 1993). The second dimension of Hauschildt's definition is the subjective dimension, that is, the issue of to whom the innovation is new. The first two of the five perspectives within this dimension will deserve special attention: from the individualistic perspective, an actor may introduce a new product, (in our context, a new policy) in his/her work environment; and from the micro-economic perspective, a new product (in our perspective, a new policy) is introduced within a particular firm (in our case, the particular organisation). For the introduction of gender mainstreaming, the European Commission adopted a top-down perspective with regard to gender mainstreaming. It is thus particularly important to take the individualistic perspective into account, i.e. whether individual actors are familiar with gender mainstreaming, whether they regard it as something new and whether they intend to actively implement it. In transferring the other aspects of Hauschildt's subjective dimension to the case of the Commission, the micro-economic aspect will be interpreted to mean whether gender mainstreaming is new to two particular Directorate Generals, i.e. DG Employment and Social Affairs and DG Administration and Personnel. The third and fourth perspectives, i.e. the sectoral economic aspect and the macro-economic perspective will correspond to international organisations. Hence, it will be examined whether gender mainstreaming plays an important role in international organisations. The fifth aspect, namely, whether the innovation is new to humankind cannot be verified with regard to gender mainstreaming since it has been shown in chapter 2 that gender mainstreaming has been transferred from the UN to the European Union.

Hauschildt's processual dimension of innovation with regard to the boundaries of an innovation is particularly important with regard to the distinction between gender mainstreaming and equal treatment and equal opportunities policies. As was shown in the section on the theoretical foundations of gender mainstreaming, it is strongly linked to equal opportunities policies, in fact, equal opportunities are defined to be a part of gender mainstreaming.

Lastly, the normative dimension of Hauschildt, that is, whether gender mainstreaming is at the same time successful as well as being new (i.e. being an innovation) can only be analysed after having examined the implementation of gender mainstreaming within the Commission. In all cases, the 'interactive process perspective' (Slappendel 1996: 118) will be used. This implies taking structures and actions into account and, in particular, examining the dynamic nature of the innovation process, i.e. that gender mainstreaming is continually transformed by the process of implementation.

5   Role and Function of the European Commission

Top officials [of the European Commission], then, are by no means above or beyond the fray of EU politics. Given the powers and responsibility they have, they are drawn into debates on the chief issues facing the Euro-polity (Hooghe 2001:8).

5.1   Introduction

The European Commission is the executive and guardian of the treaties of the European Union. A major part of its power derives from its contractually protected right of initiative on European legislation. The Commission holds the monopoly for proposing new legislation in the first pillar of the European Union, the Community dimension, comprising the arrangements set out in the EC, ECSC and Euratom Treaties, i.e. Union citizenship, Community policies, Economic and Monetary Union. Within the common policy areas of the EU, the Commission has the right to submit legislative initiatives to the Council of Ministers for discharge. At the same time the Commission acts as an implementing organ of the EU, and in the long run supervises the implementation of all measures decided by the Council in the Member States. The Commission has no analogue in national governmental systems (Dinan 1999: 205).

The following chapter attempts a summary of the current European political science literature on the European Commission, special attention is put on the description of the structure of the Commission, its relation to social society and questions about the institutional stability and change. The rules and resources which are important for the implementation of gender mainstreaming will be analysed in chapter 7.

5.2   The Role and Function of the European Commission

This subchapter outlines the early development and influences on the administration of the European Commission. As outlined by Conrad (Conrad 1992: 59), there is an important difference between a national and international administration. National administrations have grown over a long period of time whereas international administrations were set up to serve a certain purpose, often under enormous time pressure.

5.2.1   The Beginnings of the European Commission

The creation of the European Coal and Steel Community (ECSC)[72] was the foundation for the later creation of the European Economic Community and the Euratom Treaty. The High Authority, which was the administration of the ECSC and the predecessor of the European Commission was installed in office on 10 August 1952 and Jean Monnet became its first president. He thus became responsible for the administration and overview of the implementation of the decisions of the High Authority. The Treaty establishing the European Coal and Steel Community had provided for a Committee of the presidents of the four institutions, i.e. the High Authority, the Court of Justice, the Council of Ministers and the Parliamentary Assembly, to decide on the numbers of officials and their terms and conditions.

One of the first decisions of the Committee was to set up an inter-institutional committee to draw up staff regulations (*status du personnel*). Monnet was not very keen on the establishment of staff regulations, for he was apprehensive about the emergence of administrative rigidities (Conrad 1992: 65). From 1 July 1953 a provisional staff regulation applied to the staff of the Court and the Assembly which were however only applied to staff contracts that came up for renewal. Edmund Wellenstein, at that time a member of the Secretariat-General of the High Authority, describes the situation back then as 'creative chaos'. The administration resembled 'a huge pancake', presided over by the High Authority (Mazey 1992: 39)[73].

Monnet's successor, René Mayer from France promoted the drafting of the staff regulations and they were adopted in 1956. The creation of European Economic Community in 1958, which consisted in the merging of Euratom and the ECSC under one organisation, then followed. The newly founded European Commission which combined the administrations of the ECSC, Euratom and the EEC was thus a much more complex organisation than the ECSC had been in the early days. The scope of the EEC was much wider. Nine Directorates General were created (External Relations, Economic and Financial Affairs, Internal Market, Competition, Social Affairs, Agriculture, Transport, Overseas Countries and Territories, and Administration and Personnel), which were subdivided into 32 directorates. A secretariat general was created as a co-ordinating service, while the legal service, the statistical office and the press and information service were under the control of a group of Commissioners until the merger of the three Communities (i.e. ECSC, Euratom and EEC). The greater scope of the EEC also explains the creation of the Commissioner's cabinets as key actors. Of the six original member countries of the EC (France, Belgium, Netherlands, Luxembourg,

---

72   The ECSC was created with a Treaty signed on 18 April 1951 in Paris and entered into force on 23 July 1952.
73   M. Edmund's Wellenstein personal account to Sonia Mazey.

Germany and Italy), ministerial cabinets were the most developed in France, even though a system of personal advisers giving political support to Ministers was common in most of the other Member States (Ritchie 1992: 96). The basic organisational structure of the Commission as it was constructed in 1958 has remained the same until the present day.

The successor of Mayer as President of the EEC Commission was Walter Hallstein. Hallstein brought some hierarchical traditions of the German foreign office (*Auswärtiges Amt*) to the EEC[74]: he wanted the senior officials of the administration of the EEC to be on a par with the top ranks of the national administrations (Noël 1992: 150-1).

5.2.2   The Influence of National Administrative Cultures

Scholars (e.g. Spence 1997: 65; Stevens/ Stevens 2001: 30) agree that the administration of the Commission has been greatly influenced by the French administrative system. As Stevens points out however, we can also find important influences from other national administrations: for example, the procedure, under which a reserve list is used in recruitment, shows Belgian influence, while the right of the administration not to recruit in the exact order of the competition shortlists comes from the Italian tradition (Stevens/ Stevens 2001: 32). Cassese identifies three models which have mainly influenced the administration: the German model which is 'dominated by legalism, rigidity and administrative planning', the French which is symbollised by 'the rigidity of the structures and the flexibility of the bureaucracy, and the English model 'by the flexibility of both' (Cassese 1987:12-13).

5.2.3 Current Structure of the European Commission

Since the reorganisation of the Commission in September 1999 from the newly elected President Romano Prodi, the Commission is structured into 35 DGs (see table 8), which are headed by 20 Commissioners. The last internal review of the Commission's organisation and operation (European Commission 1999a) which is based on a census of staff in April 1998 concluded that 31 010 people were working for the Commission at that time. From this figure, 81.1% of intramural staff are officials from which approximately 90% are permanent and 10% temporary. From the temporary staff, 4.6% are auxiliary staff, 2.7% are casual staff and 3.4% are Detached National Experts (DNEs) (European Commission 1999a).

---

74   Hallstein himself established different hierarchies in the *Auswärtiges Amt* and subsequently exported them to Brussels. In the *Auswärtiges Amt* he served as a secretary of state which is the equivalent of a British junior Minister.

Table 8: The Directorates General and Services of the European Commission

POLICIES	EXTERNAL RELATIONS
– Agriculture	– Development
– Competition	– Enlargement
– Economic and Financial Affairs	– EuropeAid - Co-operation Office
– Education and Culture	– External Relations
– Employment and Social Affairs	– Humanitarian Aid Office - ECHO
– Energy and Transport	– Trade
– Enterprise	
– Environment	**GENERAL SERVICES**
– Fisheries	– European Anti-Fraud Office
– Health and Consumer Protection	– Eurostat
– Information Society	– Press and Communication
– Internal Market	– Publications Office
– Joint Research Centre	– Secretariat General
– Justice and Home Affairs	
– Regional Policy	**INTERNAL SERVICES**
– Research	– Budget
– Taxation and Customs Union	– Group of Policy Advisers
	– Internal Audit Service
	– Joint Interpreting and Conference Service
	– Legal Service
	– Personnel and Administration
	– Translation Service

Source: European Commission 2003j

In this book only permanent officials will be included in the quantitative illustration in chapter 7, as data is only published on the permanent officials. The temporary staff and auxiliary staff are often recruited through the DGs and not through DG Personnel and Administration which explains partly why no comprehensive data exists. The DNEs continue receiving pay from their home administration, NGO or company and all receive the same daily allowance from the Commission and again this might be the reason that the Commission might not have aggregated data on this group.

5.3 Political Cultures and political Views within the European Commission

Different scholars (e.g. Spence 1997: 65; Stevens/ Stevens 2001: 30) agree that the administration of the Commission has been greatly influenced by the French administrative system. As Stevens and Stevens points out however, we can also find important influences from other national administrations: for example, the procedure, under which a reserve list is used in recruitment, shows Belgian influence, while the right of the administration not to recruit in the exact order of the competition shortlists comes from the Italian tradition (Stevens/ Stevens 2001: 32). Cassese identifies three models which have mainly influenced the administration: the German model which is 'dominated by legalism, rigidity and administrative planning', the French which is symbolised by 'the rigidity of the structures and the flexibility of the bureaucracy, and the English model 'by the flexibility of both' (Cassese 1987:12-13).

The Commission is no longer described as a coherent unit in new institutionalist approaches, but rather understood as a 'multi-organisation' contrary to models of the classical public law theory. In particular the different organisational and administrative cultures of the Directorates-General are stressed. Michelle Cini (1996) and Lisbeth Hooghe (1998a; 1998b; 2001) examine the administrative cultures and the individual attitudes of top civil servants within the European Commission respectively. Both studies are important to understand how the Commission functions.

Cini describes the prevalence of different administrative cultures and the diversity within the Commission and comes to the conclusion that one cannot speak of a single or supranational Commission. According to Cini, describing the Commission as a supranational body would not give enough attention to the Intergouvernementalism, which takes place directly below the Commissioners in the cabinet. The efficiency of the Commission is impaired by different factors: lack of co-ordination, comparatively high number of temporary staff, unreliable communication and inadequate use of resources (Cini 1996).

Lisbeth Hooghe (1998a and 1998b, 2001) examines possible origins for attitudes of top civil servants of the Commission on the basis of 140 interviews and 106 email questionnaires. Hooghe thereby pursues two hypotheses. According to the first, the Commission employees are influenced by three different, but complementary experiences: previous experiences in foreign countries, socialisation at the job and learning in the political system in the country of origin. According to Hooghe's second hypothesis, national governments are in a position to affect whether supranational or intergovernmental civil servants occupy top positions.

The European Commission as an active Actor with regard to Equal Opportunities and Gender Mainstreaming

The European Commission is an active actor with regards to women's policies in the European Union. This might be surprising at first sight, not the least due to the low percentage of women amongst the Commissioners and in the administration of the Commission. On closer analysis, previous research has identified a variety of strategic reasons for the different activities of the Commission with regard to women's policies which will be illustrated in the following section.

Firstly, the Commission used women's policies to extend its competencies. Since the European Trade Unions and Employees Associations were not concerned with this topic in the 1970s, this area could be framed without the influence of the social partners (Hoskyns 1996: 197). Due to this, the Commission was not yet under the pressure from trade unions and employees associations and therefore relatively open for suggestions from women's groups (Mazey 1998: 138).

Secondly, since the 1970s, the Commission and the Council of Ministers have been trying to strengthen the legitimacy of the EU and to extend the social dimension of the EU. After the Paris summit in 1972, the Commission drafted an Action Programme which saw as a priority to act towards equal opportunities of women and men with regard to employment, education, promotion, working conditions and wage equality (Mazey 1998: 138). Since the Maastricht Treaty, which was signed in 1992 and came into effect in 1993, it is the declared aim of the EU to achieve a high identification of the citizens with the EU. It was intended that this would be achieved through an intensification within the social area. In 1994, it became obvious that there was a gender gap in the support for the Maastricht Treaty. In the campaigns prior to the referenda on the acceptance of the Maastricht Treaty, women's groups in Sweden, Finland and Austria campaigned against the accession of their countries to the EU, since they were afraid of a possible deterioration of the situation for women in their countries. In the aftermath of the first Danish referendum in 1992 it turned out that far more women than men had voted against the Maastricht Treaty (Liebert 1999: 206)[75]. The predominately negative voting behaviour of women, could be a reason for the increased involvement of the Commission in women's policies, i.e. that it wants to counteract the protest of women and that it wants to gain a higher legitimacy in the eyes of women.

Thirdly, since the Commission extended its competencies with women's policies, it had a high interest in strengthening civil society actors and particularly those, which are involved on a transnational level, for example, the EWL. With the referral to such transnational actors the Commission tries to strengthen and legitimate its position as a supranational organisation with regard to the Council of Ministers, which represents the interests of the

---

75   In the first Danish referendum in 1992, 40% of the voters voted 'yes', 42% voted 'no' and 18% abstained from voting. Only 35% of women voted 'yes' (men: 47%), and 44% voted 'no' (men 38%) and 21% of women abstained from voting (men: 15%) (Dahlerup 1996. Quoted in: Liebert 1999: 206).

Member States (Cram 1993: 140). Sonia Mazey describes this strategy as follows:

Thus, since its inception, the European Commission has actively cultivated close relations with the relevant policy community in an attempt to create ,constituency' support for EC intervention in a particular policy sector. This is a familiar pattern of EC policy development we and others have observed in a number of policy sectors (Mazey 1998: 138).

The finding that the Commission aims to create 'constituency' support for EC intervention was also prominently analysed by Majone (1996). He argues that the Commission is best understood as an institution, which wants to increase its influence within the EU system. Since the Commission's budget is relatively small, it concentrates on regulative policy. Contrary to distributive or redistributive legislation, which require tax increases, the regulative policy is more or less neutral for the adjusting authority. Majone explains this with the fact that

[...] the public budget is a soft constraint on regulators because the real costs of regulatory programme are borne not by the agencies but by the individuals, firms or governments who have to comply with the regulations (Majone 1996: 64).

Majone further develops the rational Choice Model of Niskanen (1971). According to Niskanen's theory, the budget size is positively dependent on the goals of administration employees like 'incomes, the conditions to the office, public reputation, power, patronage and the outputs of the office' (Niskanen 1971: 64). This model cannot be transferred in this form to the Commission, since the budget was hardly increased. Majone hypothesises that 'the utility function of the Commission is positively related to the *scope* of its competencies rather than to the *scale* of the services provided or to the size of the budget' (Majone 1996: 65). Or in other words '[...] the Commission prefers task expansion to budgetary growth' (Majone 1996: 65).

Majone illustrates his hypothesis with the expansion of the Commission competencies since the middle of the 1980s, while the budget of the Commission rose between 1985 and 1994 only from 4.35% to 4.8%. Majone explains these developments which are surprising from the view point of rational choice model with the transformation of the Commission as a regulative authority.

Laura Cram (1993) examines the regulative competencies of the Commission in the area of social policy based on Majone's model. The Commission is described as a purposeful opportunist, i.e. as an organisation which is conscious about its aims and tasks but which is rather flexible in how it achieves them. Due to this, the Commission managed to become an important actor even in areas like social policy, in which it is constitutionally weak.

Wendon (1998) transfers *the image-venue* concept of Baumgartner (1991) to the EU. Baumgartner had originally developed it for the American federal system, in order to explain political stability and changes in the policy (Baumgartner 1991: 1045, quoted in Wendon 1998: 340). Baumgartner assumes that political actors – in particular, lobby groups – can act strategically by using a binary strategy:

On the one hand, they try to control the prevailing image of the policy problem through the use of rhetoric, symbols, and policy analysis. On the other hand, they try to alter the roster of participants who are involved in the issue by seeking out the most favourable venue for the consideration of their issues. In this process, both the institutional structures within which policies are made and the individual strategies of policy entrepreneurs play important roles (Baumgartner 1991: 1045, quoted in Wendon 1991: 340). The Commission has successfully extended the number of institutional venues in which social policy and equal opportunities policies can be treated. These areas are not totally separated but rather semi-autonomous. In the past, the Commission has used the rulings of the ECJ, in particular, in the area of equal opportunities for the expansion of its competencies. This strategy holds risks however, since the judgements of the ECJ are not predictable before-hand. The other more promising strategy was developed by Delors and existed in the systematic expansion of the social dialogue. According to Wendon, the social dialogue treated as the exclusive means, could lead to policy venue dangers: if social policy is solely formulated via collective bargaining through social dialogue (i.e. through trade unions), it is only partially democratically legitimised, for the number of union members from the staff of the European institutions has strongly decreased since the founding years of the European institutions (Wendon 1998).

5.4   The Social Embeddedness of the European Commission

Sociological neo-institutionalism stresses the importance of the social embeddedness of an organisation, i.e. which interrelations and dependencies there are between the organisation and society at large. Organisations are seen as being embedded in local communities, to which they are tied by the multiple loyalties of personnel, and by inter-organisational treaties elaborated in face-to-face interaction (DiMaggio/ Powell 1991a: 12).

The social embeddedness of the Commission became particularly obvious through the public debate on European Community Humanitarian Assistance Office (ECHO) which lasted from Mai 1998 until the resignation of the Commission in March 1999. The affair had fundamental consequences for the impact and the reputation of the Commission. In the course of the matter, 2.4 million Euro were purposely alienated by means of sham contracts in favour of 27 external employees over a Luxembourg firm for the payment of personnel. Originally the money was intended for remedial measures (Rometsch 1999). Hummer and Obwexer (1999) examine the legal responsibility of the European Commission and its members for possible failure. The Commission is collectively and politically responsible in accordance with their rules of procedure as a collegial body regarding their office guidance, while Commissioners draw individually and legally responsibility. The Commission can be called to account for such actions and/or omissions, which come from the 'preceding Commission,' the so-called 'inherited liabilities'.

5.5 Institutional Stability and Change

The aim of this section is to illustrate the current aspirations to introduce an administrative reform within the European Commission.

Briefly after the assumption of the Commission by Prodi, he made all Commissioners sign a code of conduct for the Commissioners, with strict rules on defining interests and on the external activities for Commissioners. Prodi also introduced Commission working groups, in order to ensure a better co-ordination of the activities within the Commission. In his first speech before the EP, Prodi explained that he would require the resignation of individual Commissioners in the case of doubt even if the treaties would not formally provide for this. All Commissioners have accepted their office under this condition (Craig 2000).

For further reform projects a task force for administrative reform (TFAR) under the direction of Neil Kinnock, (the Vice President of the Commission and the Commissioners responsible for Administrative Reform) was created. An inter-institutional group of experts published a second report, which discusses the 'direct management' of the Commission. Direct management means that the Commission administers programmes in Member States with the assistance of private firms but without the inclusion of national administrations of the Member States. Approximately a sixth of the community budget flows into such direct management projects. Regarding direct management, the experts also addressed the difficulties involved in the outsourcing of orders and the question as to which tasks must be incumbent on the administration authority, and which could be assumed by private firms.

On the basis of the TFAR a White Paper was created, which strongly denounces the direct management system of the Commission, since half of the Commission employees spend their time with the management of projects. The execution of community programmes requires 'the structure of new forms of partnership between government actions at European level' (Craig 2000: 114). The disproportion between work input and output of the administrative action of the Commission employees was addressed partially by the introduction of a system of activity-based management, whose goal it was to make decisions on policy preferences and resources on all levels of the organisation. The Commission was requested additionally to externalise as many policies as possible, i.e. it is to delegate as many activities as possible to other institutions, without endangering the democratic legitimacy.

Spence (2000) calls the problems of the reform of the Commission the same as the last 25 years, since due to the path dependency no profound reforms would have taken place up to now (Spence 2000: 1). The present campaign to more efficiency and institutional clarity implies not only the creation of a new management culture, but also a political instrument of government action, which produces democratic legitimacy in public. Prodi began this process in 2001 with the dissolution of DG Culture, Information and Telecommunication and the redistribution of its tasks to the other DGs. Also, the DGs are not designated any more after their chronological acronyms (DG I, II, III, etc.) but rather by their functions. Although Spence calls these reforms 'dabblings', he recognises nevertheless a change in the attitude of the top officials after the resignation of the Commission (Spence 2000: 3). Spence suggests that the Commission take the EP working group as important as those of the Council due to the newly established rights of the EP which it has gained through the Maastricht Treaty.

Latest Reform Aspirations within the European Commission

As a result of the corruption scandal in 1998 which led to the resignation of the Commission in March 1999, one of the most important projects for Commission President Romano Prodi was to introduce a comprehensive administrative reform in the Commission.

The consequences of the planned reform of the Commission, which is envisaged for year 2004, were assessed very differently between management and the non-management employees. All agreed however, that some positive measures would be introduced from which especially women would benefit.

The *Comité Paritaire de l'Egalité des Chances* (COPEC; Joint Committee on Equal Opportunities for Women and Men) plays a central role in the reform process. COPEC is recognised as a Committee which advises the Commission on equal opportunities issues (see chapter 7 on a more detailed desciption of COPEC). Some representatives, especially from COPEC, thought this did not go far enough. Also, all employees below middle management said that the employees were not consulted enough in the reform process.

The timetable for the reform process is as follows: a two tier plan to implement the reform proposals is envisaged. At the end of 2001 the specific legislative proposals to amend the Staff Regulations were adopted as policy by the Commission. In the preceding concertation negotiations, the majority of staff representatives had agreed to the proposals (two out of the six staff unions, holding 59% of the votes in the staff committee elections). Amendments to the Staff Regulations have to follow the usual EU complex decision-making process.

Up until February 2001, the staff representatives were threatening to reject large parts of the drafts of the reform as they then stood. Following strike threats by the unions within the European Commission, it was agreed to set up a negotiating group comprising an equal number of Commission and staff union representatives and chaired by a mediator (Niels Ersbøll, former General Secretary of the Council). By the end of 2001, the group's conclusions were worked into proposals to amend the Staff Regulations. The Commission has drawn up a formal proposal for all requisite amendments to the Staff Regulations and presented it to the Council for decision and to the European Parliament, the Court of Justice, the Court of Auditors and the other institutions for an opinion. The Council formally has to decide on the Staff Regulations and it is planned that they will come into force in 2004 (European Commission 2002b).

The reform proposal is particularly important with regard to equal opportunities and gender mainstreaming since it transposes important elements of the equal opportunities Directives of the Council of the European Union to the European Commission. This is important since the Directives are only relevant for the Member States and not directly effective for public International Organisations like the European Commission. I shall summarise the most important changes relevant for gender, which are planned in the reform process, in the following.

– The hitherto four different hierarchical levels (A, B, C and D) will be replaced by two different levels (I and II). These two levels are not as rigid as the four categories and promotions from the second to the first level will be possible without an extra *concours* as is the case at the moment for changes between the grades[76].

---

76 Dieter Rogalla, a former MEP and civil servant who was head of unit in DG Personnel and Administration on the Unit responsible for changes in the staff regulation from 1970-1981, sees this as a way to get rid of the life-long status of European civil servants (Rogalla 2003).

- Gender mainstreaming is to be incorporated into the Staff Regulation to meet the objective laid down in the Amsterdam Treaty.
- Maternity leave is to be extended from 16 to 20 weeks. Parental leave of six months (12 months in the case of single parents) will be granted for which a fixed allowance will be paid. Also absent staff will be systematically replaced to meet the objective of gender equality laid down in the Amsterdam Treaty.
- There will be a reversal of the burden of proof in cases of discrimination, which up to now lies with the official concerned.
- Sexual harassment at work will be included as a discriminatory act in the Staff Regulations.
- The new staff appraisal policy will be closely tied to equal opportunities; the guidelines for the new mobility policy will also be applied on the basis of the principle of equal opportunities.
- Training policy will be given a key role in ensuring that traditionally under-represented groups do not remain so.
- In the area of training, women below middle management will be encouraged by their superiors to take part in preparatory courses for management duties. (European Commission 2002a).
- The upper age limit for competitions will be abolished. This was seen as an important barrier for women to enter competitions as it is mostly women who start their career at a later point due to caring responsibilities (European Commission: 2002a) or because they do not have as much support for a professional career as their male counterparts.

The main criticism from COPEC is that its members were not adequately included in the process.

One COPEC member explains:

COPEC said, look we are the experts, we want to have a word here. They [those responsible for the reform process] were asked for an opinion, of course. But they were asked after the decision was taken. And anyway you have no way to enforce your opinion. But the decision was taken anyway. COPEC was very positive and active on the reform. What I am seeing from the whole procedure is that the Vice-President [of the European Commission], he played around with us. And then he got through whatever he wanted (interview 26, female administrator).

Another COPEC member criticises the fact that the right to part-time work is limited to people with caring responsibilities and not given to those for example who want to do an extra qualification. With regard to the individual measures, especially the allowance for parental leave, these were seen as too minimal.

One particularly important proposal for the reform process was to include the implementation of gender mainstreaming in the work assessment of each employee. This would have required every single employee to think

146

about gender mainstreaming. However, this suggestion was not accepted by Neil Kinnock.

Different actors assess the actual success for the implementation of gender mainstreaming within the reform very differently. The above cited COPEC member comments in the following way:

Do you want my own personal opinion? Words. It only remains words. Vice-President Kinnock came and said I'm gonna change a system, I'm gonna go for part-time for women, and flexitime, everybody will have a baby and be a happy mother and then come back and have a happy career. I think the way it worked is that we went through huge enthusiasm in the beginning and everything was gonna change. I am now talking about working conditions in the Commission, not women in Parliament. We were promised that this would become a right for women, a right at all times. It [part time work and flexitime] remained a lot of nice words that we were going to give women the right. But now it is no longer a right. Your hierarchy has to approve it then you can be entitled. At the very end, women who choose to have children will not have the same rights. So, I don't see what changed. A lot of promises but no concrete action (interview 26, female administrator).

This actor is rather cynical about the progress achieved in the suggested reforms. She is particularly disappointed that part-time work and flexitime is still not a right for women but rather something hierarchy has to agree with.

One manager of DG Personnel and Administration assessed COPEC's role very differently by saying that according to his view, COPEC members always have the feeling to be passed over and that their positions were completely taken on board during the reform process (interview 25, manager).

5.6   Conclusion

In the founding years a lot of important administrative principles were enshrined in the Commission especially the recurrence on French, German and British administrative traditions. Various scholars like Cini (1996) and Hooghe (2001) do not regard the European Commission as a unitary actor but rather as a multitude of different organisational cultures. Both Cini and Hooghe state that the different perceptions on supranationalism and inter-gouvernementalism are one of the most important points for determining the attitude of civil servants and other employees of the Commission. A supra-nationalist or intergouvernementalist attitude of actors will determine how the importance of the Commission in relation to the other European institution is viewed. Intergouvernementalists might be more prone to argue that the Commission is one among other institutions and stress mainly the executive functions of the Commission. Supranationalists derive a special legitimacy for the Commission due to the fact that the Commission is a supranational actor, which does not represent the interest of the Member States but rather of the European Union as a whole. The European integration process suffered a set-back when the majority voted against the Maastricht Treaty in the first Danish referendum of 1992. Since women voted predominately against the Maastricht Treaty, the subsequent action of the European Commission, as regards equal opportunities and gender mainstreaming, was often argued to be motivated by the Commission's desire to increase its legitimacy and that of the European Union in the eyes of women. The Commission also used the equal opportunities and gender mainstreaming policy area to extend its own competencies by strengthening groups of civil society such as the European Women's Lobby.

The legitimacy of the European Commission was seriously challenged at the time of the corruption scandal, which led to the resignation of the entire Commission in March 1999. A number of reform proposals have been suggested since then, the most fundamental of which, is the reform proposal from Neil Kinnock which ought to be decided in 2003. Some important changes with regard to equal opportunities and gender mainstreaming were suggested within this reform process of the Commission, such as the dilution of the stiff separation of grades. The separation was seen to disadvantage especially secretaries who are often doing much more qualified work than their grade suggests. Important measures to reconcile professional and private life are included in the reform process such as the extension of maternity leave and the introduction of parental leave. However, suggestions to positively reward individual actors by including the implementation of gender mainstreaming in the appraisal of all staff were refused by management. The reform proposal is particularly important with regard to equal opportunities and gender mainstreaming since it transposes important elements of the equal opportunities Directives to the European Commission. This is important since the Directives are only relevant for the Member States and not directly effective for public International Organisations like the European Commission.

While this chapter examined the results of the social embeddedness with regard to internal changes in the Commission, the next chapter will focus on the environment of the Commission and will look at the interplay between the environment and the European Commission more in detail.

6 The Environment of the European Commission

6.1 Introduction: The Interplay between the European Institutions, the United Nations and Civil Society

Within sociological neo-institutionalism, the social embeddedness and environment of the organisation plays an important role. Organisations are seen as being embedded in local communities, to which they are tied by the multiple loyalties of personnel, and by inter-organisational treaties elaborated in face-to-face interaction (DiMaggio and Powell 1991a: 12). The importance of this was shown in the last section with regard to the corruption scandal of the Commission in 1998 which led to the planning of fundamental administrative reforms. While the last section examined the results of the social embeddedness with regard to internal changes in the Commission, this chapter will focus on the environment of the Commission and will look at the interplay between the environment and the European Commission more in detail.

Within neo-institutionalism, the environment plays an important role. Meyer and Scott (Meyer/ Scott (1992); Scott/ Meyer's (1991)) treat institutions as primarily exogenous, while Meyer and Rowan (1991 [1977] and DiMaggio and Powell (1991b [1983]) contend that the organisations can become isomorphic with their environments. The most important contentions arising from the theoretical framework (chapter 3) for this thesis will be briefly summarised in the following.

Meyer and Scott (1992) and Scott and Meyer's (1991) work has focused on causes and consequences of conformity and on the way in which the environment 'interpenetrates the organisation' (Meyer and Rowan 1977). They have come to treat institutions as primarily exogenous to organisational action. Their more recent work associates institutional pressures with the demands of centralised authorities or regulatory agencies and then, only with widespread beliefs, practices and norms.

Meyer and Rowan (1991 [1977] contend that organisations are structured in their environments by phenomena and tend to become isomorphic with them. The authors explain environmental isomorphism with the fact that formal organisations become matched with their environments by technical exchange and interdependencies.

DiMaggio and Powell (1991b [1983]) differentiate three mechanisms which bring about institutional change of organisations with regard to isomorphism: coercive isomorphism, mimetic isomorphism, normative isomorphism.

Applying DiMaggio's and Powell's (1991b [1983]) concept of mimetic isomorphism to the research question, I hypothesise that the environment of the Commission, i.e. European women's movements, European institutions and the United Nations, creates uncertainty for the Commission. The European Commission therefore copies gender mainstreaming from the UN level in order to increase its legitimacy.

Various concepts have been developed to capture those that cooperate in specific topic areas beyond the realm of one organisation and who lobby on a specific issue. Such cooperations play an important role to link the environment with the organisation or that the environment creates pressure on the organisation. Two of these concepts, namely the concept on 'advocacy-networks' and the concept on 'velvet triangles' will briefly be illustrated due to their special importance for the further course of this thesis.

An advocacy-network is characterised by the horizontal and voluntary pattern of communication and the exchange of the open and regular relation between the actors who cooperate in specific topic areas (Keck and Sikkink 1998). Actors who are lobbying for the introduction of gender mainstreaming or who are responsible for the implementation of gender mainstreaming constitute a so-called advocacy-network. Those who are directly involved with gender mainstreaming are therefore referred to as the 'gender mainstreaming advocacy-network'. Alison Woodward (2001b) developed the concept of 'velvet triangles', which is a specific form of advocacy coalition. The velvet triangle includes all three groups that are involved with gender mainstreaming on the European level: femocrats and politicians, women's movements and academics. Femocrats possess procedural knowledge, women's movements have insider knowledge, since they are dealing with grassroots movements and local actors and academics have technocratic knowledge.

The concept of velvet triangles is partly based on the concept of the 'iron triangle', which was developed in the 1970s by Theodore Löwi for the entanglement between congress committees, federal administration and industry in the US (Woodward 2001b: 36). It is also based on Ghilionis' concept of 'velvet ghettos' which targets the horizontal segregation of women in enterprises: Women are pushed to the edges of big industries, fight amongst themselves about positions and have little influence on the major policy (Woodward 2001b: 35-6).

The velvet element of the concept symbolises that almost all actors are women in a male dominated area. The softness means a considerable uncertainty with regard to the input and the loyalties. Various scholars have argued that transnational networks among non-state actors that link domestic institutional changes and international norms are the most compelling explanation for the diffusion of gender mainstreaming (Risse-Kappen 1995, True and Mintrom 2001). Thousands of women participated in the four UN women's conferences in Mexico City (1975), Copenhagen (1980), Nairobi (1985) and Beijing (1995) and New York (the so-called Beijing plus five in 2000). True and Mintrom apply Castells'(1997) concept of network society by stating:

This global women's movement extended the principles of the networked society to facilitate social change. Its decentralised form of organisation and intervention mirrors and counteracts the networking logic of domination in the information society (True and Mintrom 2001: 38).

This quotation describes the decentralised form of organisation and intervention of women's movements in a rather uncritical way since this as led to many problems of cooperation between the women's movements (Schmidt 2000). Nevertheless this form of organisation is an important point for European women's movements, since the European Women's Lobby (EWL) has strategically used the decentralised form of women's groups for their lobbying (Helfferich/ Kolb 2001).

The EU has historically been a favourable opportunity structure for women. Women achieved significant legislative gains with regard to equal treatment of women and women within the workplace during the 1970s and 1980s (see chapter 2, see also Mazey 2001, 2000, 1995; Hoskyns 1996; Helfferich/ Kolb 2001).

One important example showing how closely tied the velvet triangle appears to be is that the Commissioner for Employment and Social Affairs, Anna Diamantopoulou employed the former Secretary General of the EWL, Barbara Hellferich in her Cabinet after she became Commissioner in 1999. The Cabinets of the Commissioner consist of 10-15 advisors who are mostly employed from outside of the Commission and represent an important power base within the Commission and thus Hellferich's appointment was highly symbolic of the velvet triangle[77].

In this chapter, the relevance of different European and global institutions and social movements with regard to gender mainstreaming will be examined. I shall first of all elaborate on the influence of civil society on gender mainstreaming in the European Union, then discuss the influence of European structures and institutions on gender mainstreaming and then examine the influence of the United Nations for the development of gender mainstreaming.

---

77 Alternatively, the appointment of leading figure from a social movement could be interpreted as a strategic move by Anna Diamantopoulou to implicate a political opponent.

6.2 The Influence of Civil Society on Gender Mainstreaming in the European Union

The aim of this section is to illustrate the most important groups of civil society with regard to gender mainstreaming in the European Union. The interplay between civil society and European institutions will be illustrated by elaborating on the discussions on equal opportunities during the 1996 Inter-Governmental Conference and the inclusion of gender mainstreaming in the Treaty of Amsterdam (1997).

6.2.1 The Influence of the European Women's Lobby

The EWL was founded in 1990. It represents according to its own illustration 300 head organisations and is the largest women's NGO on the European level. Its goal is to achieve equality of women and men in Europe and to serve as a link between political decision-makers and women's organisations at EU level. The objectives of the EWL are the promotion of equal rights and opportunities for women and men and the defence of the interests of women living in the Member States of the European Union, including migrants, ethnic minorities and the most vulnerable and marginalised groups within society, in the context of a united and democratic Europe. The EWL also works to promote the implementation of a European social policy and to ensure that women are involved in co-operation between the European Union and other countries (particularly the East European countries). The role of the EWL is to represent the interests of its member organisations to the European institutions and to propose campaigns to them on the basis of information gathered at European level. The member organisations can then decide whether they wish to participate in a given campaign (European Women's Lobby 2003).

The EWL is closely tied to the European institutions and especially to the European Commission. The members of the preparation committee for the foundation of the EWL were selected by Commission employees (Hoskyns 1996: 67), therefore the EWL cannot be said to be created through a bottom-up approach by different women's groups' desire for a European head. On the contrary, it was created through a top-down approach by Commission officials' need for a European group, which in the eyes of the European Commission could represent women in Europe (Schmidt 2000). Financially the EWL is also highly dependent on the European Commission and the European Parliament, which together pay for around 80% of the total budget of the EWL (Lobby européen des femmes 2002: 2), the rest of the budget is paid for by membership fees.

The EWL aims to have positions only on 'non-controversial' topics, so that as many as possible of the member organisations are represented. The EWL has observer status with the UN and in the Committee for Human Rights of the European Council as well as two seats in the Advisory Committee for Equal Opportunities in the European Commission. An important part of the lobby work of the EWL consists in the writing of regular dossiers to the ministers in the Council of Ministers. From its self-portrayal, the EWL represents more than 100 million women in Europe (Albertini-Roth 1998: 24). This number is the sum of all women in the individual organisations, especially in trade unions and churches.

In the past, the EWL has been critical of the concept of gender main-streaming since they argue that in the past, gender mainstreaming has led to the destruction of specific structures for women (interview 29, female employee of the EWL). However, since the European Commission adopted the dual strategy on gender mainstreaming which stresses that positive action ought to be a part of gender mainstreaming, the EWL took the strategic decision that they would lobby for the efficient implementation of gender mainstreaming instead of lobbying against the concept (interview 29, female employee of the EWL). This observation was also mentioned by various Commission actors (interview 4 manageress, interview 7, female adminis-trator).

There has been criticism in the past about the internal democratic struc-ture of the EWL. This is due to the fact that the national committees sort out their own representation for the EWL. In the German context, the EWL is only represented by the German Women's Council, which represents rather traditional, close to government women's groups (Hoskyns 1996: 186), whereas the autonomous women's movement is excluded.

Heike Walk et al. (2000) warn that 'NGOs are increasingly interwoven with economic and political powers and that they get increasingly entangled with regard to their perspectives on the future' (Walk et al. 2000: 21). This does not apply to the EWL. The EWL was founded by the Commission and mainly funded by the Commission from the outset. Also its insistence on the lowest common denominator does not usually contradict the positions of the European institutions. The EWL understands itself as a lobby organisation (rather than an association with closely knit aims) which links European institutions and civil society (European Women's Lobby 2003).

Since the foundation of the EWL, it has been criticised by various scholars that a lobby organisation cannot adequately represent women (Hoskyns 1996, Schunter-Kleemann 1992. In 1982, when the German Women's Council (*Deutscher Frauenrat*) called for a meeting to found a European lobby organisation, trade unionists and feminists rejected the foun-dation due to a perceived lack of legitimacy of a European lobby organisation for women (Hoskyns 1996: 131). Despite this, the EWL is the only women's organisation which receives funding from the Commission independent of projects, so that it can be consulted as a 'women's organisation' and can represent women (Hoskyns 1996: 185). The official recognition of the EWL as representative of 'the women' and the connected support from the side of the Commission underline the relevance of the legitimacy of the EWL.

6.2.2 Other Women's Organisations on the European Level

Apart from the EWL, there are smaller and relatively specialised women's organisations on the European level, mainly Women in Development Europe.

Women in Development Europe (WIDE) is a European network of gender specialists, women active in Non-Governmental Development Organisations and human rights activists. It was formed in 1985 in response to the forward-looking strategies developed at the Third UN World Conference on Women in Nairobi. The mission of WIDE is to strive for a world based on gender equality and justice, which ensures equal treatment and political participation of women and men. WIDE aims to articulate the relevance of the principles of gender equality and justice to the development process through research, documentation, information dissemination, economic empowerment, capacity building and advocacy, networking, and the organisation of conferences. WIDE consists of twelve national co-ordinating platforms (WIDE 2003).

6.2.3 An Improved Political Opportunity Structure for Non-Governmental Organisations at the 1996 Inter-Governmental Conference

During the preliminary stages of the 1996 Intergovernmental conference (IGC), which prepared the Treaty of Amsterdam (1997), and during the IGC itself we can observe an improved political opportunity structure for NGOs and this will be analysed more in detail in the following. The political opportunity structure approach assumes that the dynamics, strategies, forms and outcomes of interest representations are shaped by different characteristics of the local, national and international context (McAdam 1998, Tarrow 1998). Helfferich and Kolb apply the more fluid aspects of the political opportunity structure approach by introducing the idea of a window of reform based on John Keeler (1993). Keeler's central assertion is that policy innovations are only possible when the various constraints, which usually prevent policy changes, open a policy window. Helfferich and Kolb argue that the EWL's activities surrounding IGC were embedded in such a window for reform (Helfferich/ Kolb 2001: 145)

Various new developments led to this changed political opportunity structure. Firstly, northern enlargement changed the distribution of power in the European Council in favour of policies conforming to the Nordic traditions, which Liebert describes as open government, participation of citizens in welfare policy and the institutional legacies of state feminism (Liebert 1999: 223-4). The enlargement also led to changes in the new Santer Commission in 1995 which included three new Member States (Austria, Finland and Sweden) 'with strong, existing commitment to equal opportunities and with considerable experience in mainstreaming gender in their own public policies' (Pollack/ Hafner-Burton 2000: 436).

Secondly, the Maastricht Treaty conferred new power to the EP, which it used as a sounding board for the public interest groups' proposals for the IGC (Liebert 1999: 227). Thirdly as Mazey and Richardson (1997) argue, the 1996 IGC – unlike previous IGCs – was characterised by extensive involvement of interest groups and a lot of 'competitive framing', which means attempts by different interest groups to ensure that their particular views and interests were represented on the agenda. The EWL was an active member of a human rights coalition of NGO's comprising Amnesty International, environmental organisations and groups representing the disabled, the elderly, gay and lesbian groups, migrants and refugees. The common policy frame for these groups during the IGC centred upon the demand to the EU to promote citizenship's rights, democracy and anti-discrimination (Mazey 2001: 32, Liebert 1999).

The ratification of the Maastricht Treaty in 1992 had provoked an unexpected rise of public opposition to European integration and the alleged undemocratic nature of Community institutions (Mazey 2001: 33). The participation by large numbers of NGOs meant that the discourse was much more characterised by normative and political debate than by legal reasoning (Sverdrup 2000: 255-260). Further, the openness of the IGC made elite control of the agenda difficult. One bureaucrat reflected this as follows: 'gone are the days when we had articles in square brackets, and the processes were purely technical; now decision-making in the IGC is open, unclear and democratic' (interview with Michel Petite, employee from the European Commission, cited in Sverdrup 2000: 260). Finally, the election of a Labour government in the UK in 1998 removed a veto that had repeatedly blocked social policy changes during the Thatcher-Major era (Helfferich/ Kolb 2001: 146).

6.2.4 The Interplay between the European Women's Lobby, the Nordic Member States and European Institutions

The adoption of the principle on equal opportunities in the Treaty of Amsterdam is an important success for two years of lobbying of the EWL on the European level, of member organisations of the EWL within Member States and the Nordic Member States. At the end of 1994 it became known that the governments of Member States called a working group on the Treaty of Amsterdam, which consisted only of men and which was referred to as the 'Group of Wise Men'. As a replica, the EWL constituted the 'Group of Wise Women' in the beginning of 1995, which consisted of lawyers and activists of different women's movements and which redrafted the texts of the treaties. The positions of Member States with regard to equal opportunities were very diverse. Generally speaking, the Nordic countries had – with the exception of Finland – little interest in a comprehensive article on equal opportunities on the European level since they were afraid that the European legislation could be levelling down the stronger national equal opportunities legislation. However, once equal opportunities became an issue at the IGC, Denmark, Sweden and Finland urged the introduction of anti-discrimination issues into the Treaty in their national provision papers presented at the beginning of the IGC. Surprisingly, Greece supported this. (Helfferich/ Kolb 2001: 146). Germany argued that the principle of subsidiarity should be applied to equal opportunities, i.e. that questions on equal opportunities should be dealt with by individual Member States or at sub-national level if appropriate. Sweden, Luxembourg and Ireland wanted to fix the principle for equal opportunities of men and women in the Treaty of Amsterdam. Spain, Portugal and Belgium took up the demands from the EWL to draft a chapter on equal opportunities in the Treaty of Amsterdam, in which positive action and gender mainstreaming would be included (Helfferich 1998: 40)[78].

In order to convince the other Member States of their position, the EWL negotiated with all national delegations and carried through a Europe wide collection of signatures for the support of their aims. The former general secretary of the EWL, Barbara Helfferich, sees the strategic alliance with the European Trade Union Congress as decisive for the inclusion of gender mainstreaming in the Treaty of Amsterdam. As a result of this strategic alliance, the European Trade Union Congress supported the demand of the EWL to have the equal opportunities principle included in the Treaty of Amsterdam. In exchange the EWL lobbied for the integration of the Social Protocol into the Treaty and for the abolition of unanimity voting in the Council with regard to social and labour legislation (Helfferich 1998: 42). Partly as a result of this concerted lobbying effort, all of the three causes

---

78   See Liebert (2002) for causes for the different positions by European Member States.

(equal opportunities, the Social Protocol and the abolition of unanimity voting with regard to social and labour legislation) were included in the Amsterdam Treaty.

6.3 The Influence of European Structures and Institutions on Gender Mainstreaming

This section examines the influence of European structures and institutions for the implementation of gender mainstreaming.

6.3.1 The Women's Networks of the Commission

The Commission has established nine women's networks in different areas such as the legal implementation of equality, employment and equal pay and critical research on 'men'[79] These networks consist of 15-30 independent experts from the different Member States (one or two representative per Member State). The networks evaluate the consequences of the existing equal opportunities policies and aggregate data which could be relevant for the work of the Commission. The aim of the network is to establish contact with national women's movements and researchers and to publish joint reports and opinions (Richardson 1996: 292). The networks only have advisory functions for the Commission. The fact that the national experts are not nominated by women's groups active in the different policy areas, but rather, that they are selected by a co-ordinator nominated by the European Commission, makes it unclear whether the above mentioned aim of a closer link to the women's groups and academic groups can be achieved. The experts are in no way accountable to the national women's movements (Schunter-Kleemann 1992: 53-4a).

6.3.2 The European Parliament

The European Parliament (EP) is the parliamentary organ of the EU, which is directly elected every five years since 1979. It has steadily acquired greater influence and power through a series of treaties. These treaties (in particular, the Maastricht Treaty, signed in 1992 and came into force in 1993 and the

---

79   The 'Network of Legal Experts on the application of Community Law on Equality between Women and Men' was set up in 1984, the 'Gender and Employment Equality' network was founded in 1995 and the 'European Research Network on Men in Europe: The Social Problem of Men' was founded in 1999 (European Women's Lobby 2003).

Amsterdam Treaty, signed in 1997 and came into effect in 1999) have transformed the European Parliament from a purely consultative assembly into a legislative parliament, exercising powers similar to those of the national parliaments. Today the European Parliament, as an equal partner with the Council of Ministers, passes the majority of European laws.

The EP is characterised by a large under-representation of women. After the European elections in 1999, the percentage of women was 29.6% compared to 26.5% in the legislative period from 1994 -1999. This small increase of the percentage of women can be explained with a much higher percentage of women in the newly joined Member States Sweden and Finland (Interparliamentary Union 2003)[80].

6.3.3 The Committee on Women's Rights and Equal Opportunities of the European Parliament

After the first direct election of the EP in 1979, the first female President of the EP, Simone Veil, inaugurated an ad-hoc Committee for the concerns of women, which was supposed to be dissolved after achieving its goal – to evaluate the implications of European integration for women. However, little progress with regard to the Equal Opportunities Directives from 1975, 1976 and 1978 led to the decision of the MEPs to transform the ad hoc Committee into a permanent Committee which was called 'Committee on Women's Rights and Equal Opportunities (Albertini-Roth 1998: 57). This Committee is one of 17 Standing Committees of the European Parliament. It is not a 'neutral' committee, i.e. the Parliamentarians who are full members in this committee can also become full members in other committees. On the one hand this has the advantage that the committee members can determine the work of different committees, on the other hand, the authority of the committee is smaller as it is not a 'full committee'.

The Committee on Women's Rights and Equal Opportunities prepares the plenary sessions. There are 40 members in the committee, whose composition mirrors the party distribution in the EP. Normally, the committee meets once a month publicly. Until the end of the legislative period in 1999 it was called 'Committee for the Rights of Women'. As mentioned in chapter 2, the Committee renamed itself to its present name (i.e. Committee on Women's Rights and Equal Opportunities) due to pressure from the Budget Committee of the European Parliament which had argued that due to the implementation of gender mainstreaming, there ought not be a Committee exclusively for women (see chapter 2).

---

80   The percentage of women in the EP is still higher than in most national Parliaments (Interparliamentary Union 2003).

The Committee on Women's Rights and Equal Opportunities has the general responsibilities of the EP concerning equal opportunities. More specifically, the responsibilities include political responsibilities, i.e. control over Community responsibilities relevant to equal opportunities legislative functions, opinions about the legislative proposals of the Commission budget control, co-decision about specific budgetary arrangements for women, international co-operation and discussion of women's issues on the global level.

The EP has repeatedly evaluated the situation of women as a result of integration. Since 1984, it is responsible for the control of the implementation of the equal opportunities directives (Schunter-Kleemann 1992: 35). The Committee passed a variety of resolutions on Equal Opportunities which are however not legally enforcing. For example in 1996, it demanded the inclusion of Equal Opportunities in the Civil Service, specifically calling on Member States at the Inter-Governmental Conference

[...] to establish in the revised treaty a new legal basis for equal treatment and rights for women and men which would provide for the legality of positive action aimed at promoting equality of opportunity between women and men;
2. Considers that there is a need for a positive definition of positive action in community law, and that the amended Directive 76/207 should explicitly include this definition, thus establishing a general framework for positive actions within the Union [...] (European Parliament 1996).

The EP thereby put pressure on the Member States to include the gender mainstreaming requirement in the Treaty of Amsterdam, which was signed one year after the above-cited report in 1997 and which entered into force in 1999.

6.3.4 The Council of the European Union

The Council of the European Union (also referred to as Council of Ministers) is the legislative organ of the EU, even though the EP has gained the right to co-decision by the Maastricht Treaty 1992 in certain areas, which were extended with the Treaty of Amsterdam (1997). All Ministers with portfolios regularly meet in the Council. With regard to equal opportunities, the ministers of employment and social affairs usually decide, even though five Member States have a special ministry for women's affairs or one that is partially concerned with women's affairs (this is the case in Belgium, Germany, Ireland, Luxembourg and Sweden). On the initiative of the British Council presidency, the women's ministries or the responsible ministers for women's affairs had a special meeting which several presidencies tried to institutionalise, however this was without success (interview 12, female administrator)[81].

6.3.5 *The Economic and Social Committee*

The Economic and Social Committee (ESC) secures the representation of the different interest groups of employers, employees and all other general interests like consumer protection, environmental protection, family interests or association interests. The ESC was set up by the Treaty of Rome in 1957 to represent the interests of the various economic and social groups and as a result the Committee sees itself as the representative of 'civil society'(Wirtschafts- und Sozialausschuss 1998). It consists of 222 members falling into three categories: employers, workers and representatives of particular types of activity (such as farmers, crafts people, the professions, consumer representatives, scientists and teachers, co-operatives, families, environmental movements). Members are appointed for four years by unanimous Council decision and this term may be renewed.

The Committee is consulted before a great many acts concerning the internal market, education, consumer protection, regional development, environment and social affairs are adopted, and it may also issue opinions on its own initiative. Since the Treaty of Amsterdam entered into force, the Committee has to be consulted on a wider range of issues including equal opportunities[82] and it may also be consulted by the European Parliament.

The Committee used the consultation procedure in December 1995 when it suggested a directive on parental rights to the Council of Ministers. This directive was later adopted by the Council. Before the adoption of this Directive, the Council itself had unsuccessfully tried to draft a Directive on this matter since 1983 (Albertini-Roth 1998: 70).

Women are under-represented in all groups of the ESC. The women's percentage within the employers' group was 30.8% in 2000, in the workers' group 20% and within the group of varied interests it was 21.1% (Wirtschafts- und Sozialausschuss 2000) [83]. The ESC has been criticised by the EWL that women's groups are not represented as special interest groups (EWL 2003).

---

81 The Council of the European Union meetings are not public and their minutes are not published, it is therefore not possible to assess why the initiative to institutionalise the women's councils was not successful.

82 Other areas include the new employment policy, the new social affairs legislation and public health.

83 It is important to note that women are better represented in the employers' group than in the employees' and varied interests group, however, no reason could be found for this.

6.3.6 The Court of Justice of the European Communities

The Court of Justice of the European Communities (ECJ), which is based in Luxembourg, consists of fifteen judges assisted by nine advocates-general appointed for six years by agreement among the Member States. Since 2000, the first woman has been appointed as a member of the ECJ. The ECJ has two principal functions: to check whether instruments of the European institutions and of governments are compatible with the Treaties, and, at the request of a national court, to pronounce on the interpretation or the validity of provisions contained in Community law. The consultations of the ECJ are not public. The majority within the ECJ is decisive; the Court does not publish minority opinions, which is customary in some Member States (like for example Germany). The ECJ as a supranational institution decides independently of the interests of Member States on the basis of interpretations of the European treaties, i.e. treaties and legislation.

The Court is assisted by a Court of First Instance, set up in 1989, which has special responsibility for dealing with administrative disputes in the European institutions and disputes arising from the Community competition rules.

The Court passed more than one hundred judgements with regard to equal opportunities until 1995 (on the results of these judgements, see Liebert 2002). The Commission also played an important role for the legal implementation of equal opportunities of women and men; the Commission filed twelve complaints against Member States due to the violation of the contract which led to a judgement of the Court of Justice (Hoskyns 1996: 25).

In 1971 the Defrenne case regarding 119 was taken to the ECJ. The 1976 decision of the ECJ was ground-breaking, for it ruled that article 119 was enforceable law since 1962[84]. The judgements since 1971 do not only concern judgements of direct discrimination but also indirect discrimination which exists when occupational regulations appear gender neutral, but which result in disproportional disadvantages for one sex like for example part time work, 80 % of which is performed by women.

The ECJ is well known for particularly stringent interpretation in the legal area with regard to equal opportunities. As a result, when the ECJ was consulted on a judgement of maternity directive, it came to the conclusion that the equal treatment directive does not aim 'to regulate the internal relations of the family or to change the division of labour between parents' (Ostner/ Lewis 1998: 201), i.e. the legal problems which went beyond the economic problems were left out.

---

84 Ostner and Lewis 1998: 204; for a more detailed account of the judgement, refer to chapter 2.

In 1995 the horticultural engineer Eckhard Kalanke went to Court against the German state of Bremen, which gave preference to a female applicant. This was explained to Kalanke by referring to state law which states that women with equal qualification should be positively discriminated. The Court ruled that a general and automatic positive action policy on recruitment and promotion contravened Article 2(4) of equal treatment Directive 76/207 (Council of the European Union 1976). The Kalanke judgement led to a lot of insecurities within women's organisations, who were afraid that positive action in general was put into question (Albertini-Roth 1998: 47). This led to a Commission communication on the interpretation of the judgement of the ECJ, which states that

The Commission considers that the Court has not condemned the implementation of positive action measures in general, but has ruled only on a specific feature of legislation applied by the Land of Bremen whereby women are automatically given absolute and unconditional priority for purposes of appointment or promotion in sectors where they are under-represented. The Commission therefore takes the view that the only form of positive action condemned by the Court is the rigid quota system under which there is no possibility of taking particular individual circumstances into account. It believes that there are many forms of positive action which are not affected by the judgement in question, and that Member States and employers may avail themselves of a wide range of positive measures such as State subsidies granted to employers who recruit women in sectors where they are under-represented, positive training-oriented action, vocational guidance, child care and flexible quotas (European Commission 1996: 1).

In 1997, the Kalanke-judgement was differentiated by the Marschall judgement. In 1997, the teacher Hellmut Marschall went to court against the state North-Rhine Westphalia in Germany, because his application for a better paid position was denied with the argument that as long as women are under-represented, they are generally granted priority. According to the Court, in the working world a male candidate will tend to be promoted even if a female candidate is equally qualified for the post in question. Certain deep-rooted prejudices and stereotypes as to the role and capacities of women in working life still persist. The Court concludes from this that the practice of giving priority to equally qualified women, designed to restore the balance, is not contrary to Community law, provided that an objective assessment of each individual candidate irrespective of the sex is assured such that promotion of a male candidate is not excluded from the outset. The Marschall judgement was seen as a general affirmation of positive action within the EU.

Another important judgement of the ECJ also concerned a German citizen. Tanja Kreil, who was trained in electronics, applied in 1996 for service in the weapons electronics maintenance service of the German Armed Forces (*Bundeswehr*). Her application was rejected by the German Armed Forces on the ground that German law bars women from military posts involving the use of arms. After the rejection of her application Tanja Kreil brought an action in the Administrative Court (*Verwaltungsgericht*) in

Hanover. She claimed in particular that the rejection of her application on grounds based solely on her sex was contrary to Community law. The German Court asked the ECJ for an opinion on this matter and the ECJ replied that German legislation barring women outright from army jobs involving the use of arms is contrary to the Community principle of equal treatment for men and women. However, derogations remain possible where sex constitutes a determining factor for access to certain special combat units. This judgement was highly controversial in the German women's movement and the German left because important parts were in favour of the abolishment of the army. The judgement however shows the scope of the judgement of the ECJ for equal opportunities policies.

On a more general account, the Court was criticised for interpreting the vague treaties rather extensively. For example, the academic lawyer Hjalte Rasmussen referred to the ECJ as 'running wild' with its interpretations. He examined the extent of judicial policy making and its impact on the process of European integration. According to Rasmussen, judicial activism might be a social good if it agrees with the wishes of Member States. However, Rasmussen came to the conclusion that during the 1960s and 1970s, this was not the case. He accused the Judges that they had une certaine idée de l'Europe of their own (Rasmussen 1986). According to Rasmussen, the Court thus pushed forward their own interpretations, rather than the spirit of the Treaties, which undermined the Court's authority.

6.4 The Influence of the United Nations for the Development of Gender Mainstreaming

The following actors and events are utmost important for the implementation of gender mainstreaming in the EU: United Nations, the inclusion of gender mainstreaming in the Platform of Action in the Women's Conference in Beijing in 1995, and the description of gender mainstreaming in the conclusion of the Women's Conference in Nairobi in 1975. In the following section, the importance of the above mentioned actors and events regarding the terms 'women' and 'gender' for the development of gender mainstreaming norms and rules will be elaborated.

6.4.1 The United Nations International Women's Conferences

1975 was declared a UN 'Women's year and the 1975 First International Women's conference in Mexico City laid the foundation for the later gender mainstreaming policies. The conference decided that all governments should establish agencies dedicated to promoting gender equality and improving the status and conditions of women. This provided the impetus for the diffusion of 'national machineries', the term used to refer to these agencies (Rowan-Campbell 1997: 141-2). The decade following the UN Women's year and the first Women's Conference was declared a 'Decade for Women' by the United Nations, which took place from 1976-1985.

In two decades, permanent gender equality machineries[85] with different power basis have been adopted by an overwhelming majority of nation-states world-wide, with some exceptions[86]. Even countries where women suffer considerable amount of gender injustices have instigated institutional changes to advance the cause of women and gender equity. This rapid global diffusion of a state-level bureaucratic innovation is unprecedented in the post-war era (True/ Mintrom 2001: 30). It is an example of the increased role of the state in an era where economic globalisation is expected to diminish rather than enhance the scope for state policy-making (Reinicke 1998).

The UN's Third World Conference on Women in Nairobi in 1985 reviewed the achievements of the United Nations decade for women from 1975 until 1985. The final declaration of the Third World Conference does not utilise the term gender mainstreaming but the content, especially, of article 114 can be seen as a basis for the later development of gender mainstreaming:

114. The incorporation of women's issues in all areas and sectors and at the local, national, regional and international levels should be institutionalised. To this end, appropriate machinery should be established or strengthened, and further legislative action taken. Sectoral policies and plans should be developed, and the effective participation of women in development should be integrated both in those plans and in the formulation and implementation of mainstream programmes and projects and should not be confined solely to statements of intent within plans or to small-scale, transitory projects relating to women (UN 1985).

The exact wording of the Platform for Action of the Beijing conference ten years later with regard to gender mainstreaming is as follows:

189: In addressing the inequality between men and women in the sharing of power and decision-making at all levels, Governments and other actors should promote an active and visible policy of mainstreaming a gender perspective in all policies and programmes so that before decisions are taken, an analysis is made of the effects on women and men, respectively (UN 1995).

---

85 For a distinction between different types of policy machineries, see Stetson and Mazur 1995).
86 Jacqui True and Michael Mintron list the following countries as exceptions: Afghanistan, North Korea, Kuwait, Iraq, Congo, Libya, Sierra Leone, Yugoslavia, United Arab Emirates, Bahrain, Saudi Arabia, Poland and Singapore (True/ Mintron 2001: 30, footnote 85). In 2002, Afghanistan established a Minister for Women's Affairs.

The Platform also defines gender mainstreaming with regard to specific policy areas. Different policy areas are described in different articles and then the above or very similar definition of gender mainstreaming is stated in each article[87].

The European Community, represented by the Commission, was a negotiator and signatory of the Platform for Action at the Women's conference in Beijing. According to the EP resolution on gender mainstreaming

Gender mainstreaming was explicitly endorsed as a strategy to achieve the goal of gender equality by the UN Fourth World Conference on Women (Beijing 1995). The EU played a key role to this effect (European Parliament 2003: 13).

In the 'national strategies for the implementation of the women's conference in Beijing, the European Community committed itself to check the introduction of gender mainstreaming and to develop a concept for the implementation. Due to the signing of the Platform for Action at the UN Fourth World Conference on Women, the European Commission also specifically committed itself to the regular budgetary concept from the point of view of a gender specific perspective.

Ever since the UN's Fourth World Conference on Women in Beijing in 1995, gender mainstreaming has been an integral part of equal opportunities policy in many parts of the world. In June 2000, a special session of the UN General Assembly, the so-called Beijing plus five Assembly, met to assess the implementation of the Beijing Platform for Action, the agreements reached during the 1995 conference. The session ended by reconfirming the importance of gender mainstreaming, since it is not yet automatically incorporated into policy-making and implementation. The complementarity between mainstreaming and special activities targeting women was stressed in the final document. Certain areas were identified as requiring focus and attention. These included education; social services and health, including sexual and reproductive health; the HIV/AIDS pandemic; violence against women and girls; the persistent and increasing burden of poverty on women; vulnerability of migrant women, including exploitation and trafficking; natural disaster and environmental management; the development of strong, effective and accessible national machineries for the advancement of women;

---

87 The following policy areas are defined in the articles mentioned: 79: education; 105: health status; 123: violence against women; 141: armed or other conflicts; 164: economic potential and independence of women; 187: policy development and the implementation of programmes; 201: central policy co-ordination unit inside of government; 202: mechanism for promoting the advancement of women; With regard to national governments, the platform for action demands mainstreaming with regard to: 205 a: policy making; 229: human rights; With regard to relevant organs, bodies and agencies of the United Nations system, the platform for action demands mainstreaming with regard to: 231 b and c: human rights; 238: media; 252: management of natural resources and the environment; 273: children and youth; 292: monitoring and evaluation of programmes; 326: office of the Secretary General.

and the formulation of strategies to enable women and men to reconcile and share equally work and family responsibilities (UN 2000: article 38).

6.4.2 Conceptual Shift from 'Women' to 'Gender' in International Organisations

The shift from the usage of the term 'women', via 'empowerment' to the term 'gender' can best be observed in technical cooperation (Braunmühl 1997; Braig 1999). Both the UN women's year and the UN Decade for Women (1975-2000) can be seen as fundamentally important for the newly articulating transnational movements (Newland 1991: 122-132) since an increasing number of governments recognised the transnational movements in one way or another (Braig 1999: 282). Under the umbrella of the United Nations the transnational movements played an increasingly important role. This was also obvious through the double structure of the women world conferences where special meetings were arranged for NGOs next to the official government delegations. Despite various conflicts between NGOs and government delegations, the pragmatic approaches of the NGOs particularly with regard to the Women in Development (WID) approaches convinced the government agencies with the result that women's policies were institutionalised. In 1973 the governmental agency for economic and humanitarian assistance world-wide of the United States of America (USAID) established a WID office. In 1976 the International Research and Training Institute for the Advancement of Women (INSTRAW) was founded, which is the UN International Research and Training Institute for the Advancement of Women.

The WID approach was criticised by women from developing countries since it was allegedly developed based on western life styles. Women from the South criticised that they felt homogenised and victimised to 'third world women'. Thus the empowerment approach was developed by women's movements and groups from the South which led to foundation of various international women's networks at the end of the women's decade, especially 'Development Alternatives with Women in a New Era' (DAWN).

The gender mainstreaming approach was mainly introduced into development work by female economists. They demanded that the gender specific consequences of structural adjustments were examined in order to get a clearer understanding of the impact of economic theories and also to achieve a higher efficiency. Gender mainstreaming also allowed to examine gender specific exclusion mechanisms (GTZ 1997).

The German sociologist Ilse Lenz (2001) distinguishes two different discussion patterns with regard to globalisation and women. Some authors focus on 'economic globalisation and examine particular structures of inequality and processes of inequality' (Lenz 2001: 8, for an example for the described discussion pattern see e.g. Mies 2001). Another discussion pattern concentrates on the question

[...] to what extent international organisations and global women's networks and women's movements in the UN decade on women were able to establish women's issues as a central theme and to succeed in some areas. This discussion pattern adopted the global governance approach, which assumes that negotiations between global and national institutions and civil society can lead to new international norms and rules (Lenz 2001: 8)[88].

6.5 Conclusion

The European Commission is interdependent on its environment in various ways. The development and control of the implementation of gender main-streaming within the Commission is closely interwoven with European women's movements, European institutions and the United Nations. The European Women's movements, the EP Committee on Equal Opportunities for Women and Men and the United Nations all create uncertainty for the Commission by publishing resolutions and comparative reports on the progress of gender equality in the European Union. The European Commission implements gender mainstreaming to increase its legitimacy with regard to its environment. The implementation of gender mainstreaming in the Commission can be seen as an example of mimetic isomorphism (DiMaggio/ Powell 1991b [1983]). The environment of the Commission with regard to gender mainstreaming consists of European Women's movements, European Institutions and the United Nations.

The most important lobby group within European Women's movements is the EWL. The foundation of the EWL has proved to be of utmost impor-tance for the development of equal opportunities and gender mainstreaming policies in the European Union. The campaigning of the EWL in favour of positive action led to the inclusion of positive action in the gender mainstreaming approach of the Commission in the so-called 'Commission method' or 'dual track approach'. The 1996 IGC in the preparation for the Treaty of Amsterdam demonstrated that an improved political opportunity structure for NGOs and the strategic lobbying of the EWL led to the inclusion of gender mainstreaming into the Treaty of Amsterdam. The European institutions, particularly the Women's Committee of the EP and the Advisory Committee have emerged as important players for the monitoring of gender mainstreaming. The UN and the World Conference of Women in Nairobi (1985) and Beijing (1995) have been particularly important for the

---

88   Translation by the author.

inclusion of gender mainstreaming on the global level which led to the introduction of gender mainstreaming on the European level.

7 The Construction and Implementation of Gender Mainstreaming within the European Commission

7.1 Introduction

This chapter will explore the research questions in the empirical setting, i.e. to what extent gender mainstreaming can be seen as an innovation and an institution in the European Union. I shall first summarise all the main findings of the theoretical chapter in order to link the theoretical and empirical parts closely together.

Jepperson (1991) defines an institution as a social order or pattern that has attained a certain state or property; whereby *order* or *pattern* means standardised interaction sequences. Jepperson stresses that institutions need to be self-reproducing, i.e. their persistence is not dependant on recurrent collective mobilisation. With regard to gender mainstreaming we thus need to examine the extent to which gender mainstreaming has led to standardised interaction sequences and whether these are self-reproducing.

Giddens' structuration theory (1984) will be used to analyse how action taken by different actors within and outside the Commission affects gender mainstreaming and why its diffusion remains somewhat limited. The structuration approach also enables the internal power struggles of actors on gender mainstreaming to be studied.

The following hypotheses, in particular, will be thoroughly examined in this chapter: The higher the degree of vested interests that are opposed to the transformation of gender relations, the greater the likelihood of organisational resistance to gender mainstreaming.

The following hypothesis, partly derived from Oliver (1991: 160-170) and DiMaggio and Powell (1991b [1983]) (see chapter 2) will be scrutinised:

The higher the degree of voluntary diffusion of gender mainstreaming by actors within the European Commission, the lower the likelihood of resistance from the Commission as an organisation to institutional pressures from the United Nations.

The following two thesis, derived from chapter 3, will also be examined: The more powerful the position of one of the two groups of actors, i.e. either the gender mainstreaming coordination unit or the individual organisational units which implement gender mainstreaming, and the greater the power each has to define its own position as legally given, the more this particular group will be able to influence the negotiating process in a particular way. A legally strong position held by gender mainstreaming responsible officials can be confronted with an avoidance power by the lower ranking implementing group.

The fact that various Member States implemented gender mainstreaming despite a missing legal obligation can be seen as an example of coercive isomorphism as explained by DiMaggio and Powell (1991b [1983]: 67).

I shall argue that the limited success of the hitherto used equal opportunities policies is one important reason for the implementation of gender mainstreaming in the EU.

The most important single indicator on the implementation of gender mainstreaming is to examine the construction of gender mainstreaming by different actors. The first part of the chapter will examine how actors perceive the changes that have taken place due to mainstreaming. This part will examine how the actors construct gender mainstreaming, what they think are success criteria for gender mainstreaming and the most important changes that have taken place due to gender mainstreaming. The second part will examine these changes in more detail according to the categories that emerged from the theoretical framework. Thus the resources that exist as a result of gender mainstreaming will be examined. Furthermore barriers to the implementation of gender mainstreaming will be illustrated. As one of the concluding points the question of whether the implementation of gender mainstreaming can be seen as an innovation will be assessed. Finally, the main research question of this book will be elaborated, i.e. to what extent gender mainstreaming has been structured or institutionalised within the European Commission.

7.2 The Social Construction of Gender Mainstreaming within the Commission: Actors and their Interests

7.2.1 The Understanding and Association of different Actors regarding Gender Mainstreaming

Since there are many different perceptions and understandings on the concept of gender mainstreaming, it is first of all important to see how gender mainstreaming is viewed by different actors within the Commission.

One important finding is the discovery that there is a great difference in understanding between the gender mainstreaming advocacy-network and those who are not directly involved with gender mainstreaming. Those from the gender mainstreaming advocacy-network all recited the spirit and many made reference to the official gender mainstreaming definition of the Commission which can be found in the 1996 Communication: 'Incorporating

Equal Opportunities for Women and Men into all Community Policies and Activities' (European Commission 1996).

However, those interviewees not directly involved with gender mainstreaming form the large majority of those working in the Commission and in general they had a very imprecise idea of gender mainstreaming. Only one male interviewee came close to the official definition of gender mainstreaming by saying:

I don't know much about it [gender mainstreaming]. As far as I know, gender mainstreaming means the permeation of all policy areas with regards to equal opportunities and positive action. These should be considered in all laws or action programmes (interview 3, male administrator).

Even though his definition of gender mainstreaming is closest to the official definition of the Commission in the 1996 Communication (European Commission 1996), his insecurity is still shown by his introductory sentence when he says that he doesn't know much about gender mainstreaming.

Other actors' comments on gender mainstreaming that it has something to do with 'equal opportunities of both sexes' (interview 25, manager), the 'proper equilibrium of the sexes' (interview 6, manager[89]) and 'reconciliation policies for professional and private life' (interview 15, female administrator) cannot as definitions be distinguished from positive action policies (refer to chapter 2) and indeed when they were prompted on the difference between positive action and gender mainstreaming, they saw none (interview 6, manager; interview 24, manager).

However, even some of those who are directly responsible for gender mainstreaming are sometimes unclear about its meaning. As one assistant recounts:

I was supposed to be responsible for gender mainstreaming technically, that is, in my job description. But I've never really understood what it means. And when I asked what it means the only explanation I got was that I should try to ensure that more female staff are recruited and promoted. And that there are a lot more men than women and we should try and recruit more women. Also that the women should go before the men, but I don't think this is a good idea. In the beginning they took it quite seriously and [...][90] [a former Director General] also took it seriously. I made a comment about it but I am not sure if it made an impact.
Author: And now you are not responsible for gender mainstreaming any more?
I still am, but it is very difficult if the Heads of Unit argues that the man is excellent and has the right profile for the job what can I – as a personnel person – say? (interview 19, female assistant).

This quotation is revealing in various respects. The actor actively tries to find out her responsibilities with regard to gender mainstreaming. However, the

---

89 The term 'manager' denotes a male manager, while manageress is the female equivalent.
90 She quotes the name of a former Director General, which is omitted here for the sake of anonymity of the interviewee.

explanations she gets are not very precise. In fact the point she raises, that she is supposed to give preferential treatment to women over men, is not part of the gender mainstreaming policy in the Commission. It might be that she misunderstood this point or that the person explaining to her had misunderstood the gender mainstreaming policy of the Commission, or indeed that the internal interpretation on gender mainstreaming is different to the official one. After various frustrating experiences, the fact that the assistant no longer feels responsible for gender mainstreaming is suggested by the use of past tense in the phrase 'I was responsible for gender mainstreaming' even though she later acknowledges that she is still responsible.

According to the majority of interviewees, the most important requirement for the implementation of gender mainstreaming is commitment from the top level. However, the top-down implementation of gender mainstreaming in the Commission is also criticised by one actor:

I think it's commitment and also commitment from the top. That is essential. But it's not enough. They organised a gender training for the Heads of Unit and the Directors. But I don't think it's sufficient. It is important to change the attitudes of the personnel. It's not only the hierarchy which has to change. For all the documents that are issued, it is not the hierarchy who are drafting them. And when the hierarchy intervenes it might be too late to do something. I don't agree with the approach that we should train Heads of Units and Directors and leave the rest. I think we should start from the bottom. For me it's a bottom-up approach. You have to have political commitment. And the political commitment is there (interview 10, female administrator).

This administrator does not believe that the hierarchy will adequately pass the gender mainstreaming requirement on to the other hierarchies. Therefore, in her view, trainings should not be limited to the hierarchy. She thinks that gender mainstreaming could be implemented more effectively with a bottom-up approach. Her last point that there is political commitment in the European Commission is much disputed and will be elaborated in the section on authoritative resources.

Several male employees voice an association of equal opportunities with tensions between men and women which is illustrated in the following quotation as an example:

Mainstreaming means that there ought to be equal opportunities between the sexes. I don't see this as an issue solely between men and women, but also for disabled people and different races. I see mainstreaming as much more general than the tensions between men and women (interview 6, manager).

Indeed, this would be in line with two Directives adopted by the Council of the European Union to prohibit discrimination in the Member States in employment with regard to racial and ethnic origin, religion and belief, disability, age and sexual orientation[91].

Another important association with regard to gender mainstreaming was the introduction of quotas which was mentioned by various male and female interviewees and which is exemplified in the following quotation.

I associate with gender mainstreaming the proper equilibrium between the two sexes. I am not saying that in every circumstance we should have 50:50, because I am not sure if we have 50:50 in the world. What I associate with it is that we should have the human perspective, the woman perspective, the man perspective and that we should not discriminate men against women, nor women against men. I think that sex has no importance in the way we manage, in the way we do things. Of course we are in a public administration. I am not saying that if you carry heavy loads of course there should be no differentiation, of course we are different physically. But in our more intellectual activities, sex should not play any role (interview 24, manager).

One reason for the association of gender mainstreaming with quotas might be the decision of the Commission to gender balance all Committees and Expert Committees set up by the Commission with 40% of each sex (European Commission 2000). This decision was being discussed intensively during the period when the interviews took place and had enormous effects on those in the Commission who were dealing with Committees, as they were sometimes made responsible for the implementation of the decision, though often it were Member States which nominating delegates to the different Committees. It is thus not surprising that, for a few interviewees the quotas were one of the first associations made with regard to gender mainstreaming. The above quotation seems exemplary as an expression of the opinion of a variety of officials who see no structural discrimination between men and women. The particular manager cited above is saying that sex should have no importance in the way that processes are managed and run at the Commission. He acknowledges physical rather than socially constructed differences with regard to women and men. However, in the last phrase of the quotation he says that these differences *should* not play a role in the work at the Commission since the work does not require physical activity, rather than

---

91   The first Directive prohibits discrimination on the grounds of racial and ethnic origin and prohibits discrimination in the fields of employment, education, social protection (including social security and health care), social advantages and access to goods and services (including housing) (Council of the European Union 2000a). The second Directive (Council of the European Union 2000b) prohibits discrimination in employment on the grounds of religion and belief, disability, age and sexual orientation, i.e. covers all grounds for discrimination named in Article 13 of the Treaty of Amsterdam (1997) except for gender which is covered by the amended Directive on Equal Treatment (Council of the European Union 2002a, see annexe). These Directives still have to be transposed into national law before they take effect. The Member States have until 19 July 2003 to transpose the Racial Discrimination Directive and until 2 December 2003 to transpose the Employment Discrimination Directive (with a possibility of an extension of up to further three years for the provisions on discrimination on grounds of disability and age).

that they *do not* play a role. This might be interpreted as an indication that he is not entirely convinced of his previous statement i.e. that sex has no relevance in the management and way of working. Alternatively, the latter statement could be meant as a moral statement, that there ought not to be any differences between men and women even though there might be.

Ambiguity on the possible difference between both genders which was voiced also by other actors was expressed by the following secretary:

I don't take it [differences between both genders] into account in a terribly conscious way. I don't think I take it into account. Linguistically I notice. Written language, I sort of notice, when women haven't been taken into account. Or in committees which are in no way balanced. So I am probably subconsciously very aware of the issue. [...] And that is since I worked in the Equal Opportunities Unit. And I notice language. I notice language when a text refers only to 'he' but I also notice language when it is so convoluted because it is full of 'he/she' (interview 1, female secretary).

On the one hand this actor notices if women are omitted in spoken language or if they are underrepresented in meetings. She notices if women are omitted in written language but on the other hand she also finds that some texts containing references to both sexes 'convoluted'.

The following administrator sees another problem with the concept of gender mainstreaming in that, by making everyone responsible for gender mainstreaming, in the end no one feels personally responsible. This point was indeed also raised by various other actors.

Gender mainstreaming means 'gender' and 'mainstreaming'. Mainstreaming means not being responsible for anything personally. Gender means to have equal chances for men and women. That is the same as the integration of the disabled and the same recognition of races. It is a political approach, at the end of the day it is the responsibility of others. (interview 3, male administrator).

Indeed this view corresponds to the criticism of parts of the women's movement and various scholars elaborated in chapter 2, that by mainstreaming the responsibility of gender, gender becomes less obvious at the end.

One manager with a linguistic background comments on the term gender mainstreaming in the following way:

I hate the term gender mainstreaming. I am a linguist. Gender is a thing that by definition is not attached to a person. So it is a depersonalisation. It does not attract anyone. It reduces to der, die, das[92] and undervalues the person behind. On the streets, I don't go up to someone and think what gender the person has (interview 25, manager).

This manager is not in favour of the term 'gender mainstreaming' because he feels the term is depersonalising and undervalues persons. He also says that gender has no practical meaning since he himself does not think about it.

---

92   German definite articles denoting the male and female gender and neutral.

Indeed, women of the global South and ethnic minorities in the global North have highlighted the fact that white men are often not aware of their sex, – while ethnic minority women as a potentially repressed group are usually very aware of theirs. The US-American sociologist Michael Kimmel cites the example that when a woman is asked whom she sees when she looks into the mirror, she will say a woman. Women of ethnic minorities might also be aware of their ethnic background. Whereas when a man is asked the same question he will say a human being. He is not aware of his gender or ethnic belonging since he does not feel any discrimination (Kimmel 2002: 3)[93].

Another important question on the understanding of gender mainstreaming is whether it is perceived that actors in different DGs and actors working in other areas and in different hierarchical steps of the Commission have a shared understanding of gender mainstreaming. The large majority of those interviewed saw no common understanding. This difference was seen firstly between people who were involved with gender mainstreaming or not and between different DGs. The first point is illustrated by the comment of the following administrator:

The people who are directly involved with gender mainstreaming do have a common understanding, they can pass on their understanding to other people. Those who are not directly involved might have an idea; they may perhaps know that it has something to do with equal opportunities. (interview 7, female administrator)

This quotation raises an important point regarding the differentiation between those who are part of the gender mainstreaming advocacy-network and those not directly involved with gender mainstreaming. The identity of belonging to one of the two groups is often described with terms like 'we', other actors not working directly within gender mainstreaming and equal opportunities are referred to as 'they' (interview 21, female administrator; interview 7, female administrator). One actor says that

I don't talk to such people who argue against gender mainstreaming. [...]. What is important are actions, there is too much talking (interview 4, manageress).

This interviewee recounts that she does not communicate with people who are opposed to gender mainstreaming, which emphasises the existence of different communities 'pro-gender mainstreaming' and 'anti-gender mainstreaming'.

This positive and negative identification suggests a point that has been invoked before, i.e. that gender mainstreaming has not so far, reached the point at which everyone feels responsible for gender mainstreaming.

---

93   This example is taken from a Northern context. A white middle class man who wakes up in Zimbabwe in 2002 and 2003 where expulsions of white farmers took place might also see a white person in the mirror, rather than 'just' a human being.

One way to find out how a policy is seen by actors is to examine their associations with other policies. With regard to policies comparable to gender mainstreaming most actors mentioned environmental policy as being closest since sustainable development is also regarded as a horizontal issue (interview 13, male administrator). One administrator says that there are many similarities between gender mainstreaming and a knowledge society in that both are horizontal issues which are supposed to permeate all areas. However, he thinks that gender mainstreaming has many more resources and more political backing than a knowledge society (interview 9, male administrator).

The difference of knowledge between those who are actively involved in the gender mainstreaming policy structures (or who used to be in the past) and those who are not directly involved with gender mainstreaming would suggest that gender mainstreaming might only be institutionalised amongst the 'gender experts' within the Commission and not the whole of the Commission. This will be further examined in the following sections.

At first sight, with regard to knowing of what gender mainstreaming consists of, no significant difference could be seen between the sexes, nor between the different hierarchical levels[94]. However, male actors appear to have far more 'loaded' and negative associations with gender mainstreaming than their female counterparts. The aim of this section was to summarise the construction of meaning with regard to gender mainstreaming by different actors, the next section will examine the understanding of actors in different Directorates General.

7.2.2 Understanding across different Directorates General

The significant differences in the understanding of gender mainstreaming between people in the different DGs is exemplified by the following statement:

There is no common understanding [between the different DGs]. Even though we are not very advanced here [in DG Employment and Social Affairs] I see that they are much less advanced in DG Competition (interview 19, female assistant).

Several interviewees named DG Competition as a negative example for the understanding and implementation of gender mainstreaming.

One actor talks specifically of the different understanding of DG External Relations:

In Relex [DG External Relations] they consider that mainstreaming issues are those dealing with human rights because they tend to know that women's rights are human rights. But

---

94 Since the sample of the interviewees is not representative, and since a clear typification of the degree of knowledge is problematic, no detailed figures are provided for these different categories.

other than these rights I don't think they ever thought of this being an issue (interview 10, female administrator).

One possible reason for this is explained by another actor in the following way:

But for example gender mainstreaming and development cooperation and international co-operation. They were running into serious cultural difficulties. And I have the perception that you are just up and against something so entirely different to a western society. And the Commission's mainstreaming policies, they were thought for the women in the Commission but the differences between the West and other areas are huge, and the priorities are very different. Perhaps it is a luxury of the rich, to be able to focus on gender issues. If you only have a dollar a day, you have other problems (interview 1, female secretary).

Both actors agree that gender mainstreaming is not high on the agenda of DG External Relations. The second one is saying that the gender mainstreaming policies were developed for European standards and that the employees would encounter a lot of resistance form non-Western countries even if they implement the policies internally.

The following manageress is talking about missing support from other DGs, particularly DG External Relations:

If I just take the Barcelona process which is the programme for the Mediterranean; we had a session last year a big event in July and then there was a ministerial meeting in Novem-ber. And the idea in the new Medec programme was that, we have a strand on women. And we might, it's not happened yet but we might actually succeed in that. But that's not gender mainstreaming. That's specific action. And I think if we wanted to mainstream the Barcelona process itself we would meet with a lot of resistance. So all we got there is specific action, as opposed to gender mainstreaming.
VS: And from whom would you say that you meet resistance?
Well in something like that we do tend to get a lot of resistance from External Relations [DG External Relations]. Because if you think about it for a minute, you are going to the rest of the world, say the United States and Japan and your position is totally different. So if you come with European norms on gender equality and you talk to the Mediterranean countries or the Asian countries, you will certainly meet a lot of resistance. And since the colleagues there already meet a lot of resistance, the last thing they want to do is to come up with another issue where they meet even more (interview 2, manageress).

This quotation shows that the officials in DG External Relations whom the actor refers to drop gender mainstreaming from their agenda in order to avoid confrontation with countries outside of the EU.

One official from the Equal Opportunities Unit from DG Employment and Social Affairs sees the problem as a lack of common understanding on gender mainstreaming.

There is no common understanding on gender mainstreaming, and part of the difficulty is to some extent, our own in that we haven't yet managed to identify a good definition or explanation in simple words. With all the definitions you find on gender mainstreaming, you need a dictionary to understand them. We have been struggling with that. How do you

177

say it in very simple words to make it clear? We often find that we can only explain it by giving an example (interview 10, female administrator).

This perceived lack of common understanding has led to a new strategy from the Equal Opportunities Unit in DG Employment and Social Affairs. Since 2001 they have deliberately stopped saying that gender mainstreaming is easy to implement. Instead, they stress how complicated and difficult it is. Since then, they have given training to the Heads of Units from DG Employment as well as the Regional and Structural Funds and the geographical desks within DG Employment and Social Affairs which deal with the implementation of gender mainstreaming in the European Social Funds in individual Member States.

This shift in strategy can be explained by normative isomorphism developed by Larson (1977) and Collins (1979). As has been elaborated in chapter 3, normative isomorphism is closely associated with professionalisation, which is the collective struggle of members of an occupation to define the conditions and methods of their work, to control 'the production of producers' (Larson: 1977: 49-52) and to establish a cognitive base and legitimisation for their occupational autonomy (DiMaggio/ Powell 1991b [1983]: 67). The new approach by the Equal Opportunities Unit has been explained by the above cited actor herself as an attempt to increase the legitimacy of gender mainstreaming and also by extension the work in the Equal Opportunities Unit. The training carried out by the Equal Opportunities Unit itself allows the unit to define gender mainstreaming and establish a cognitive base for gender mainstreaming. It also enables members of the Equal Opportunities Unit to increase their competencies since their actual task is to implement gender mainstreaming in the programmes and measures of the Commission vis-à-vis the outside world.

7.2.3 Motives for the Implementation of Gender Mainstreaming within the European Commission according to the Actors

The motives seen by individual actors, as being behind the introduction of a new policy are important for the motivation of the actor to implement that policy. There are four main reasons seen by actors for the implementation of gender mainstreaming: Firstly, the World Conference on Women in Beijing (interview 4, manageress; interview 2, manageress), secondly the pressure from the EP and the EWL (interview 2, manageress; interview 11, manageress; interview 19, female assistant) thirdly a notion of political correctness (interview 1, female secretary) and fourthly the conviction that gender mainstreaming leads to a more efficient policy (interview 4, manageress).

The Beijing conference can be seen as a 'critical event' (Bourdieu 1984). The French sociologist Pierre Bourdieu introduces this term with regard to

178

the analyses of protest events in Parisian Universities in May 1968. According to Bourdieu, important signs of critical events are synchronising effects, i.e. not the addition of different crises, but their recursive entanglement. The various critical events will result in a 'general crisis' and:

Paradoxically, it is not probably conditional in the reinsertion of critical moments back into the series, that the intelligibility lies. It is in the nullification of what is in a sense the singularity, that one can understand, in its own right, what defines the critical situation, if not as a 'novel creation out of the unforeseeable' then at least as the sudden appearance of the possibility of innovation. In brief, just as in clear weather every kind of future is possible and in this very measure, they are partly so (Bourdieu 1984: 212)[95].

When interviewees were asked to give the reasons why they thought gender mainstreaming was implemented in the Commission, the single most important factor offered was the UN World Conference on Women in Beijing:

Without Beijing we would never have gender mainstreaming as a principle. Beijing was a turning point for women's policies world wide (interview 26, female administrator).

Even though various actors stress that they were not responsible for gender mainstreaming at the time or that they were not sure of the reasons for the implementation, they still mentioned that they thought the Beijing conference had an important impact.

This is in clear contradiction to the publication of the Commission (European Commission 1996) and the EP (European Parliament 2003) which state that the Commission played an active part in the 1995 UN World Conference in establishing gender mainstreaming in the first place. Gender mainstreaming is thus perceived very differently by the actors within the Commission than in the official publications of the Commission. This confirms the hypothesis that due to the low degree of legal coercion, the Commission framed gender mainstreaming in such a way that it must be implemented and used the normative pressure from an institution like the United Nation to create coercive isomorphism.

The second most important motive for the implementation of gender mainstreaming was the lobbying of the European Parliament and specifically the women's committee and the European Women's Lobby (see chapter 6), on equal opportunities for men and women. A third motive for the implementation of gender mainstreaming is thought to be a notion of political correctness:

---

95   Translation by the author. The French original is: 'Paradoxalement, c'est sans doute à condition de réinsérer les moments critiques dans les séries où réside le principe de leur intelligibilité, annulant ce qui en fait en un sens la singularité, que l'on peut comprendre ce qui définit en propre la situation critique, sinon comme « création d'imprévisible nouveauté », du moins comme surgissement de la possibilité de la nouveauté, bref, comme temps ouvert où tous les avenirs paraissent possibles, et le sont pour un part, dans cette mesure même.'

[Gender mainstreaming is implemented...] to be politically correct. For me it is not normal. It is just to be politically correct (interview 22, female secretary).

This actor does not see gender mainstreaming as part of her normal routine, but rather only implements it to be politically correct.

The German sociologist Simon Möller (1999: 197-205) examined discourses of 'sexual correctness'[96] and concluded that two different types of discourses can be distinguished: Firstly the presentation of 'sexual correctness' feminism as a 'political functional construction of the enemy', which means that anti-'sexual correctness' authors are able to define themselves in delimitation of feminists. Secondly, 'anti-sexual correctness' as a 'repudiation of justice of distribution', i.e. the authors of 'anti-sexual correctness' are in favour of the deconstruction of the welfare state since this as well as feminists are seen as patronising. Even though Möller suggests that 'anti-sexual correctness' discourses are a 'special fight by men (as a social group) for the maintenance of their traditional dominating economic and social position' (Möller 1999: 197) they are nevertheless also brought forward by women as the interview citation suggests.

Other motives for the introduction of gender mainstreaming cited by individual actors were for example: pressure from the women's movement[97] (interview 19, female assistant); the Scandinavian countries (interview 2, manageress); the women's unit in DG Administration and Personnel (interview 19, female assistant); DG Employment and Social Affairs (interview 11, manageress); social movements and social partners (interview 22, female secretary); the Advisory Committee on Equal Opportunities (interview 11, manageress) and the commitment of Anita Gradin and Monika Wulf-Mathies, two former Commissioners[98] (interview 3, male administrator).

Even though the actors see a wide variation of motives for the introduction of gender mainstreaming, it is noteworthy that none of them mentions the framings from the publications of the Commission, i.e. the reference to equality and the reference to increased economic efficiency (refer to chapter 2).

---

96 Möller refers to the discourses on 'political correctness· in German media as 'sexual correctness' in an 'exaggerated manner' (Möller 1999: 19).

97 As elaborated in chapter 3, there is a dispute among scholars whether the European Women's Lobby should be treated as being part of the women's movements, or whether they should be rather seen as a quago (quasi governmental organisation) or quango (quasi non-governmental organisation).

98 Anita Gradin from Sweden and Monika Wulf-Mathies from Germany both served as European Commissioner from 1995-1999. Anita Gradin was responsible for Immigration, Home Affairs and Justice; relations with the Ombudsman; Financial Control and Fraud Prevention. Monika Wulf-Mathies was responsible for Regional Policies; Relations with the Committee of the Regions and the Cohesion Fund.

7.2.4 Success Criteria for Gender Mainstreaming

An important indicator for the different conceptions of a policy is how the actors define the criteria for success for this policy. While it is important to think in general terms as well as in the abstract about the flaws and contradictions of gender mainstreaming in the Commission, I shall focus on the implementation of gender mainstreaming from the point of view of the aims set by the Commission and thus the implementation can only be measured by these aims. I shall thus define success criteria for gender mainstreaming as a close fit of the implementation of the gender mainstreaming Communication (European Commission 1996) and the implementation of gender mainstreaming by the individual DGs and actors.

The interviewees stressed different points; the most important being the dispersion of gender mainstreaming across the Commission and the changes in the organisational culture and measurable indicators such as quotas.

The latter point about the introduction of quota is bitterly disputed. Some interviewees felt so strongly about the introduction that when they were questioned about success criteria they made a negative reference to quotas in that they would not constitute a criterion for success. Other interviewees who favoured quotas mentioned different figures for possible quotas. The 25% quota mentioned by the interview partner below might be a reference to the 20% target for middle management posts in the year 2000. Other interview partners mentioned 40% as a quota, which might be a reference to the Commission Communication on a 40% representation in all committees set up by the Commission (European Commission 2000). A 50% quota might be a reference to the demands of various women's movements for equal representation for men and women.

The following actor stresses the relevance of qualitative success criteria of gender mainstreaming rather than quotas for different areas which illustrates the ambivalence of various actors towards a quota:

Well, that is a difficult question. Success criteria. Well, there are measurable things, i.e. that more money is granted for gender mainstreaming, that more people work on it, that more women are in decision-making positions and that we [the Commission] now say that we want to increase the employment rate to 60% by 2010. The criteria for this are that firstly the employment rate will be 60%, and also the quality of the jobs. [...] We could get many women into part-time employment by 2010, but that doesn't mean anything. Gender mainstreaming goes beyond the quantitative analysis, it's quality that counts (interview 4, manageress).

This manageress stresses that the success of gender mainstreaming cannot be assessed by the indicators such as the employment rate for women, but that normative factors like the quality of jobs play an important role. This refers to the critique of the women's movements, trade unions and the ILO which all demand that the quality of new jobs should be stressed rather than their quantity (see e.g. Baccaro 2001).

7.2.5 The Importance of Culture within the Commission

The importance of culture for GM is viewed very differently within the Commission. Some actors claimed that because of the different cultural backgrounds of employees in the Commission, it would be easier to implement gender mainstreaming. Others said that there is an important North-South divide between the perceptions of equal opportunities. These views will be elaborated in what follows, but firstly it is important to explain the concept of culture within organisations.

Ulrike Berger (1993: 12) differentiates between two different camps in the literature on organisational cultures: Firstly, that the one within management studies is primarily interested in the contribution of organisational culture to the success of enterprises. The authors in this camp conceptualise the enterprise culture as a variable which can manipulate and explain the actions of organisational members. In this context, cultural system and social system are analytically separated (compare Parsons 1951). The corporate culture camp is close to the economic management camp and has functional intentions and many consultancies adhere to this approach.

The second camp refers to the 'social construction of reality' (Berger/ Luckmann 1966). The scholars in this camp are mostly interested in understanding and interpreting the meaning of organisational phenomena. Texts in this context interest themselves in the symbolic qualities of organisational phenomena such as managerial behaviour or organisational symbolism. Authors starting from this viewpoint base their work on symbolic interactionism and ethnomethodology. Organisational culture is thus not a variable but rather a root metaphor of a culturalistic organisational analysis (Smireich 1983, Ebers 1985), i.e. in this context, organisational culture is not merely one indicator amongst others but rather a central point in the analysis. As has been implicitly stated in the theoretical framework, this study is clearly based within the second camp.

One actor explains the importance of culture in the following way:

One issue that is important at least here at my level for the personnel policy is that we did not properly explain to male colleagues why it is important to have mainstreaming. I think this is not specific to the Commission. There has been a big change in the role models in society with regard to gender. Now we have to give time to society to readapt to this new situation. Okay we have our culture, we have our pre-conceived ideas, and little by little this changes. And I don't think that the Commission or an institution would change alone. We would change at the same rate and at the same time as societies (interview 11, manageress).

This manageress emphasises the emebeddedness of the Commission within society. As elaborated in the theoretical framework, this is an important pre-condition for both theoretical strands underlying this book, i.e. neo-institutionalism and structuration theory. She addresses various problems regarding culture. Firstly she is saying that the raison d'être of gender mainstreaming has not been adequately explained to men working in the Commission. She is saying that it will take time until society has readapted to the new gender roles. She sees a recursive process between society and the organisation in that changes can only take place simultaneously.

The next actor also stresses the importance of culture, but in addition, says that:

For me culture is the key aspect. And the other thing is acceptance. More than imposing. Convincing. Real arguments. The only way you can have a process change is to have people on board. And this is the way you change things. Of course it depends on society. But globally there are no major discriminations. There are people who are completely against gender mainstreaming of course. The only way is to change the way of thinking rather than imposing by law (interview 24, manager).

This manager is saying that the culture can only be changed by convincing people of a certain cause and that these changes also depend on society. He does not believe that a law can change the way of thinking within the organi-sation. According to his view, there are no major discriminations globally so indeed there is no need for any fundamental changes.

The importance of having the point of view of each gender in the discus-sion is stressed by various interviewees. One male official from the management level stresses that it is important to have, for example, both men and women to deal with the public, since each gender finds 'it is easier to deal with certain issues' (interview 24, manager). This symbolises a function-al understanding of gender difference, that women can relate better to certain issues and vice versa. He elaborates further:

I don't think gender mainstreaming should mean the achievement of a quarter of women everywhere. Of course if you have very few women for example in the hierarchy, you can think about that. But we also need to think about the evolution. I believe that in the future, there will be no discrimination. I don't think that this will be achieved by law. This is more a cultural achievement. If you say we need to have this because we are all equal, you will have more success than if you impose. It's like any policy. You will have more success with a policy if you have everybody in favour than if you impose. It's the same with an innovation or a change. If you want any change in an organisation will be successful you need to have commitment. So I think the main aspect, the main indicator of the success of this policy is that everybody accepts it and applies it (interview 24, manager).

In his view, gender mainstreaming should not be enforced by the organisa-tion; rather, he believes that the Commission will evolve to be more equal by way of 'cultural achievement'. He thinks that every new policy should evolve from within the organisation rather than being imposed upon it.

The following administrator stresses the importance of cultural change:

As I said, there is still a lot of ground to cover; it is not just finished by introducing regulations. Rules and regulations by themselves will not change anything. People need to become aware of what they do. People say that we have been living in a democracy for 200 years. But I tell them that it was not a democracy in that women only got to vote after the World War. Before that it was not a democracy. Then people are shocked. But afterwards he realised that I did have a good point. So there is always improvement (interview 10, female administrator).

This actor also stresses that regulations alone will not change anything. Rather it is that people need to be more reflective of their actions. She is also saying that the cultural change can only be brought about by individuals trying to change the situation.

The actor in the following quotation suggests that any change in culture is difficult compared to changing the regulations.

There is a culture of long working hours. To change that is relatively difficult. To change the staff regulations is much easier. But to really change such things, such customs, is very difficult, especially with the difference in culture. Those who come late, can stay later in the evening (interview 25, manager).

This manager also mentions the importance of cultural differences with regard to long working hours. This has become particularly important since the introduction of flexitime in the Commission. DG Employment and Social Affairs introduced a system of flexitime, which allows employees to arrive any time up to 9.30 a.m., on Mondays until 10.30 a.m. They should remain at work until at least 5.30 p.m. from Monday until Thursday and until 4 p.m. on Fridays[99]. Some southern European employees in the Commission openly stress that they prefer to arrive late in the morning and/ or prefer to take long lunch breaks and stay later in the evening[100].

The culture of long working hours has a lot of consequences for family life. One actor comments on this in the following way:

I think gender mainstreaming really only comes about when men's attitude towards children change. It's not just to enable women to look after their kids it's also to get men to take their share of responsibility for the kids. Then in the long run you'll start to see changes in the working culture (interview 10, female administrator).

The administrator in the following quotation denies the relevance of cultures, although in fact in a direct manner she says that cultures are important. According to this actor, Scandinavians are more familiar with gender mainstreaming. She gives the example of the Portuguese in that they feel they are

---

99 The relatively late ultimate arrival time on Monday and early leaving time on Friday can be explained by the fact that many employees use Monday morning and Friday afternoon as commuting times from their home country to the Commission.

100 For the sake of anonymity, the interview numbers are not provided in this context, since the cultural background of the interviewees is mentioned.

184

left behind with regard to the implementation of equal opportunities, while Germans on the other hand don't appear very attentive according to this actor, since they perceive themselves as progressive in this respect.

No, cultures don't play any role. There is no North- South divide as one could think. The only difference that exists is there because of Scandinavia. Scandinavian people are more familiar with the mainstreaming concept. Other than that it is vice versa. People from Portugal have an inferiority complex and think that the South is behind on everything, whereas the Germans think they are so progressive and believe that the reason why so few women work professionally in Germany is not the result of missing kindergarten places but because they do not want to work. Thus they don't make any effort and don't do anything for equal opportunities (interview 26, female administrator).

Various actors mention the importance of the input of Scandinavian Member States for the implementation of gender mainstreaming (interview 2, manageress; interview 7, female administrator). In the view of other actors, the existence of different cultures within the Commission was, in fact, positive for the implementation of gender mainstreaming, since the different cultures were seen as 'very enriching' (interview 12, female administrator) and 'since people are more outspoken because they work with people from different national backgrounds' (interview 7, female administrator). Another administrator comments that

[...] some Member States are more advanced than others [with regard to the implementation of gender mainstreaming]. [...] So we should benefit from them. So above all, we should be able to use the best standards (interview 11, manageress).

The use of best practice is a sensitive issue within the European Commission since 'cultural differences' between the Member States are often put forward by Member States that do not qualify as best practice cases in a particular area.

One administrator says that 'it is difficult to work in an international environment in any case' (interview 9, administrator). However, according to him, the implementation of gender mainstreaming within the Commission is not more or less difficult than the implementation of other policies. This view was also shared by other actors (interview 24, manager; interview 1, female secretary).

Another manager stresses the special importance of Eastern European enlargement of the EU[101].

[...] maybe [the implementation of gender mainstreaming is] a bit more difficult than in other organisations. Even though people here have more of an international point of view which makes it easier. Maybe with the Eastern European countries it will be more difficult. I don't know how it will be with Polish society, and whether equal opportunities is

---

101 The following countries joined the EU in 2004: Estonia, Latvia, Lithuania, Malta, Poland, Slovakia, Slovenia, Czech Republic, Hungary and Cyprus.

achieved there. With regard to the current 15 EU Member States, I do think that it is an aquis[102] (interview 6, manager).

Sanctions with regard to Gender Mainstreaming

The most far-reaching concept discussed in the Commission with regard to implementation of gender mainstreaming is the introduction of sanctions. As has been elaborated in chapter 2, sanctions only apply when gender mainstreaming is not implemented within the European Social Funds (ESF) which principally concerns ESF project applications within the Member States. Gender mainstreaming within the ESF is thus implemented by means of monetary incitements.

Within the framework of the reform process in the European Commission in 2001-2002, the introduction of both positive and negative sanctions for Commission employees were discussed. The interviewees were split equally into three groups regarding sanctions, i.e. roughly one third say that there should be no sanctions with regard to gender mainstreaming, one third was in favour of positive sanctions (i.e. rewards) and one third supported negative sanctions (i.e. some form of 'punishment'). All groups will be examined in turn.

Of those opposed to sanctions with regard to gender mainstreaming, the actor in the first quotation asserts that they are a bad idea because he thinks that gender mainstreaming in general is badly run. He stresses that it ought to be shown that gender mainstreaming is important for the survival of the Commission as a whole.

I think sanctions are a very bad idea. Not everybody should be penalised for a badly run programme. First of all it would be important to show that the Commission can only survive with gender mainstreaming. You shouldn't give up the aim. Gender mainstreaming does not only mean the publication of opinions and reports. It must be shown that gender mainstreaming is a question of survival for the Commission (interview 3, male administrator).

The actor in the next quotation thinks that people cannot be forced to something they don't like. Instead, she suggests the introduction of positive sanctions. She also says that due to budgetary and human resources constraints, many employees don't have the proper resources to implement gender mainstreaming and therefore cannot be held responsible for an improper implementation of gender mainstreaming.

The question about sanctions is a quite delicate one. I don't think that by introducing sanctions we can make things move. Because this is like forcing people to do things they

---

102 Aquis is the short form of 'aquis communautaire', that is, possession (acquisition) of the Community, in other words, more or less a 'given' in a way. The aquis refers to all common laws and treaties in the European Union.

don't want to do. This is kind of a reverse of awarding a medal. I think that maybe it would be more effective to reward. Rewarding, giving people the tools to use this concept of mainstreaming. Because anyway, in the Commission, I don't think sanctions would ever work. Because we have so many constraints. We have budget constraints. We have human resources restraints. So how can you force people, how can you really sanction people who are not doing this, when they don't have the tools to do it? So I think that in some cases it would be unfair (interview 11, manageress).

As elaborated later in the section on resources, there is no special budget in the Commission to implement gender mainstreaming, which causes problems according to the above-cited manageress.

Other actors who are opposed to sanctions in general argued first of all that it is not possible to monitor a proper implementation of gender main-streaming for individual actors (interview 25, manager; interview 14, female assistant). Another actor argued secondly that there are no effective sanctions for gender mainstreaming (interview 10, female administrator).

From those actors in the second group who are in favour of positive sanctions, the secretary in the next quotation believes that providing incentives for individual actors is the only way to change people's behaviour.

No, they [negative sanctions] are not going to work. You can't force people, you have to teach them. There are other ways of making people do things rather than punishment. Probably the only way you get anyone to do anything is by showing them what's in it for them (interview 1, female secretary).

The following actor's view is exemplary for the third group of actors who are in support of negative sanctions:

Everybody should be in fear of the Lord. There need to be consequences when gender mainstreaming is not implemented. I am not talking about people who are totally convinced of mainstreaming but rather about what any good bureaucrat is doing, i.e. that he understands what it is, how to do it, and that it is something I have to do, otherwise I am held to account. [...] That means that in the thinking and in the daily planning of humans who implement it, that it has a high priority and that as a consequence, I will be promoted. Whereas if I don't do it, I will not be promoted. That is the precondition (interview 4, manageress).

This approach might reflect a Weberian image of a bureaucrat as a 'paragraphs machines', whose work results can be calculated in the same way as 'one can calculate the expected output of a machine' (Weber 1988 [1921]: 322). Indeed, the Commission is following a top-down approach with regard to gender mainstreaming (Schmidt 2001b). The following two actors are critical that despite this top-down approach there is no sanction or monitoring from the top level for implementing gender mainstreaming:

And I would have a police force on mainstreaming based in the Secretariat General whose job was basically a gender mainstreaming audit unit and who would report directly to the Cabinet of the Commissioners. But when I say gender police, if you have a Commission Decision on mainstreaming it would mean that we would be able to ensure that gender mainstreaming is really implemented in every single programme. It wouldn't be a problem, it would be automatic (interview 2, manageress).

You can tell who thinks it [gender mainstreaming] is important or not. If people see it as unimportant and they have more important things to do, then they will not do anything about it. If they keep doing it systematically without being sanctioned or without being rewarded, they will continue to do it that way. So there was the idea of including in the regular appraisal of civil servants and mainly of the management, their willingness to make equal opportunities and mainstreaming move forward. This would be considered as criteria for a good or a poor manager. But the hierarchy has not retained this idea (interview 11, manageress).

Both mangeresses argue in favour of sanctions. The first actor quoted is in favour of a centralised monitoring system of gender mainstreaming which reports to the highest-level administrative section within the Commission, i.e. the Secretariat General which is directly below the President of the Commission. According to her, the monitoring of gender mainstreaming should contain a clearly defined sanctioning system symbolised by the mentioning of a 'gender police'. She is also suggesting a Commission Decision which would require gender mainstreaming to be implemented in every programme of the Commission (interview 11, manageress)[103]. The second actor quoted stresses the importance of individual incitements for the personnel of the Commission in order to achieve a proper implementation of gender mainstreaming.

7.2.6 Suggestions by the Actors for changing Gender Mainstreaming

This section will be split up into two parts, rules and resources. With regards to rules, three sets of suggestions were made about how the actors would change gender mainstreaming. The first set of suggestions revolved around the issue of language and reconciliation. The ongoing battle over using gender neutral language within the Commission was mentioned by one actor who suggested that this could only be changed with a clear Commission Decision (interview 11, manageress). The second set of suggestions revolved around reconciliation policies. One actor demanded an obligatory working time (without overtime) which would stop the culture of long working hours (interview 10, female administrator). Another suggested the introduction of flexitime in DGs other than Employment and Social Affairs. She stressed that this is particularly important for employees in the 'A' category, since problems usually arise in this group. If secretaries want to have flexitime, the

---

103 The demanded Commission Decision should not be confused with Commission Communications. Commission Decisions usually give more detailed descriptions of how the content of the Decision is to be implemented in the administration of the Commission, while a Commission Communication (which already exists on gender mainstreaming) is a rather general announcement on a topic.

188

administrators and assistants can always ask other secretaries from the department for assistance, but this is usually not possible for 'A' officials who often have specialised duties (interview 26, female administrator). An assistant who is dealing with personnel says that more flexible arrangements with regard to maternity leave are important, i.e. that the time is flexible on when maternity leave is taken and that both parents can split up the maternity leave between them (interview 19, female assistant).

With regard to resources the most radical suggestion was the introduction of a strict monitoring and control system, which was discussed in the section on sanctions.

Furthermore, a clearer statement on gender mainstreaming was demanded by means of a new Commission decision. This would enable gender mainstreaming to be 'automatically' integrated into management training and it would make the data collection from other DGs easier, a point which was also raised by another actor (interview 7, female administrator). It would also enable gender neutral language documents to be produced.

Several actors stressed the importance of better human resources. This point was first raised in the context that the workload in the Commission is perceived to be very unevenly distributed within the Commission. The other suggestion was that there is a need for better resources with regard to training people for gender mainstreaming and its implementation. The importance of training was raised by various actors (interview 7, female administrator; interview 10, female administrator; interview 26, female administrator; interview 4, manageress). One explanation will be given as an example:

Well I think that first of all what is missing is the human resources, to really cope with the different burden of work that is needed. Because what we find here and what is the most difficult part is that you must have people working on it and secondly to have sufficiently prepared people. We have tried, but it was quite modest. We have tried to organise some modules as training, because mainstreaming is something much more complicated than what can be said over a cup of coffee. To repeat my two elements: First of all to make people available and in charge of this job, and secondly to train these people to know how to do their job. Only then we can really say what should and what should not be done in the different policies. Not only in the personnel policy, I emphasise that my job is only concerned with personnel matters, but of course gender mainstreaming should also have regard to mental structure and the mental attitude required for all the different activities in all the other policies (interview 11, manageress).

The manageress is saying that to really implement gender mainstreaming in the 'mental structure' it is important to make people feel responsible and knowledgeable on gender mainstreaming. Another manageress states that training would be particularly important for all higher-level and top-level civil servants:

I would send them all to school I would send all the Directors and General Directors and all higher-level civil servants to school. Then I would call them all to a meeting and give a speech to them and require that they develop a programme, an annual programme, outlining the extent to which he or she could implement gender mainstreaming in the particular area. Then I would expect that a budget be allocated and that sufficient personnel be allocated and that gender mainstreaming becomes a normal item on the agenda, and that at the end of the year a report will be written on the implementation of mainstreaming (interview 4, manageress).

Her point, that gender mainstreaming ought to be a 'normal agenda item' is particularly interesting in the framework of this study since it is a demand for the institutionalisation of gender mainstreaming.

Another actor comments that it would be ideal to have gender training for the Commissioners but that this would not be feasible politically (interview 26, female administrator).

One actor suggested that when the human resources are examined with regard to women's representation, a study should also be made as to where women are in the majority, since in some areas, even amongst 'A' officials, women are over-represented (interview 7, female administrator).

Finally, the importance of introducing elements of 'good management' are mentioned for the implementation of gender mainstreaming:

I would examine how gender mainstreaming is perceived by individuals. I would do that in the manner of market research. I would examine where it benefits people. You invite them to participate. I would implement the principles of good management (interview 3, male administrator).

7.3   Resources for Gender Mainstreaming

One of the key questions for the implementation of a new policy is how many resources in the form of direct funds or human resources are allocated to the implementation of this new policy. The Commission has no special budget for the implementation of gender mainstreaming within their own house, a number of resources are, however, made available and these are examined below. One manageress describes the importance of resources for gender mainstreaming by linking them to a functioning monitoring system and sanctions, as discussed in the previous section:

An important condition [for gender mainstreaming] is that sufficient means are available to implement it. And you need really independent monitoring, a surveying system in which you monitor what is done in which way and what the implications are. Yes, and the other thing which makes it [gender mainstreaming] difficult is how to assess what would happen if you brought in the gender perspective a priori. That means that with every policy you take into account all the implications that policy has on both genders (interview 4, manageress).

7.3.1 Allocative Resources

The following allocative resources of gender mainstreaming will be discussed in this section: gender reports, recruitment of officials, monitoring of the gender composition of the existing staff and gender training.

7.3.1.1 Gender Reports

The Inter-Service Mainstreaming Group decided in 1997 that each DG should publish an annual report outlining the most important changes on the implementation of gender mainstreaming in that particular DG in the previous year and how they plan to implement gender mainstreaming in the following year. These gender reports are published internally by the Commission.

The importance of gender reports is assessed very differently within the Commission. The following actor says that everyone is conscious of gender mainstreaming because of the gender reports:

First of all, these reports are published each year and they summarise the positions occupied by women, and indeed there have been more nominations of women. Thus, everyone is conscious of this topic (interview 25, manager).

Another actor is, however, very sceptical about changes resulting from the reports:

These reports don't lead anywhere. You write something in them and it doesn't achieve anything. I am sceptical about changes (interview 3, male administrator).

Even though these two quotations appear contradictory at first sight, they are not necessarily so. The first actor is saying that the reports make people conscious of gender mainstreaming. The second actor is sceptical about changes as a result of the reports. His criticism is that the gender reports do not have any consequences. Indeed, there are no incitements or sanctions for particularly good or bad advances made with regard to gender mainstreaming in the different DGs. His remark, that the reports don't achieve anything, might refer to actual changes in the structure of the Commission. However, the first actor appreciates the changes made in the consciousness of individual actors. The following administrator stresses that due to the report, different DGs have to be concerned about gender mainstreaming.

Surely it is an important criterion of success that classic DGs take account of mainstreaming. It is also important that individual DGs are generally concerned with gender mainstreaming [...]. For example the contribution of different DGs to the work on mainstreaming. All DGs are required to submit a report on what they have achieved with regard to mainstreaming so that you can see the changes at the end of the year. Of course some DGs don't have much to say (interview 7, female administrator).

When prompted on which DG she was referring to with the remark 'classic DGs', she explained that she was talking of DG Agriculture, DG Competition, DG Economic and Financial Affairs and DG Budget.

One manageress shares this view by saying that the gender coordinators who write the gender reports in the DGs are often not really committed to gender mainstreaming:

They look more at which mainstreaming measures were introduced within the DG. But they haven't even changed their own mentality (interview 27, female administrator).

Her comment, that they just look at 'which measures were introduced' might suggest that they adopt a 'ticking the box approach' to gender mainstreaming, i.e. that they put the least possible information into the reports, without reflecting much on the issue (see chapter 2).

Other actors stressed that the fact that because they were asked each year by the gender mainstreaming official to state what they had done to implement gender mainstreaming effectively within the particular unit or DG, this actually made them think about the situation (interview 13, male administrator; interview 20, male administrator).

7.3.1.2 Recruitment of new Officials

One of the most important measures for the introduction of gender mainstreaming, according to the majority of interviewees in DG Personnel and Administration, was seen to be the screening of competitions in order to increase the number of newly recruited women[104]. Even though the applicants for the A6-A8 entrance competitions were predominantly female in 2001[105], the number of women who won the competitions for the A6-A8 reserve list was only 33% in that year, with 31.6% of women actually being recruited (European Commission 2002a).

As a result of this, all parts of the competitions are now screened to find out the extent to which they disadvantage women. One example which given was that in the Multiple Choice section of the competitions, one question asked which country had won the (men's) European soccer championship in

---

104 The organisation of entrance examinations is an important task of DG Personnel and Administration. The majority of civil servants working in the Commission join by means of a competition (the exception being the parachutists (refer to in a later section of this chapter)). The competitions run by the Commission usually have three parts; the first round consists of a multiple-choice test on the area for which the competition is advertised. A certain number of those who score best in the first round qualify for the second round, which usually consists of an essay written on the special field applied for. Those who score best in the second round can qualify for the third round which consists of an oral examination.

105 Grade A6-A8 is the grade for university graduates with little or no previous work experience.

a particular year, a fact more likely to be known by men than women (interview 11, manageress). Another example is that research carried commissioned by the Commission has shown that men are likely to do better in tests which are intended to measure logical reasoning if this is tested by means of number series test, whereas if tests with non-numerical answers are carried out the results are gender neutral, as, for example, testing sequences with different symbols[106] Commission (interview 11, manageress).

For the oral part of the competitions, attention is now also paid to ensuring that the applicants do not face an all male jury which might intimidate women. The following manageress describes the different aspects of the competitions as follows:

It was through the everyday work that I saw and understood that gender mainstreaming was important. And the first aspect that really struck me is the question of competitions. As you know, DG Admin [Administration and Personnel] organises the competitions for civil servants. Of course in the competitions, if we don't take into account the differences of gender, we are discriminating negatively. My first experience was that we received some complaints and some calls for help, some women that were just about to give birth or who had just given birth and who had small children to breastfeed so they could not be considered to be the same as the mass of the other candidates. They needed to have some specific arrangement in order to be able to pass the competition and to be respected as mothers- to-be or as young mothers who had just had a baby. So in that case we needed to try to provide some specific arrangements for them. That was the first thing (interview 11, manageress).

The manageress is bringing up the issue discussed in chapter 2; that in some cases, gender mainstreaming can mean that both sexes are treated unequally in order to take account of the special needs of women. The manageress quotes examples of women who need special protection because of birth-related requirements and breastfeeding. It is important to note that she does not suggest any other protectionist measures for women that might ultimately be discriminatory (an example of this could be the argument that for medical reasons women should not be allowed to participate in the competition during their maternity leave).

One administrator comments on the difficulties with regard to changing the competitions in order to increase the number of successful female candidates:

I have also been involved in the concours [competitions]. However, when women arrive at the concours at the oral stage, they tend to 'block'. Initially they said it was because of an

---

106 In the United States of America, this method is referred to as 'Differential Item Functioning' procedure. It was developed by the Educational Testing Service researchers in 1986 using a methodology adapted from medical research, which is applied to tests with sufficient samples of examinees. The procedure assumes that if test takers have approximately the same knowledge (as measured by total test scores), then they should perform in similar (though not identical) ways on individual test questions regardless of their sex, race or ethnicity (Educational Testing Service 2003).

all male jury. But now we have a mixed jury with an equal number of men and women. I think we are more self-conscious, more aware of our disabilities. Men don't think that way, they don't think that they might not know something. So you need to change the whole system of recruitment if you want to achieve better results for women, because I don't accept what some say i.e. "Because there are only old men in the jury". That is completely false. All this 'Could more women on the board change something?' I don't think that makes any difference (interview 10, female administrator).

The administrator in the above quotation is arguing that the different results for men and women in the oral part of the competitions originate in differences in the behaviour of men and women rather than in the fact of having all male juries. According to her, women are more 'self-conscious' and talk more of their 'disabilities'. As a consequence she says that the whole system of competitions needs to be changed if better results are to be achieved for women.

7.3.1.3 Monitoring of the Gender Composition of existing Staff

Unequal pay within public administrations can only be studied if one examines the differences in their different classifications for grades and echelons and gender imbalances. Within a specific grade and echelon, women and men receive the same salary. One manager describes this as follows:

What we have here is a big advantage in the public administration: equality of income. But also equal conditions with pension insurance. There is no differentiation between women and men. With our *statut* [staff regulations] there are some problems, *le fonctionnaire* [a male civil servant], *la veuve* [a widow], you see what I mean. That can still happen today and are things that need to be changed. That is a different way of thinking. But that is the terminology, the consequences are neutral (interview 25, manager).

The manager is stating that there is no direct or indirect discrimination in the staff regulations. He argues that gendered language which designates a civil servant as male and a widow as female reflect a different way of thinking and ought to be changed.

There are five different grades within the Commission and indeed in all European Institutions, since Staff Regulations cover officials in all European Institutions[107]. However, there is a difference from institution to institution in job description, and the one which follows concerns the European Commission: The A grades are composed of Senior Management (Director-General/Deputy Director General (A1), Director/ Chief Advisor (A2), Middle Management (Heads of Unit/ Advisors (A3-5) and Administrators/Assistant Administrators (A6-8). The B grade consists of principal assistants, the C

---

107 As explained in chapter 6, only Civil Servants will be analysed with regard to the quantitative analysis due to lack of data for the other groups.

grade of secretaries and the D grade of qualified workers. The LA grade consists of Heads of linguistic units; interpreters and translators.

Figure 8: Composition of Commission Staff by Category in May 1998

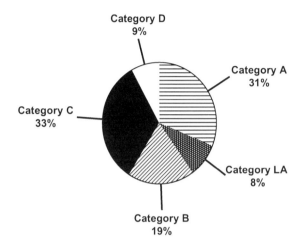

Source: Own illustration. European Commission 1999a

The intramural staff of the Commission (22 496 persons) can be broken down into 6945 persons in category A (equivalent to 31%), 4218 in category B (equivalent to 19%), 7421 in category C (equivalent to 33%), 1990 in category D (equivalent to 9%) and 1922 in the LA category (equivalent to 8%) (refer to figure 8) (European Commission 1999a: 9-10).

The pay, which varies considerably according to these grades as can be seen in table 9, is often described as very high compared to that of national civil servants. This is due to the 'levelling up' process, which means that the salaries must be attractive even to those countries where civil servants are relatively well paid as in Denmark and Germany, since, for reasons of equality, there can be no discrimination between officials from different Member States. A comparison with wages from the private sector is also an important factor (Stevens 2001: 50).

Newly recruited employees begin at step 1 and can be promoted upwards within their grades. The lower the number of the grade, the more seniority the employee has. If employees want to change grades, they have to win a competition. The actual difference of work tasks between A, B and C grades is difficult to assess. One administrator comments on this issue by saying:

It is absolutely ridiculous if you look at the wage difference between A and C grades. With changing technologies and changing work requirements in general, many secretaries do exactly the same work as A grades (interview 9, administrator).

According to this administrator, the large difference in wage between especially A and C grades is not justified.

The basic income of a newly recruited secretary is roughly 26% lower than that of a newly recruited A employee (see table 9). More importantly, the highest salary a secretary can reach is about 65% lower than that of the most senior position in middle management (B1, step 8, compared to A3, step 8)[108].

Table 9: Basic monthly Salaries in Euro for selected Grades and Steps (valid as of July 2002)

Grade	Description	Lowest Step	Highest Step
A1	Senior Management	11.940,71 (Step 1)	15.112,21 (Step 6)
A8	Assistant Administrator	3.998,94 (Step 1)	4.160,21 (Step 2)
B1	Senior Assistant	5.252,79 (Step 1)	7.258,99 (Step 8)
B5	Junior Assistant	2.951,34 (Step 1)	3.324,87 (Step 8)
C1	Senior Secretary	3.367,66 (Step 1)	4.318,26 (Step 4)
C5	Junior Secretary	2.276,47 (Step 1)	2.556,31 (Step 4)
D1	Senior Qualified Worker	2.572,75 (Step 1)	3.360,18 (Step 8)
D4	Junior Qualified Worker	2.058,62 (Step 1)	2.311,88 (Step 4)

Source: European Commission 2002a

In addition to this basic salary, household allowance (5% of the basic salary), child allowance (237,73 Euro per child), schooling allowance, expatriation allowance (16% of the basic salary), installation, resettlement and travel expenses are added. Officials of the European Institutions do not have to pay national taxes but must pay Community taxes, a progressive income tax, which rises to 45% on salaries earned in the top band and is 8 % at its minimum, depending also on individual situations such as the number of dependent children. Two insurances are also deducted: 8.25% of the basic salary for pension and 1.8% of the basic salary for health and accident insurance.

We can observe an increase in the percentage of women in all grades between 1984 and 2000 apart from the B grades where a small decline took place (refer to table 10 and 11 and figure 9 and 10).

---

108 As the number of senior management positions is very low, the most senior position of middle management is compared to the most senior position of a secretary.

Table 10: Gender Composition within the European Commission:
Percentages of Women from all Employees

	1.1.1984[109]	1.1.1994[110]	31.12.2000[111]
Composition of Commission staff			48
Senior management: (A1)	4,4	1,9	7,4
Senior management: (A2)	0	2,5	11,8
Middle management: (A3-A5)	6,6	10,7	13,2
Administrators, Assistant Administrators (A6-A8)	16,5	19,3	28,5
A grade (total of above)	9,3	13,5	20,6
B grade (Assistants)	39,9	37,4	39,7
C grade (Secretaries)	80,7	80,4	81,5
D grade (Qualified workers)	11,2	22,1	22,3
Language Service (LA)	45,5	50,1	64,3

Source: Based on European Commission 1994a and 2002a

Note: The figures include those civil servants who are relevant to the
operating budget.

Figure 9: Gender Composition of different A grades: Percentages of Women
from all Employees

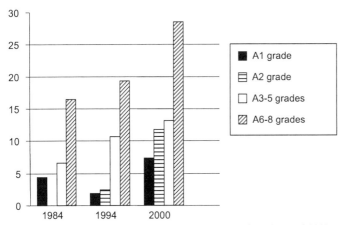

Source: Own illustration. Based on European Commission 1994 and 2002

109 Commission of the European Communities 1994
110 Commission of the European Communities 1994
111 Commission of the European Communities 2002. Note the different time periods between
    1984, 1994 and 2000.

Figure 10: Gender Composition of different Grades: Percentages of Women from all Employees in different Grades in 1984, 1994 and 2000

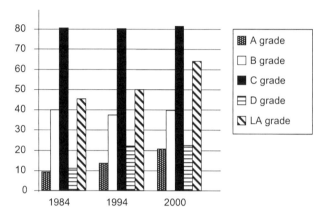

Source: Own illustration. Based on European Commission 1999a and Women in Decision-making 2003

Looking at figure 10 on the gender composition of different grades, the largest change can be seen within A and D grades where the percentage of women roughly doubled in the time period studied. The percentage of women in the C grades increased slightly from 80.7% to 81.5%, while that of the Language Service moved from 45.5% to 64.3%. When looking at the A grades more specifically, the largest increase in the percentage of women can be seen in top management, where the percentage of women at Director General and Deputy Director General increased from 4.4% to 7.4%and that of Director and Chief Advisor from 0 to 11,8%. However these large increases have to be compared with caution, as the total figure is very small, for example the total number of A1 personnel was only 45, while that of A2 was 119. Thus a few promotions for women change the statistics considerably. In comparison, A3-5 was composed of 1494 persons, A6-8 of 722 people.

Important changes can also be observed in middle management, where the percentage of women more than doubled from 6.6% to 13.2%. The Administrators and Assistant Administrators who are normally the newly recruited university degree holders almost doubled from 16.5% to 28.5%.

To evaluate the changes in gender imbalance between the different grades, it is especially important to look at promotions and recruitment within a given year, since the gender imbalance can be changed only gradually. For example, the number of those who enter the Commission by means of the so-called 'parachuting', i.e. occupying top positions in the Commission by being appointed from high positions in private industry, lobby organisations or national administrations, is limited, although it would be worth analysing the gender balance of the parachutists, despite their small number. Unfortunately, however, these figures are lacking, and also, since the parachutists are usually nominated by Member States, the Commission has only limited power to change this situation[112]. The representation of women in top management can thus be achieved mainly by first increasing the percentage of women recruits in the A grades and by increasing their percentage in middle management. Since the Second Positive Action Plan (European Commission 1994) the Commission has set annual targets. The most recent available data on targets are for the year 2000, and the results, are illustrated as an example in table 10. We can see that the appointments at Senior Management level have exceeded the target while those for middle management and newly recruited A6-A8 recruits have not been met.

Table 11 summarises the percentage of women in the grade for administrators and management in the different Directorates General. We can observe a big difference between the different DGs with regard to their gender composition among A grades. The difference in gender composition could be analysed in different ways: One reason could be the subject matter of the different DGs: Those DGs which cover 'soft' subject areas such as education and culture, development aid, translation and social affairs have a relatively high percentage of women. However, in the General Inspectorate of Services, which has a very low percentage of women, the total number of A staff is only 15 and therefore the percentage figure should be looked at with caution. Another reason might be how long the DGs are in service and at which period when their main recruitment took place. We would expect that those DGs which have recently come into service have a higher percentage of women because of higher gender awareness and because of positive action plans. Another reason might be their gender mainstreaming policies, however it is not possible to analyse all these in the realm of this book.

With regard to the two DGs which serve as case studies for this book, we can see that DG Employment and Social Affairs has the fourth highest percentage of women amongst their A grades with 33 % of women amongst their A staff, while DG Administration and Personnel represents the average with 19.8 % of women amongst their A staff.

---

112 The importance of those parachuted can be seen with regard to Germany. There was not a single woman among the last 50 senior management positions (A1 to A5 grades) Germany (up to November 2001) nominated. One administrator comments that the reason for the gender imbalance is that such positions are often given to party cronies as favours and those cronies are usually men (interview female administrator 26).

Table 11: Percentage of Women in the Directorates General –Category A
(aggregated positions grade 1-8)

	Total	Women	Men	Women %
Education and Culture	206	76	130	36,9%
Europe Aid - Co-operation Office	91	33	58	36,3%
Translation Services	9	3	6	33,3%
Employment and Social Affairs	**200**	**66**	**134**	**33,0%**
Humanitarian Aid Office	37	12	25	32,4%
Internal Market	163	51	112	31,3%
Secretariat General	100	27	73	27,0%
Enlargement	80	21	59	26,3%
Environment	173	42	131	24,3%
Transport	91	21	70	23,1%
Justice and Home Affairs	44	10	34	22,7%
Health and Consumer Protection	229	52	177	22,7%
Joint Interpreting and Conference services	9	2	7	22,2%
Legal Services	108	24	84	22,2%
Customs and Taxation	106	22	84	20,8%
Competition	205	41	164	20,0%
Personnel and Administration	**222**	**44**	**178**	**19,8%**
Press and Communication	86	17	69	19,8%
Enterprise	295	55	240	18,6%
Agriculture	302	54	248	17,9%
Regional Policies	150	26	124	17,3%
Eurostat	190	32	158	16,8%
Common Service for External Relations	180	28	152	15,6%
External Relations	519	80	439	15,4%
Internal Audit Service	75	11	64	14,7%
Trade (DG Commerce)	184	27	157	14,7%
Budget	89	13	76	14,6%
Fisheries	84	12	72	14,3%
Development	325	43	282	13,2%
Economic and Financial affairs	166	20	146	12,0%
Research, technological development and integration	75	9	66	12,0%
Office for Official Publications of the European Communities	35	4	31	11,4%
Information Society	110	12	98	10,9%
Energy	175	17	158	9,7%
General Inspectorate of Services	15	1	14	6,7%
Fraud Prevention Office	49	3	46	6,1%

Source: Women in Decision-Making Database 2003

Table 12: Annual Targets and Outcome of Recruitment in 2000

Target Groups	Annual targets 2000	Outturn by end December 2000
Target 1: Senior Management: A 1 A 2	Appoint 2 women Appoint 5 women	Three women appointed Seven women appointed
Target 2: Middle Management	Appoint 20 % women to middle management posts	14,3 %
Target 3: A6-A8	Recruit equal number of men and women from the reserve list	31,6

Source: Own illustration. Based on European Commission 2002b

Many different factors need to be taken into account when comparing women in the different grades: The most important would be to include the number of female and male applicants for the competitions and their success rate, also the impact of enlargement on the recruitment policies, especially of the Nordic countries, since it can be expected that they would employ a higher percentage of women than EU average. Another important factor would be the introduction of competitions during the 1980s. Before this people were recruited on the basis of formal qualifications and interviews. However, one interviewee reported that women were automatically graded as B assistants regardless of their qualifications and merits (interview 13, male administrator). Unfortunately the data accessible on female and male staff does not allow for calculations to be made as to how the introduction of formal competitions influenced the gender balance of the recruitment.

7.3.1.4 Gender Training

In DG Personnel and Administration and in DG Employment and Social Affairs, gender training is organised to raise awareness on gender issues (for the aims of gender training, refer to chapter 2). This was aimed at Directors and Heads of Unit, but some employees were critical, stating that in general they themselves did not come but would send a female substitute and there was also criticism of the fact that the training took place during lunchtime.

The majority of the conference was made up of women. It was very interesting but. it took place around lunchtime. It was a bit of a toss up, either eat or go to the conference (interview 14, female assistant).

The fact that the training took place during lunchtime is seen as a provocation by another interviewee (interview 10, female administrator). However, some respondents also say that lunchtime was specifically chosen in order to increase the participation rate of management who attend many meetings at all other times (interview 25, manager; interview 26, female administrator).

Furthermore, since 2000, DG Employment and Social Affairs has included gender mainstreaming in its induction courses for all newcomers to the DG in the grades A, B and C regardless of their hierarchical level within these grades. Gender mainstreaming is the only horizontal policy of the Commission to be explained in the induction courses.

7.3.2 Authoritative Resources: Gender Mainstreaming Structures within the European Commission

There are a number of procedures and monitoring groups in place to implement the gender mainstreaming strategy within the Commission. One important structure for the implementation of gender mainstreaming is the reorganisation of working time. The most important groups within the European Commission for gender mainstreaming are the Group of Commissioners on Equal Opportunities, the Inter-Service Group on Gender Equality, the High-Level Group on Gender Mainstreaming, the Commission Advisory Committee for Equal Opportunities for Women and Men, the Comité Paritaire de l'Egalité des Chances, Equal Opportunities Units and the Organisation of C Grades which will all be examined in the following.

7.3.2.1 Gender Mainstreaming of working Hours

Two rules have been implemented within the Commission to take account of the different working habits of both men and women.

In both DG Employment and Social Affairs and DG Personnel and Administration a rule exists that no training or meetings is to take place on Wednesday afternoons. The reason for this is that in Belgium, where most of the Commission services of these two DGs are located, schools and kindergartens are closed on Wednesday afternoons. It was seen as a specific disadvantage for women if meetings and training took place during this time since many women who work part-time take Wednesday off in order to care for their children.

In 1998, the Committee on equal opportunities within the Commission (COPEC) introduced a rule that no internal meeting in the Commission was to start after 4 p.m.[113]. In DG Employment and Social Affairs the then Director General Alan Larsson implemented this rule very vigorously.

---

113 COPEC's role will be analysed more in detail below.

Employees were encouraged to refuse to attend meetings after 4 p.m.[114]. This rule was specifically introduced in order to implement gender mainstreaming by changing the late working hours and thereby changing the working culture. Two interviewees regard this rule as one of the most important changes since the introduction of gender mainstreaming within the Commission (interview 19, female assistant; interview 15, female administrator).

The following two actors emphasise that people with carer responsibilities suffer most if late meetings are called. The first one is saying that resources could be much better used by exploiting new technologies like video-conferencing efficiently. Since travelling abroad for meetings might be particularly difficult for those who have caring responsibilities (who happen to be mostly women), the use of alternatives to inefficient missions abroad could, first and foremost, be advantageous for them. The second interviewee is asserting that due to the culture of long hours, the hierarchy is still positively rewarding those who stay late, regardless of what they have achieved during the day.

[...] which is another thing, the long working hours. Calling meetings at 5 [p.m.] and 5.30 [p.m.] shouldn't be allowed. It happens all the time. It always leaves you with a bad feeling. I don't care what people think of me since a long way back. But if my career depended on it I'd have a very different view. The rules that there should not be any meetings after 4 p.m. should be applied. We have video-conference facilities, but no one uses them. We have a culture to just go over to other countries. There are far more effective ways to use resources (interview 21, female administrator).

I must say that nowadays the management, the higher management, is more aware, but there are still meetings that start after 4.30 or 5 p.m., the fact is that they look down on you because you want to leave early to take care of your kids. This is not my situation any more but I see it from others. Now they don't say it, but the prejudices still exist. The bosses have to see that – the view is that someone who stays late is willing and motivated. Whether you have coffee all the time and start working at 6 p.m. is irrelevant (interview 14, female assistant).

The following actor gives an example of how little the rule is institutionalised in the Commission as a whole: a meeting of the Inter-Service Mainstreaming Group was called on a Wednesday afternoon after 4 p.m.

I remember the first meeting [of the Inter-Service Group] I attended was on a Wednesday at 5 p.m. I made a frivolous remark about what the equal opportunities committee had achieved a) that no meeting is to be scheduled after 4 p.m. and b) no meeting is to be scheduled on Wednesday afternoons as the kids leave school early. So this was the first point I mentioned to the speaker of the Inter-Service Group (interview 25, manager).

---

114 Other DGs also implemented this rule though with different timings, for DG Justice and Home Affairs it is also 4 p.m. (interview male administrator 9), for DG Internal Market it is 5.45 p.m. (McDonald 1998: 40).

Even though the rule remains in place in the Commission as a whole, in DG Employment and Social Affairs it is not adhered to any longer since Alan Larsson was replaced by Odile Quintin as new Director General in 2000 (interview 2, manageress). This might be explained in part by the cultural backgrounds of the Directors General: Alan Larsson comes originally from Sweden where gender mainstreaming was introduced by law in 1994 and where people are perceived to work most efficiently when they get their work done within their working time. The Director General who followed Alan Larsson, Odile Quintin, comes from a French background, where gender mainstreaming has only begun to be introduced in recent years and where there is a culture of long working hours in public administration[115].

. One measure implemented by DG Employment and Social Affairs to, potentially, improve and reconcile the gap between caring responsibilities and professional life has been the introduction of a pilot project on tele-working. This was started in early 1999 with 50 employees of both sexes; however it is still under review.

7.3.2.2 Group of Commissioners on Equal Opportunities

At the highest level, the Santer Commission established the 'Group of Commissioners on Equal Opportunities' in 1995 chaired by Commission president Jacques Santer and attended by Commissioners Pádraig Flynn, Anita Gradin, Erkki Liikanen and Monika Wulf-Mathies. Other Commissioners were invited to attend according to the subject discussed.

One member of the Committee on Equal Opportunities for Men and Women of the European Parliament, describes the reasons for the inauguration of this group as follows:

We put so much pressure on the old Santer Commission that the Commission President, Santer, started a working group on gender mainstreaming and equal opportunities with five, six Commissioners, who were responsible for the implementation of gender mainstreaming and who decided to give it top priority by taking the chair of this group. The Group of Commissioners also co-operates with our Committee [EP Committee for Equal Opportunities for Women and Men] and the Parliament [EP], and invites us to their meetings and the EWL is also integrated into the process. Of course, Prodi [Commission President Romano Prodi] cannot go back on this decision, he also had to take over the Chair, which he did. I was present then and noticed that his heart is not in this topic but he at least signalled that he got the message (interview 28, female MEP).

The MEP stresses the role of the Committee for Equal Opportunities for Men and Women for the inauguration and continuance of the Group of Commissioners.

---

115 Odile Quintin has however worked in the Commission since 1971 and therefore these culturalistic explanations should not be overestimated.

As mentioned in the above quotation, the Prodi Commission kept this group running, and it is now chaired by Commission President Romano Prodi, its other members are the Commissioners Anna Diamantopoulou as Vice-President, Neil Kinnock and Viviane Reding. The meetings are also attended by the Directors General and a representative from the Cabinet (i.e. the political advisors of the Commissioners) of the other DGs. The Commissioners Group meets two to three times a year. According to its own presentation, the Group plays a major role in giving political impetus to the Commission's gender mainstreaming and equal opportunities strategy and actions. It also helps to ensure co-ordination between the departments involved and monitors progress being made in the implementation of the Framework Strategy on Gender Equality and, if necessary, makes recommendations. Once a year the Group holds a joint meeting with representatives of the European Parliament, the Council Presidency, the Advisory Committee on Equal Opportunities and the European Women's Lobby, to discuss the progress of equal opportunities and gender mainstreaming measures. In the period following September 1999 the Group has paid particular attention to the problems involved in promoting equal opportunities in the applicant countries, preventing the trafficking of human beings, and mainstreaming equal opportunities in the internal reform of the Commission.

The influence of the Group of Commissioners is much disputed between Commission officials, with one interviewee from the Equal Opportunities Unit of DG Employment and Social Affairs complaining:

In my opinion they are not doing anything. They need to take more responsibility regarding objectives and follow up. They don't even have a proper work programme. I think you can only achieve an outcome on the basis of the work programme. [...] The Commissioners Group only meets twice a year and then they have discussions with Parliament and the Advisory Committee. However, in order for gender mainstreaming to work, the highest level must take the responsibility. I haven't seen anything important coming from the Commissioners' Group of Mainstreaming yet (interview 10, female administrator).

The administrator criticises the effectiveness of the Group of Commissioners which she sees as a structural problem, that is, their not having a work programme.

In contrast, another person from DG Employment and Social Affairs at Management level says that:

The group of Commissioners gave gender mainstreaming an enormous political impulse. Especially politically, because suddenly the highest level was involved, formally involved, and they could not say, we don't want to meet any more, they have to meet and discuss issues, which they would not normally discuss. This has given a big impulse both to the public and inside the Commission (interview 4, manageress).

Regardless of how effective this group actually is, its mere existence shows a high-level commitment, and in principle also provides a means for the co-ordination of gender mainstreaming in all DGs and in all policies.

7.3.2.3 Inter-Service Group on Gender Equality

Below the Commissioner's Group, *the Inter-Service Group on Gender Equality* was founded. This is a merger of two groups that existed previously, i.e. the Inter-Service Group on Equal Opportunities for women and men (which was set up in 1996) and the Group of Gender Mainstreaming Officials. The secretariat of the Inter-Service Group is located in the Equal Opportunities Unit in DG Employment and Social Affairs. The Inter-Service Group serves two main purposes:

1. As an interface with the Group of Commissioners on Equal Opportunities; the Inter-Service Group assists the preparation of its meetings and receives political guidelines for implementation at services level.
2. Co-operation and exchange of experience between all Commission services with regard to the implementation of the dual-track approach towards gender equality.

Inter-Service Groups exist on a number of issues that are of relevance to a number of DGs. They are supposed to be attended by Heads of Unit and Directors. Many, however, send their subordinates and the great majority of those attending the meetings are women. In fact, the problem of sending subordinates also exists in other Inter-Service Groups; the Inter-Service Group on Equal Opportunities is described as one which is very well attended. Nevertheless, the status of some of the participants of the Inter-Service Group is criticised by some participants of the group:

How serious a DG is regarding gender mainstreaming becomes obvious when you look at who is participating in the Inter-Service Mainstreaming Group. Who they send and, the level of the participant. They are, to some extent, token people. Some of them cannot contribute anything (interview 7, female administrator).

But, it tends to be either the ardent feminist in the DG who takes this [gender mainstreaming; V.S] as her issue, or it's the last female stagiaire to have arrived (interview 2, manageress).

Two of her colleagues go further in their criticism:

From our point of view more than half the group is wrongly chosen. They are people from Personnel who don't have enough of an overview of the policies. When they ask for it they get information from within their DGs but often they do not know of the existence of papers. With some members of the group, their only qualification is to be a woman (interview 26, female administrator).

The most difficult thing with the Inter-Service Group is that everybody has a full-time job and they are supposed to do gender mainstreaming along the way (interview 11, manageress).

Different issues are mentioned in these quotations. Even though the membership of the Inter-Service Groups is defined as being at the level of Directors and Heads of Unit, those who actually attend the meetings are described as a far from ideal group of people. In addition, the members of the group do not get extra time to implement gender mainstreaming; on the contrary it is added to their normal workload.

Further, the general power structure of gender mainstreaming is criticised:

The Inter-Service Mainstreaming Group is – I want to be very frank here –rather feeble as it is not supported from the highest level and the highest level is not interested in this group. Those DGs that have understood the concept such as DG Research, have already implemented gender mainstreaming. I know DG Development would like to implement gender mainstreaming but they lack the resources. However, they are also too concerned with women in development (interview 4, manageress).

Odile Quintin, the Director General of DG Employment and Social Affairs addressed this problem by sending a letter to all the Directors General in the other DGs reminding them that Directors ought to be attending the Inter-Service Group. One manageress notes:

Only half of the DGs responded and sent at least some directors, the other half did not respond. You can tell from that how seriously individual DGs take gender mainstreaming (interview 4, manageress).

Another structural problem is the co-ordination between the Commissioners' group and the Inter-Service Group. There are no individuals who attend both groups, since the Inter-Service Group is chaired by a Director of DG Employment and Social Affairs and the Director General of the DGs attends the Group of Commissioners' meetings. It is, thus, difficult to co-ordinate them.

But now, the Inter-Service Group on gender mainstreaming is like any other Inter- Service Group, it only concerns the happy group and not the rest of us. For me that is the negative part of having an Inter-Service Mainstreaming Group. On the other hand, we cannot just say we will leave it there. We cannot just say it is a horizontal issue endorsed by every-body. Because if you leave it, it will disappear. Maybe the Swedes see it differently, but the Greeks and others see it in another way (interview 10, female administrator).

On a more positive note, several actors emphasised the steering function of the Inter-Service Group, particularly with regard to DG Regional Policy. They stressed that DG Regional Policy only implemented gender mainstreaming as a result of the discussions at the Inter-Service Mainstreaming Group (interview 7, female administrator; interview 2, manageress)[116].

---

116 Since the interviewees are referring to changes in Regional Policy rather than the organisation of the Commission, the actors are not cited in this context.

7.3.2.4 High-Level Group on Gender Mainstreaming

The High Level Group on gender mainstreaming is introduced in the Framework Strategy on Gender Equality 2001-2005 (European Commission 2000). Before the implementation of the Framework Strategy, the Netherlands first organised an informal high level meeting in 1996 during their presidency, and these meetings were continued by other presidencies. Since the Framework Strategy has been in place, the Commission has organised a high-level meeting once a year with senior officials from the Member States with responsibility for gender mainstreaming. However, since the high level group is only concerned with the implementation of gender mainstreaming within the Member States it will not be further discussed here.

7.3.2.5 Commission Advisory Committee for Equal Opportunities for Women and Men

The Commission Advisory Committee for Equal Opportunities for Women and Men (which will be referred to as the 'Advisory Committee' in what follows was set up by the Commission in 1981 as an institutionalised framework for the purpose of regular consultations with bodies having special responsibility in the Member States for promoting equality of opportunity (European Commission 1982, 1995a).

Its aims are to help the Commission formulate and implement Community measures aimed at promoting equal opportunities for women and men, and to encourage the continuous exchange of information on experience gained and policies and measures undertaken between the Member States and the various actors involved.

The Committee has 40 members with a three-year, renewable, term of office. It is composed of one representative from each Member State appointed by the respective national Governments from among the officials of Ministries or Government Departments responsible at national level for promoting equal opportunities, one representative from each Member State is appointed by the Commission from among the members of national committees or bodies specifically responsible for women's employment and/or equal opportunities, five members represent employers' organisations at Community level, and a further five members representing employees' organisations at Community level are appointed by the Commission on the basis of a proposal from the social partners. Two representatives of the European Women's Lobby attend committee meetings as observers; representatives of international, professional and membership organisations may also be admitted as observers following a reasoned request.

The Advisory Committee produced a variety of opinions; one in 2002 on the 'Implementation of Gender Mainstreaming in EU Policies' concludes with the following statement on the implementation of gender mainstreaming within the European Commission:

Gender mainstreaming is not applied in a coherent and efficient way. We call, therefore, for a stronger high-level commitment and a goal-oriented systematic approach to gender mainstreaming. Through the opinions we communicate our vision of this extremely challenging and multi-faceted operation, which is one of the core elements of the Community Framework Strategy on Gender Equality 2001-2005 ("the Framework Strategy"), the other means being specific actions in favour of women (The bracket is included in the original) (Advisory Committee 2002: 2).

The Committee's deliberations are based on requests for Opinions made by the Commission and on Opinions delivered on its own initiative. They are not followed by a vote. The role of the Advisory Committee was confirmed in the Framework Strategy 2001-2005 which states that:

The Commission Advisory Committee for Equal Opportunities for Women and Men will continue to assist the Commission throughout the implementation of the framework strategy. Its role will be vital in providing expertise and information on Member States' gender related policies, in particular as regards the benchmarking, monitoring and reporting exercises of the framework strategy (European Commission 2000: 15).

7.3.2.6 Comité Paritaire de l'Egalité des Chances

Another group important for the implementation of gender mainstreaming within the Commission is the *Comité Paritaire de l'Egalité des Chances* (COPEC). The predecessor of this group, the ad hoc working group *Egalité des Chances* was founded in 1978 and was transformed into a committee in 1981 in accordance with the Staff Committee. In 1992 COPEC was officially acknowledged as a committee by the Commission.

COPEC's aims are to implement the equal opportunities policies within the Commission and it is responsible for the supervision, the implementation, and the evaluation of the positive action programme of the Commission. The Committee also gives an opinion on the budgetary needs of the equal opportunities policies within the Commission. COPEC consists of 28 members, of whom 14 are chosen by DG Personnel and Administration and 14 from the Central Staff Committee. The president is chosen by the Director General of DG Personnel and Administration in consultation with the Central Staff Committee. The Vice-President is nominated by the Central Staff Committee in co-operation with DG Personnel and Administration (see chapter 5 for COPEC's role in the reform process).

Even though COPEC was formed to implement equal opportunities rather than gender mainstreaming in the Commission, it was, nevertheless, mentioned as a very important structure for the implementation and monitoring of gender mainstreaming by various actors (interview 24, manager; interview 11, manageress).

7.3.2.7 Equal Opportunities Units

On a more institutionalised level, the Commission has two Equal Opportunities Units, one in DG Personnel and Administration, one in DG Employment and Social Affairs.

The Unit in DG Personnel and Administration is called the Non-Discrimination and Equal Opportunities Unit and was set up in 1991. It is responsible for incorporating and monitoring the implementation of an equal opportunity and discrimination-free dimension into the Commission's staff policy. The Unit cooperates closely with departments and organises awareness raising and information activities for staff. It also cooperates in the implementation of pilot projects relating to gender issues in certain Directorates-General. The Equal Opportunities Unit in DG Employment and Social Affairs is responsible for coordinating the implementation of gender mainstreaming in all the policies of the Commission.

On a decentralised level, all DGs have gender mainstreaming officials who are responsible for drafting the gender report for their DG, several other DGs have gender desks which are also supposed to coordinate the gender mainstreaming policies in the particular DG. The staffing of the gender desks is very different, however, some have full time positions, others are staffed with people who have gender mainstreaming added to their normal workload.

7.3.2.8 Organisation of C Grades

Another important measure taken to introduce gender mainstreaming within the Commission was the organisation of C grades, which are composed mostly of secretaries. The tasks of secretaries altered tremendously with the change to word processing and the use of modern technologies. The organisation of C grades, staffed predominantly by women, was seen as an important step towards addressing issues such as part-time work and parental leave. It was initiated by the former Director General of DG Employment and Social Affairs, Alan Larsson and is supported by his successor, Odile Quintin in the name of mainstreaming.

The initiation and support of the organisation of C grades is explained as a gender mainstreaming measure because management saw that the work of secretaries could be organised in a much more flexible manner which would accommodate their caring responsibilities and thereby increase their work motivation (interview 1, female secretary). Indeed, this is an example of the Commission attempting to achieve economic advantages with the implementation of gender mainstreaming measures.

The C grades within DG Employment and Social Affairs meet on a monthly basis and organise an 'away-day' once a year when they discuss issues of concern to them, and have further training on issues such as time management. The Group co-ordinating the different organisations of C grades in other DGs meets four times a year. The Inter-DG group of C grades has published a guide to administrative procedures and they exchange ideas on best administrative practice. They have also forwarded suggestions on reform and, according to one active member of the C group organisation, several problems have been taken on board, 'such as access to part-time and more family friendly work' (interview 1, female secretary). They have also officially welcomed the fact that this DG Employment and Social Affairs offers Flexitime as a policy to its entire staff.

One of the organisers of the C grades explains, however, that the C grade organisation is not seen primarily as a gender specific organisation:

When the C grades got together, it was to raise awareness, to get them engaged, to create networks, to create a better working situation. Normally they work alone. And they don't have any natural networking. And it is also an exchange of knowledge. [...] But we try to steer away from feminising – you know saying we are C grades, we are women and we want special treatment because we are women. C grades talk about specific problems they have with childcare and because they work part-time, but it is difficult to say that this is because they are C grades, it is more because most of them are women and many have children (interview 1, female secretary).

Even though she stresses the importance of the C grade organisation for enabling her to better organise her work, she stresses that the organisation of C grades is not part of her job description. Despite the importance that was attributed to the organisation of C grades by various interviewees, the organisation depends entirely on individuals organising the meetings and activities.

7.4   Barriers to the Implementation of Gender Mainstreaming

The actors saw different barriers to the implementation of gender mainstreaming, these were principally: that gender mainstreaming is not discussed openly, the attitudes of employees, long working hours, short maternity leave and no parental leave, no replacement for those on maternity leave and a lack of work reorganisation when employees change to part-time work.

All interviewees agree that in general, gender mainstreaming was a positive asset for the Commission. However, one male interviewee interprets the problem with finding support for gender mainstreaming by saying:

You will not find anyone who says publicly or even just to you that gender mainstreaming is a bad thing. I'm not saying that either. But for that reason it is very difficult once there is a campaign, because no one will dare say publicly that he is against it. However, only few people will actively support it (interview 4, manageress).

There seems to be a problem that gender mainstreaming is not discussed openly within the Commission and that some actors do not dare to voice their opinion. Another actor comments on the barrier to the implementation of gender mainstreaming:

Attitude. Attitude of people. Not having it properly resourced. Lack of leadership. If the right leadership is there they will make sure that the right people get employed and that the resources are in place. Everybody could point them in the right direction. Some people want to do good things, but they don't have the right resources or the interest and flexibility (interview 12, female administrator).

Mistakes are made in being too aggressive and also in ignoring the general picture and being too concerned with details. A gender mainstreaming document makes all this huge hoo-hah if somebody has written chairman instead of chairperson. I think that this sort of thing immediately causes antagonism because people see the detail and the bigger picture is forgotten (interview 1, female secretary).

The single most important barrier to gender mainstreaming was described as the culture of long working hours in the Commission (see above). Both men and women found the balance between private and professional life unsatisfactory. One male interviewee also described a difference in conception between women and men regarding family responsibilities:

When a woman leaves a meeting early because she has to pick up her child from school at 6 p.m., she will have a very bad conscience. When a man says the same thing, everybody in the meeting will say oh that's great, he's taking care of his children (interview 9, male administrator).

Whether the bad conscience he observes is actually justified by the thoughts or reactions of the other participants at the meeting, i.e. if they do think differently of a woman leaving early, remains open to question. The fact that women do have guilty consciences was described by several interviewees as a serious problem.

Another official talks of the problem of reconciliation on a more personal level and describes the traditional role model, which persists in many families, as one in which it is woman's responsibility to take care of the children. The interviewee is sceptical that women will change once they reach positions of power.

I am the only one in my unit who has small children. And it is difficult. I have to leave early, I take my work home but you know [...] as a child I suffered because of my mother's absence. So I did set my priorities. You should see my husband for example. When I ask him "why don't you come home?" he says ah! Because everyone else is here. That is the argument. He does not think that because he has children he should come home, he expects the women should do that. So I think that disappoints me. People who don't have direct responsibility tend to neglect the problem. And I personally don't see that women will change anything (interview 10, female administrator).

Another major obstacle to reconciling family and career is the short maternity leave allowance, which is currently only 16 weeks, and the missing parental leave. When women or men want to care for their children they have to go on sabbatical, which means that they are not covered by social security and that they lose all the social benefits, including free schooling and kindergarten for the children, available to the dependants of European officials. Since the employees of international organisations are not covered by national social security, they are, thus, not be entitled to any state benefit either.

Furthermore staff on maternity leave, or on sabbatical, or who work part-time, are not systematically replaced and thus this is viewed very unfavourably by middle management and by colleagues who must compensate for the workload. Also, there is no right to part-time work; it is always up to the Heads of Unit to decide whether part time work is possible and since a replacement is usually not available they are reluctant to grant part-time work. Even if people are allowed to work part-time, their workload is generally not reduced. One person from Personnel observed that since the Director General is in favour of part-time work, it is usually possible to obtain it (interview 19, female assistant), despite the problems which were described above. However, evidence suggests; that unfortunately, this is not always the case, especially not for DNEs[117].

As outlined in chapter 2, another important precondition for the implementation of gender mainstreaming is the degree of top-level support and from other DGs.

One administrator comments on the involvement of the Commissioner for Employment and Social Affairs, Anna Diamantopoulou, in the following way:

Diamantopoulou is the vice-chair of the group. However, she is not very active on gender mainstreaming. She is more active on trafficking and Afghan women. She is not very interested in gender mainstreaming. It is boring for ministers, it is not very flashy and they won't get on the news with it. It is very technical. So mainstreaming is a difficult subject. It is not very hot stuff (interview 12, female administrator).

---

117 There is a pending case with the European Ombudsman, the institution responsible for complaints against European institutions. The complaint concerns the rules adopted by the European Commission with regard to national experts on secondment to the Commission. According to Commission rules, such national experts must work on a full-time basis throughout the period of secondment. The complainant, a UK civil servant who has a small son, applied for a post as a national expert at the European Commission. However, she wished to be able to work there on a part-time basis in order to be able to look after her child. When informed that national experts had to work on a full-time basis, she had reluctantly withdrawn her application. She then complained to the European Ombudsman, arguing that the relevant rule was discriminatory on the grounds of sex (European Ombudsman 2000).

7.4.1 Problems with the Implementation of Gender Mainstreaming

This section is divided into two parts. The first examines problems that arise due to the particular implementation of gender mainstreaming in the Commission, while the second elaborates on more fundamental problems with the implementation of gender mainstreaming.

One administrator explains that the Women's information unit was dissolved when the tasks of DG Information, Communication, Culture Audiovisual (DG X) were decentralised in the general reorganisation of the Commission in September 1999.

Then DG X [DG Information, Communication, Culture, Audiovisual Media] collapsed and the Commission decided to put together all the women's issues in the Equal Opportunities Unit, which I now think was wrong. I used to be very much in favour of it [making all units responsible for gender mainstreaming] because I thought it would work better. But the danger of mainstreaming is that when you mainstream, you might lose things. Whereas, when you have them specifically for women, you keep something. It is a double tranchant [French term for blade] if you say, why do we need information for women, it's stupid, we don't get the same information, but then you can do more things for women if you have this. It's like having a minister for women, a big backing for major action, saying 'I'm here, I wanna see results'. Whereas if you mainstream something, it might get lost (interview 23, female administrator).

The actor describes her ambiguous opinion about the dissolution of the Women's Information Unit. Even though she was initially in favour of the dissolution, she now sees the danger that special achievements for women might be lost.

The issue of quotas is most relevant on actors' when they are prompted on the subject of gender mainstreaming.

Well, I don't like it when gender mainstreaming is organised in a fanatical way. When men are repressed. Or when the biological differences between men and women are denied. Or, in other words, when you conduct it fanatically (interview 6, manager).

He enlarges on this issue, stating that another fanatical implementation of gender mainstreaming is the introduction of quotas.

Well sex should not play a role. Of course if you look at the different posts that we have and insist that we need to achieve a quarter I am not very much in favour of this quarter principle, because if you follow it you are already discriminating against people. From my perspective, we should not say we need a man or a woman. In specific cases we should encourage equilibrium. But if you have two people for a post, what should determine the outcome is the professional capacity of the applicants (interview 24, manager).

The actor in the above citation argues that any form of quota system results in discrimination in favour of the over-represented group.

Some female actors were in favour of quotas. However, they also stress that it is far more important to change the work culture rather than just intro-duce quotas (interview 4, manageress; interview 15, female administrator).

The following two actors stress the biological and social differences between men, respectively:

I am opposed to gender mainstreaming when the biological differences between men and women are renounced. If you formulate the whole issue ideologically, then I think that testosterone leads to more aggressiveness and aggression is important for an organisation. Often a defence is very important, sometimes in a very tough way. Some women can do that, but many women don't like doing it because they are biologically designed like that. I don't think it is by chance that for centuries the situation has been as it is today (interview 6, manager).

In contrast to this actor who argues that genders are different because of distinguishing biological pre-conditions, another male administrator stresses that:

Women and men have different conceptions about their career. Women do not want to make top careers. They also want to have a family and take care of the family (interview 3, male administrator).

In analysing this comment with the help of insights from theory of structuration, it is interesting to note that the role of co-actors as well as the interplay between agent and context are lacking. As Wolffensperger comments on such a context:

As a consequence, the properties of the organising system are overlooked, and reflection on access to resources, differentiated according to gender, as well as on gender-specific employment of rules, becomes difficult. Gendered facilities, norms (double-standards) and interpretative schemes (gender stereotypes) are rendered invisible, as are the related organising principles. Legitimation (assumed biological differences) and signification (socially constructed gender identities) together produce gender inequality. Although the rules are different for women and men, female agents are held responsible for their own fate (Wolffensperger 1991: 97-8).

Women, either due to assumed biological differences, or due to socially constructed gender identities, are thus rendered responsible for their situation. Men are seen as the norm to which women are expected to adapt. We can observe an important gender difference here however: none of the female actors described the situation in those terms, rather, they stressed the importance of gender mainstreaming for reconciliation measures, and those whose husbands and partners work in the Commission stressed that they hoped that gender mainstreaming would motivate their husbands to contribute more to their caring responsibilities. The absence of a conceptualisation of systems with both constraining and enabling properties can have unintended consequences.

One manageress stresses that gender mainstreaming can have negative consequences, particularly for women. She provides the example that if you were to fully gender mainstream health care costs, it would be much more expensive for women, because women generally use health care more than men according to the interviewee. For this reason, she was opposed to it (interview 2, manageress).

Besides these contradictory issues with regard to the implementation of gender mainstreaming, there are also more fundamental problems which might be inherent in the implementation of gender mainstreaming.

The boundaries between problems of the particular implementation within the Commission and inherent problems of gender mainstreaming are fluid. There are three reasons, as stated by actors, which seem more general than the points raised in the problems with implementation. The three points raised were that gender mainstreaming is too flawed; that there is legal insecurity with regard to gender mainstreaming, and that the economic situation is difficult at the moment. Each point will be examined in turn.

One administrator with a legal background stresses that lawyers are usually opposed to gender mainstreaming since they find it too flawed.

With positive action you have concrete guidelines and regulations. With gender mainstreaming you rely on the goodwill of others, on how others take up their issues (interview 10, female administrator).

The continuing legal insecurity even within the Commission with regard to gender mainstreaming becomes apparent in the following quotation:

The most important barrier is that it might contradict the existing laws, depending on how you interpret it. That is why there are all these court proceedings (interview 7, female administrator).

The legal insecurity the actor is probably referring to may relate to the Kalanke and Marshall cases of the ECJ (see chapter 6).

Lastly, the next actor refers to the worsening economic situation and believes that gender mainstreaming is less popular now:

I also have to say that the gender equality issue was much more en vogue than now. And also perhaps the international conjunction and the economy. I think that things have not slowed down, but it is not the same (interview 10, female administrator).

7.4.2 Commitment to Gender Mainstreaming

As was elaborated in chapter 3, it is important to examine the extent to which actors have created gender mainstreaming as an institution. Institution was defined to mean whether the negotiations on gender mainstreaming have led to 'generalised expectations' and 'interpretations of behaviour' or 'typifications of habitualised actions that constitute institutions [which] are always shared' (Berger/ Luckmann 1966: 72).

One important indicator of the extent to which there are shared typifications with regard to gender mainstreaming, is whether men are also involved with gender mainstreaming, i.e. whether only women or only men amongst themselves have shared typifications on this issue or whether there are cross-gender typifications.

In many interviews, women stress the importance of gender mainstreaming for both genders, as this would also enable changes in men's behaviour towards families in that men might want to redefine their gender roles and take on more responsibilities for the family.

At the other extreme, one official cannot see how men can be committed to gender mainstreaming. He says:

How do you imagine that men are committed to mainstreaming? That is not meant as a nasty question. What does it mean to say a man is committed to mainstreaming? That he says once a week in his meeting 'mainstreaming is important'? I am also committed. I just held two job interviews with a man and a woman and I selected the woman. I thought this was quite important for us. We are a small team. I could have chosen a man but for me it was important to have the point of view of a woman. Does that mean I am committed? Maybe (interview 24, manager).

This interviewee seems uncertain about the aims of gender mainstreaming and especially his role or the role of any man in the gender mainstreaming process. From the Commission's point of view, both genders should benefit from gender mainstreaming, however in the implementation process this might be difficult to achieve.

Another manager comments:

One question is, what you want to achieve with gender mainstreaming. I think it's good that there are women who want to achieve higher positions. But I am a man. There ought not to be too many women. The reason is that it is hard to reconcile private life and professional life. If you really want to change something, you need to do something in this area. I would also prefer to be at home. I have two children. I would rather spend more time with them. Thus this 'gender mainstreaming', or the reconciliation between private and professional life is something very general. It is also valid for men. You should change something there. If you do that, it is also good for gender mainstreaming. That would indirectly help women to take up the challenge of higher positions (interview 24, manager).

This manager is describing an aspect of the aims of the gender mainstreaming policy in the Commission quite accurately, i.e. that gender mainstreaming is supposed to be beneficial for both men and women. However, he does not appear aware that his ideas are in fact the stated aims of the Commission's gender mainstreaming policy (European Commission 1996).

One manager, in answer to the question about what he personally thought of gender mainstreaming, said that it was not important for him, since no woman applied for the position he is in (interview 6, manager). He is implying that the only impact gender mainstreaming could have on him would be that a woman receives a job instead of him, as a result of positive action measures. The only association he has with gender mainstreaming is thus the notion of increased competition from women. One manager thought that in some cases men are disadvantaged; for example, over adoption rights.

Under staff regulations in place at the time of interviewing, only female officials who had adopted a child could apply for special leave, while this was not the case for male officials (interview 25, manager).

Those who work in either of the Equal Opportunities Units are seen by all interviewees as being committed to gender mainstreaming regardless of their sex. Several stated those who work in the two Equal Opportunities Units are the only men committed to gender mainstreaming. However, there seem to be a lot of prejudices around those men that are working in the Equal Opportunities Unit at DG Employment and Social Affairs:

It tends to be homosexual men. No I think that is interesting. All those that have worked there since I have dealt with the unit were either homosexual or completely weird. They were not completely weird but, yeah they were. They come in orange robes and they go and hug trees at weekends. They're not mainstream people. You don't get lawyers from DG Competition wanting to work in Equal Opportunities, which is a shame. It adds to the perception of this crowd of left wing feminists who are sort of eating this. And this perception would change if you had a more advanced participation (interview 1, female secretary).

This official stresses the perception of men working in Equal Opportunities as being 'weird or homosexual'. She does not argue that they are weird from the mere fact of their working there, but that they are either weird from the outset or that they become weird while working because they do not dress or behave according to the norm. She also has the perception that the others who work in the Equal Opportunities Unit are seen as a crowd of left wing feminists, so in fact, in her view the whole unit is marginalised. Indeed, this corresponds to the criticism with regard to equal opportunities, that the Equal Opportunities Units tend to be marginalised.

This problem is acknowledged by the Equal Opportunities Unit within DG Employment and Social Affairs:

Yes, the single biggest problem I have with mainstreaming is that it is labelled as a women's thing. And we are having difficulty in getting our male colleagues to feel that they too are being covered by our activities. That's why this year they have as our priority thing, the reconciliation of work and family life. And the sub-theme is giving fathers back to the families. So it is clearly around the issue of parental leave (interview)[118].

This administrator stressed that those men that work in the Equal Opportunities Unit in DG Employment and Social Affairs, or those that have worked there in the past, have usually worked on the legal aspects of gender mainstreaming and not on the policy-making side.

One official also states that it is not common for men to be committed to gender mainstreaming. He goes even further by stating that any involvement

---

118 The number and the status of the interviewee is not provided here since it would not be possible to retain anonymity as the Equal Opportunities Unit is relatively small.

218

with gender mainstreaming would be a barrier to the furtherance of their careers.

No, if they are committed, they don't show it. Otherwise they would be seen as weird by those who are not committed. In general it is like that with innovations, that others, who are not ready to implement them, see them as weird. For a man, a commitment to gender mainstreaming would be seen as luxury and also as a barrier to his career. It would have the same value as if someone was committed to green paint in his office. Or if someone was committed to disabled people. It is very much dependent on how the hierarchy is behaving. If they were strongly committed to gender mainstreaming that would be quite different. For anybody who wants to make a career in the Commission it is not a good idea to be committed to gender mainstreaming (interview 3, male administrator).

This administrator confirms the view of the above-cited actor, that those who are committed to gender mainstreaming are seen as weird. However, while the previously cited actors state that those who agree to work in the Equal Opportunities Unit are weird from the outset, this actor says that they are seen as weird per se by those who are not committed to gender mainstreaming.

Another potentially contradictory effect of gender mainstreaming is the perceived effect it has on the actors involved in it. Those who are directly involved with gender mainstreaming largely agree that it might have a negative effect on their future career:

I would not say it's [the involvement with gender mainstreaming] negative. I would not say it's positive either. I would say it's neutral. I would say that for someone who is dealing with Equal Opportunities I don't think it benefits their careers at all. I think that if I were doing other things, I would be much better rewarded, or my career would advance faster. But I would not say that it is negative. Now in terms of promotion, of course it can be negative if they promote other people doing things than me doing this. [...] But on the other hand, equal opportunities and mainstreaming are part of the political aims and political objectives set out by the Commission. So in theory it is something important, it is something that we should be doing [...]. There are two issues there. You have, let's say, somebody who is in a policy area of, let's say, environment or whatever. If they are active in gender mainstreaming does it impair their prospects? Probably not, depending on how you do it. Because normally when you gender mainstream, you do make your policy more precise. So normally in such circumstances, the policies improve. So it is unlikely to be perceived negatively. However, if you are directly involved with gender mainstreaming there does tend to be a negative label (interview 2, manageress).

The citation of the above actor also demonstrates the contradiction that, on the one hand, gender mainstreaming is official policy in the Commission and on the other hand, that it might impede career prospects.

Another actor comments on the same issue:

It can be disadvantageous to be involved too much with gender mainstreaming, because it can easily happen that one is pushed into a feminist ghetto and it is then difficult to advance (interview 26, female administrator).

Various officials stressed the importance of men being committed to gender mainstreaming. One administrator states this in the following way:

The women tend to appreciate those men that are involved. They think that the men will change something. When you look at [gender mainstreaming] conferences, 99.9% of participants are women, which is also a problem because it concerns men as well (interview 7, female administrator).

In DG Regio [Regional Affairs] there is a male head of research regarding gender equality. And they have achieved a lot. And it is also important to have this issue taken up not only by women. In my view they become even more credible if there are men who are taking them up. But I am not in favour. I don't think that it can make a change in mentalities (interview 10, female administrator).

It is not possible to assess whether the involvement of the previous inter-viewees actually did have a negative impact on their careers. However the perception of these actors, that it would have a negative impact, maybe an important indicator of how they see their work valued. Also, this perception might result in these actors not even applying for other positions in the future.

Several employees stated the perception that gender mainstreaming is bad for the career of officials. Some differentiated between both genders with regard to the opportunities for careers. According to some, a commitment to gender mainstreaming would hinder only women's careers, while it would benefit men. It is difficult to assess any of these statements with regard to whether they are actually correct. It is, however, noteworthy that individual actors perceive the situation in this manner.

7.5 Structuration/ Institutionalisation of Gender Mainstreaming

7.5.1 Importance of Gender Mainstreaming

Another important indicator as to the extent to which gender mainstreaming can be seen as an institution is how other units apart from those that are directly dealing with gender mainstreaming are dealing with the issue. None of the officials interviewed in units outside the Equal Opportunities Units find that gender mainstreaming plays an important role in their unit. However, some actors see important changes due to the introduction of gender mainstreaming. One official who, amongst other things, is responsible for checking whether gender mainstreaming is implemented horizontally in various geographical areas comments:

Well, if nothing else, gender mainstreaming had as a consequence that I am concerned with it. But I cannot generalise about that. At the moment, 10% of the budget in the ESF is granted to positive action measures. In addition, there is the horizontal process of gender mainstreaming. Everybody who wants to have money has to at least pretend to implement gender mainstreaming. That gives hope that mainstreaming will be implemented properly one day (interview 20, male administrator).

Even though this statement is not concerned with the implementation of gender mainstreaming within the Commission but rather with the implementation of gender mainstreaming in the ESF, it nevertheless raises two interesting points. First of all the official admits that no real checking takes place with regard to the implementation of gender mainstreaming in the ESF by saying that project applicants have to 'pretend' that gender mainstreaming is being implemented. Secondly he raises the notion that despite the missing will to implement gender mainstreaming at the moment, it might nevertheless be implemented later on.

One actor makes the criticism that commitment only exists at the rhetorical level and that it has no impact on policy-making and the internal organisation of the Commission (interview 13, male administrator). A different interviewee claims that the commitment only exists for policy-making and not for the internal policies (interview 21, female administrator). Yet another official states that the operationalisation is usually the problem:

In any case on the political verbal level and in the general documents, gender mainstreaming is always integrated and that is a big progress. The problem starts when it is operationalised. Let's say we had good communications about mainstreaming in development politics, that was great, but where is the gender perspective and then how we do it? The result is that there is a frustrated person at the gender desk who does not know what she is supposed to do (interview 4, manageress).

The following actor also thinks that gender mainstreaming exists merely at the rhetorical level. Additionally, she is also sceptical about any changes in organisation once more women are in the organisation.

I picked up gender mainstreaming since I started with the gendering of international relations. But what I have realised is that on paper everybody writes that they are in favour of gender mainstreaming and that they take the needs of men and women into consideration you know. But in practical terms, especially with development co-operation and trade and external relations, women's problems are not even recognised. It's still on paper, but when you look at projects in place [...] On the other hand, one should not go to the other extreme. I am against the notion that a minority group should get their rights by any means. Having more women in the decision-making process won't change things. I know that from my professional life and also from my personal life. I don't think that by pushing more women to the top, we will have more resources for women (interview 10, female administrator).

The importance of 'pretending' to implement gender mainstreaming should not be underestimated. This is also an important element in neo-institutionalism. According to Oliver (1991), when an organisation expects that conformity will increase social or economic fitness, the most likely response will be acquiescence. As has been shown in chapter 2, gender mainstreaming is framed by the Commission to increase social and economic fitness, thus we could expect that the organisations will acquiesce to the gender mainstreaming concept.

With regard to co-operation by the Equal Opportunities Unit with other units, it was stressed by individual actors who define gender mainstreaming as important for their work that they regularly co-operate with the Equal Opportunities Unit. Employees from within the Equal Opportunities Units confirm this, stressing that sometimes it is very time-consuming for them to consider the impact of gender mainstreaming in often very specialised policy areas. One actor also stresses that the requirements with regard to gender mainstreaming have increased considerably and that the workload of the Equal Opportunities Unit has been greatly extended (interview[119]).

One employee from the Equal Opportunities Unit in DG Employment and Social Affairs stresses the importance of informal networks:

There is a loose network of colleagues, who are responsible for gender mainstreaming in geographical desks. And I try to keep in touch with them. It is important that the information does not go to the gender desks but rather goes directly to the geographical desks. We meet according to need; the network is very informal, we have only met once so far. The network is not institutionalised. It [the instutionalisation] does not make so much sense (interview)[120].

This actor points out the importance of informal networks since it allows her to talk directly to those colleagues who are responsible for actually implementing gender mainstreaming in the policies, rather than just cooperating with people from the gender desks.

The importance of gender mainstreaming in the work of the Commission is assessed very differently by the interviewees. On the one hand there is a greater awareness amongst the employees of gender issues, however, gender mainstreaming has not yet resulted in a change of everyday routine for most actors.

7.5.2 Special Position of Gender Mainstreaming

One way to measure the institutionalisation of gender mainstreaming is to examine whether it is perceived as something special or is seen as being a part of the daily routine. Most interviewees agreed that gender mainstreaming still has a special position, i.e. that it is not a normal part of the routine. Giddens describes routinisation in the following way:

---

119 Ibid.
120 Ibid.

The concept of routinisation, as grounded in practical consciousness, is vital to the theory of structuration. Routine is integral both to the continuity of the personality of the agent, as he or she moves along the paths of daily activities, and to the institutions of society, which are such only through their continued reproduction. (The emphasis was added in the original; Giddens 1984: 60).

The 'shared typifications' developed within neo-institutionalism are also closely linked to the concept of routines.

One middle aged administrator who comes from a Member State where the women's movement is particularly strong, argues that:

For the majority of A level employees, gender mainstreaming is normal. That it is, in fact, not a new topic. It was already there during their student days. Certainly, it is also a question of generation, 30 years ago, it was different. Today it is not an issue (interview 3, male administrator).

This interviewee does not see gender mainstreaming as a new issue, since he says that it was a new issue for him in his student days. However, being prompted on the difference between gender mainstreaming and equal opportunities, he saw none. There is also evidence that for some administrators gender mainstreaming is an entirely new subject. One interviewee spoke of an occasion where an administrator was substituted at a meeting on gender mainstreaming and the substitute said at the meeting 'You'll be relieved to know that I won't be talking about gender mainstreaming because I don't know anything about it.' The others in the meeting laughed about the comment and the meeting went ahead. It is not so surprising that individuals don't know much about gender mainstreaming. However, that they openly say so at a meeting on gender mainstreaming is a different issue. The phrasing that the others would be 'relieved to know that she was ignorant of the issue' might suggest that she thought everyone there was opposed to it in any case. This example shows that gender mainstreaming is still not taken seriously by everyone. If the above example happened with regard to a more institutionalised topic, for example the budget, i.e. if someone said in a budget meeting 'you'll be glad to know I won't talk about the budget because I don't know anything about it', this might have caused an outcry and could have led to disciplinary proceedings.

Several actors stress that while equal opportunities was in place, whenever a policy concerned women, they passed it on to the Equal Opportunities Unit, whereas now that they know that equal opportunities is their responsibility as well they simply ask the Equal Opportunities Unit for advice and then implement it on their own.

Those who are not directly involved with gender mainstreaming did not generally know the difference between equal opportunities and positive action.

I think it's still seen as outside of normal procedure. I think people still need to be reminded. But it's not new [...] people just have to get their head around it. Maybe the

aggressive approach will work – eventually.
There is a perception of a puuh and peng and you do it. And I know, especially as someone coming from being inside the unit that was doing it and now being outside, that there is a perception. And you know there are a lot of comments in the couloirs [French term for corridors]. 'Oh bloody hell, here they are going on about that sort of thing all the time. Gender mainstreaming this and gender mainstreaming that, haven't they got enough to do'. There is a certain antagonism, but maybe that is normal (interview 1, female secretary).

This quotation includes a lot of the contradictory opinions with regard to gender mainstreaming. From other comments it is apparent that this secretary is in favour of gender mainstreaming. However, she is uncertain about how to best implement it. On the one hand she suggests that the 'aggressive' approach, as she perceives it, might work (i.e. the approach currently in place in the Commission). On the other hand, she sees that a lot of people are opposed to gender mainstreaming because of its prevalence in many different areas.

One official stresses that even though gender mainstreaming is not on his mind all the time, he is not opposed to it:

If I may be very frank here then I would say that gender mainstreaming is something that is sometimes forgotten. And if the Head of Unit of the Equal Opportunities Unit is not calling, then it is something that is forgotten (interview 25, manager).

This manager expresses a 'neutral' view towards gender mainstreaming. However, since it is not part of his normal routine, he sometimes forgets it. The actor in the following quotation confirms his view:

Oh no, it's still regarded as something confined to those people who deal with it and the rest of us are not really involved. Even the training. When you join DG Employment you receive training on what gender mainstreaming is. I think that is good because everybody gets acquainted with the idea. And they also begin to feel that that affects them on a personal level. Also, people in the services tend to say, well, she is the one responsible for gender mainstreaming, we don't care about it. But as for me, I never thought about it like that (interview 15, female administrator).

This administrator mentions a general problem with gender mainstreaming. As was shown in the general framework on gender mainstreaming, one of the major differences with regard to equal opportunities is that every actor involved in the process is supposed to implement gender mainstreaming.

Another indicator with regard to the institutionalisation of gender main-streaming is the extent to which people in other DGs feel responsible for gender mainstreaming. The following opinion; that some DGs do not feel at all responsible for gender mainstreaming and indeed do not see a link between their work and gender mainstreaming, is voiced by several administrators working in the Equal Opportunities Units.

Although it is becoming more normal I think it still has a special position because some DGs do not feel responsible when prompted on gender mainstreaming. If you ask them, you get as a response, 'we are not responsible for that'. If you hear something like that you know that for many people no internalisation of gender mainstreaming has taken place. Neither within the hierarchy, nor for individual employees (interview)[121].

7.6 Gender Mainstreaming as an Innovation

According to the Communication from the Commission 'Innovation policy: updating the Union's approach in the context of the Lisbon strategy', innovation is defined in the following way:

Innovation can be incremental or radical, it can result from technology transfer or through the development of new business concepts, it can be technological, organisational or presentational' (European Commission 2003a: 2).

In the Communication, a concise definition of innovation is given as 'the successful production, assimilation and exploitation of novelty in the economic and social spheres' (European Commission 2003a: 2). The Communication refers to a Green Paper of the European Commission which presents a more detailed definition:

[…] innovation is the renewal and enlargement of the range of products and services and associated markets; the establishment of new methods of production, supply and distribution; the introduction of changes in management, work organisation, and the working conditions and skills of the workforce (European Commission 1995a: 4). These definitions continue to be a valid basis for the Commission's approach to innovation policy, and are consistent with the Lisbon European Council's perception of the importance of innovation to competitiveness (European Commission 2003a: 2).

In this section, the actors' attitudes towards innovations are not limited to gender mainstreaming and equal opportunities. This allows us to assess the relevance they give to gender mainstreaming as an innovation, whether or not gender mainstreaming comes to their mind when thinking about innovations in the Commission.

The political opportunity structure is one important indicator as to the likelihood of an innovation being implemented within an organisation. As described in chapter 6, the political opportunity structure approach assumes that the dynamics, strategies, forms and outcomes of interest representations are shaped by different characteristics of the local, national and international context (McAdam 1998, Tarrow 1998). Two managers when interviewed agreed that in fact the time was right to implement a new policy (interview 11, manageress; interview 25, manager). This was partly accounted for by the reform process which was then in the process of taking place. They argued that since many parts of the staff regulations were under consideration, it

---

121 Ibid.

would be easier to implement new policies. Others, however, said that the time for introducing a new policy not directly linked to improving economic performance was not good, since the economic situation was perceived to be deteriorating[122] (interview 3, male administrator). One actor argues that the European convention and the preparations for the next enlargement are the ideal situation for implementing gender mainstreaming further:

> Now with the European Convention and the preparation for enlargement we should use the chance. I think that enlargement poses exactly those questions, i.e. how many commissioners, how many DGs we shall have. We could make a clean sweep and say we should do that now. Well that is one possibility. That is definitely a political change of structure. The more difficult question is how you implement it in the practical sense, how you can work practically with 28 states (interview 4, manageress).

Another argument is that the Commission has not, so far, really established a management attitude to the question. One manager explains that now all employees are supposed to be seen as clients, not as 'annoying colleagues who have a problem' (interview 24, manager). However, as in any organisation which implements New Public Management approaches, this leads to radical changes in the running of the organisation. The above cited actor explains this as follows:

> If our main role is to serve our customer, it is a managerial approach. So innovation should first address the managerial approach in the unit. Secondly we need to use all the tools we have in order to provide the service, i.e. computers, internet, the new potential means of multimedia, to provide the service. For example we have created a call centre to enable everybody to phone in and obtain the information they want. But we are also involved in e-commission, i.e. providing the service in an electronic way. We need to be very careful. Social means human, humans treat human aspects, human issues not only by means of electronics. We need to make a balance. There are a lot of things we can do through electronics but we still need to have human contact. So innovation means finding the right balance between the traditional way of having only individual contact and providing the service only through the internet (interview 24, manager).

Four actors say that fundamental changes are needed before any innovation can be properly implemented in the Commission. One says that the Commission ought to be split up into different compartments, like national ministries, that the Commission is otherwise too big to meaningfully introduce innovations (interview 4, manageress). In contrast, another actor demands that the Commission be organised more horizontally than vertically, since otherwise everybody only thinks about their own departments and DGs (interview 3, male administrator).

Finally, one actor says that it is of the utmost importance to have a full transition to technology, which according to her has not happened yet (interview 2, manageress).

---

122 As we have seen in chapter 3, there is a dispute between academic commentators as to whether gender mainstreaming can be linked to an improved image of the organisation.

The actors had very different ideas as to which innovations were needed within the Commission. Most suggestions circled around reconciliation policies (interview 10, female administrator; interview 19, female assistant) and different models for working hours, like flexitime (interview 22, female secretary) and a shortening of the 'real working times' (interview 25, manager). In general, the existing patterns of working time, i.e. either full or part-time and the difficulties of changing between the two models were criticised (interview 19, female assistant). One actor demands the 'humanisation of working times' (interview 15, female administrator). Others demand a further orientation towards a customer attitude within the Commission (interview 24, manager), more incentives for effort (interview 3, male administrator) and a better working environment. The latter point was argued firstly, that there needs to be a 'comfortable' cafeteria where employees can sit down (interview 19, female assistant) and also that there need to be facilities specifically for parents with small children (interview 10, female administrator).

The actors responded very differently with regard to successful innovations within the Commission. The question was framed rather generally, and the response was not required to be related to equal opportunities. The most radical reaction was that 'innovations are not possible in the Commission'. It was argued that even the promised introduction of showers and the supply of bikes for travelling from one Commission building to the next was not possible (interview 13, male administrator). Three other actors say that they could not think of any successful innovation in the Commission (interview 24, manager; interview 3, male administrator and interview 15, female administrator). Several others say that e-mail or the use of computers in general was regarded as innovation (interview 24, manager; interview 27, female administrator and interview 22, female secretary). One actor did say state more specifically that she regarded using a common drive in her unit as an innovation (interview 1, female secretary). One person mentioned the financial reform, implemented in the Commission in the 1990s, called SEM 2000, which was about regrouping the financial circuit and introducing 'sound and efficient management' (interview 14, female assistant). Another thought that the Transeuropean Networks, i.e. building European highways and railway lines was an innovation (interview 20, male administrator). One actor mentioned that she thought equal opportunities within the commission were innovative. She explains this as follows:

I have difficulties with the term innovation, because everybody wants to make innovations, everybody wants to be creative. Though I would say that there was an innovation with regard to equal opportunities. Because of the pressures from the EP, the President of the European Commission, Santer more or less got a vote of no confidence from the EP. Then he said innovatively, 'okay, we will found a Group of Commissioners for Equal Opportunities between Women and Men'. This led to many changes. Thus I would say that the innovation was worth it. It would be worth copying. In this context you can say equal opportunities are something very positive (interview 4, manageress).

Even though she has a critical attitude towards the term innovation, since she thinks that it has a normative connotation and might therefore lose meaning, she says that due to external pressure, innovations were introduced with regard to equal opportunities by the creation of the Commissioners Group on Equal Opportunities. Another actor who is involved in the programme on innovations in Member States also points out that it is important to take the context into consideration:

> In general, the Commission claims innovation for all its projects. Whether they are really innovative is often difficult to say. What is an innovation? I think that on a European level, it is difficult to tell [...] What is innovative in Cologne does not have to be an innovation in northern Finland. You really have to look at every concrete situation in the Member States (interview 15, female administrator).

She is referring to the contextual dimension explained in chapter 4 and indeed, this plays a role within the Commission since some DGs are dominated or led by a particular nationality. There is also the question of the perception on how gender mainstreaming changes are to be implemented.

When the actors were asked about unsuccessful innovations in the Commission the majority responded on issues relating to equal opportunities. One person stated that the reform aspiration during the Santer commission could not be realised partly because the Santer Commission had to step back (interview 13, male administrator). Two actors mentioned the introduction of quotas as an unsuccessful innovation. One argued that this was the case because very few women applied for higher-level positions, even after the introduction of quotas (interview 23, female administrator), another contends that quotas need a long time before changes can be seen and that so far not many are evident (interview 22, female secretary).

Finally, it is important to see whether actors perceive the implementation of gender mainstreaming in the Commission to be an innovation. The views were much split on this. Seven interviewees say that it does not constitute an innovation, while four think that it could be regarded as an innovation. These opinions will be examined in turn. Three of the actors who rejected it as a form of innovation say that it does not create anything new, or indeed any philosophy. A further three contend that its implementation within the Commission did not constitute an innovation. Those who say it could be regarded as innovative had very different views on why this was the case and these will be analysed separately. One of the actors who said that gender mainstreaming was not new enough to constitute an innovation at the time of interviewing explains:

> Not today of course. Back in the middle 90s, when it came after Beijing it would have been an innovation. But today it is no longer considered to be so. It is not as well established in the Commission as I would like it to be. But when you talk about gender mainstreaming or the issue of gender, it's not as though you have fallen from the sky, 'Oh what are they talking about or, here they come again'. But it is not a binding innovation. So I don't think

gender mainstreaming is an innovation today (interview 2, manageress).
No, because it is nothing new. They have been talking about equal opportunities for a long time. It is just a new vocabulary. The Commission changes its vocabulary quite regularly. They do the same for people with disabilities; there is not even a statistic on disabled people (interview 14, female assistant).

The first actor is saying firstly that gender mainstreaming is not an innovation any more, since it has been around since the mid-90s and secondly that she cannot think of it as an innovation since it is not binding. Since the second actor sees no difference between gender mainstreaming and equal opportunities it cannot, therefore, be seen as an innovation in her view.

Another actor says that:

I have a problem in to recognising mainstreaming as a philosophy; it ought to be a matter of course. It must be possible to get into a situation where the question does not arise. An enterprise has a financial interest to get the best people into a particular position and not to ask, is it a woman or is it a man. There are areas where they cannot make changes, for example maternity leave. And you can be as good as you want but if somebody is not there for a couple of months or half a year you need to ensure that the negative consequences are limited. In areas where you cannot correct the cause you need to correct the consequences. Equal treatment. In most countries, 90 to 95% of all prison inmates are men and only 10% women. So you could also say that this is a scandal, we need a quota here (interview 25, manager).

This actor does not regard gender mainstreaming as a distinct policy since it ought to be part of rational decision-making. Thus he does not see it as an innovation. Yet another actor says that gender mainstreaming is fully accepted within society and therefore cannot constitute an innovation.

Three other actors say that the way gender mainstreaming is implemented in the Commission could not be seen as an innovation.

On the positive side, three more say that it could be regarded as an innovation. They explain their views in the following way:

Yes. It is totally changing the culture, the working culture. The culture of the Commission, on how we look at things. The acceptance of family-friendly practices, new ways of working, part-time, teleworking, all of these are integrated into the concept of gender mainstreaming: They have completely revolutionised the situation. Part-time, you know if you used to do that, it was the end of your career. But now, it is not a problem. Higher managers are working part-time, higher managers are teleworking. It is no longer a hindrance to one's career (interview 19, female assistant).
Gender mainstreaming is a very radical system change. It alters the whole structure. Policies have to plan society in a differently way. For example, only a government and administration can change the transport strategy. At the moment transportation is organised so that men can best reach their offices (interview 12, female administrator).
Yes, innovation in the sense that gender mainstreaming is something we should think about but have not considered it in the past. In that sense yes. But I would also say that in some cases we should not be sceptical, but neither should we be orthodox, in applying any kind of policy. In that way gender mainstreaming is a good thing but its implementation is not if other aspects are not thought about (interview 24, manager).

The first actor quoted regards gender mainstreaming as an innovation since it has changed the working culture in the Commission, particularly the working hours. The second administrator also thinks it is an innovation, since it radically changes the system. The manager in the third quotation believes that gender mainstreaming might be an innovation, but he also warns that the policy should not be implemented in an orthodox manner.

I don't know, that needs to come little by little. One cannot do it slowly today and then it's the great revolution. It is not like an innovation, which is instantaneous; it is something done little by little. So you cannot say it is an innovation. If you talk of a fixed period, 20 years later maybe you will see a change. But it is not something that you see right away. It is a slow revolution (interview 26, female administrator).

She refers to gender mainstreaming as a gradual change policy, which Hauschildt (1993) describes as an incremental innovation (see chapter 4).

7.7   Conclusion

Even though gender mainstreaming was formally introduced into the Commission at the time of the inception of the Commission Communication (1996) and the 'Third Action Programme' in 1997, the diffusion of gender mainstreaming has remained somewhat limited. Not surprisingly, most actors who are directly involved with gender mainstreaming are familiar with the concept and define it according to the Commission Communication of 1996. For the gender mainstreaming advocacy-network, gender mainstreaming has clearly become an institution as defined by Jepperson (1991) (see chapter 3). For them, gender mainstreaming is a social order, i. e. standardised interaction sequences that has attained a certain state or property. Gender mainstreaming is also self-reproducing within the gender mainstreaming advocacy-network, i.e. its persistence is not dependant on recurrent collective mobilisation.

However, the institutionalisation of gender mainstreaming has not spread beyond the relatively small group of gender experts. For actors not directly employed in the Equal Opportunities Unit but who have gender mainstreaming as one responsibility amongst others, the commitment to gender mainstreaming is up to the individual. The understanding of the hierarchy about gender mainstreaming remains limited despite training opportunities for Heads of Unit and Directors. Various actors made the criticism that the opportunity for training was seized only by a few of the target group of the hierarchy and that a lot of (often female) substitutes were delegated to attend the training instead. The limited knowledge about gender mainstreaming is, thus, unsurprising.

Many actors outside the relatively small gender mainstreaming policy machinery are not familiar with the concept of gender mainstreaming. They remain unable to distinguish between gender mainstreaming and positive action policies. Indeed according to one employee of the Equal Opportunities Unit in DG Administration and Personnel (who is responsible for the implementation of gender mainstreaming), the most important changes that took place due to gender mainstreaming could have been part of the positive action policies which had been in place in the Commission before the introduction of gender mainstreaming.

One of the biggest failures in the implementation of gender mainstreaming lies in the fact that men are not sufficiently included in the concept. The majority either don't see any advantages for themselves, or feel threatened by the concept of gender mainstreaming. With the introduction of targets about the recruitment of new officials which aims to gender balance the work force in the Commission, some men will clearly have to endure some disadvantages due to the introduction of gender mainstreaming. The first hypothesis established in this chapter that the higher the degree of vested interests that are opposed to the transformation of gender relations, the greater the likelihood of organisational resistance to gender mainstreaming could be confirmed. The management of the Commission acknowledged this problem and particularly has men as fathers as a target group for the internal gender mainstreaming policies in 2002.

The second hypothesis of the empirical chapter, i.e. the higher the degree of voluntary diffusion of gender mainstreaming, the lower the likelihood of resistance from the Commission to institutional pressures could also be partially verified. Gender mainstreaming has not yet diffused from the small gender mainstreaming structures to the general structure of the Commission. The 'resistance' consisted in conscious refusal to learn about and adopt gender mainstreaming policies. Various other actors feared negative effects on their careers due to an involvement with gender mainstreaming.

Gender mainstreaming measures in the Commission, such as increasing the access of women to the Commission and improving women's promotional chances are monitored from the highest level in the Commission. No interviewee stated they are against gender mainstreaming. However, until today, very few employees seem to actively search for ways to implement gender mainstreaming in their day-to-day routines.

The hypothesis that the lower the legal coercion behind gender mainstreaming, the higher the likelihood of organisational resistance to gender mainstreaming could be verified. Even though the Commission Communication (European Commission 1996) and the subsequent guidelines on Gender Impact Assessment (European Commission 1999c) clearly define gender mainstreaming as an organisational aim of the Commission, there is no legal coercion behind the concept. There are no incitements or sanctions for the implementation of gender mainstreaming within the Commission, for either DGs or Units, or at the individual level[123]. The main actors pushing for the implementation of gender mainstreaming are the gender mainstreaming coordination units. However it is up to the individual organisational units to actually implement gender mainstreaming. Even though the gender mainstreaming coordination units have the weight of the Commission Communication (European Commission 1996) behind them, the implementing units often avoid the implementation and ignore the gender mainstreaming goal.

Gender mainstreaming thus appears to be an example of an institution which, at least at the time the interviews took place, remains 'without concomitant changes in interaction orders' (Barley and Tolbert 1996: 111). This means that a significant proportion of Commission employees adopted gender mainstreaming as a formal policy without producing obvious shifts in their daily routines (Meyer and Rowan 1977). However, as gender mainstreaming is a very complex programme in that it involves the reorganisation of many work processes and a lot of work organisation, it is, after only six years[124], too early to assess conclusively whether its implementation can be regarded as merely symbolic.

---

123 Monetary incitements for gender mainstreaming only exist for applications for the Structural Funds, but not within the European Commission.
124 As outlined in chapter 1, the interviews with Commission employees took place between Summer 2000 and Winter 2001/2002.

8   Conclusion

This book examined gender mainstreaming from two different perspectives. From a policy analysis standpoint I examined to what degree the definitions and interpretations of the European Commission can be seen as a policy innovation. From an organisational point of view I studied to what extent the implementation of gender mainstreaming in the European Commission can be seen as an organisational institution and innovation.

Gender Mainstreaming as a Policy Innovation

Gender mainstreaming was strategically framed by the Commission in McAdam et al.'s (1996) definition to fashion 'a shared understanding of the world'. All four frame alignment processes that were initially developed theoretically by Snow et al. (1986) for social movement organisations and transposed to public administrations by Rein and Schön (1993) took place with regard to gender mainstreaming in the European Commission.

Firstly, frame bridging took place in the EU when Article 119 was included into the Treaty of Rome in 1957 which stipulated the principle of 'equal pay for equal work'. This constituted a new paradigm as until then social policy (including the principle of equality) had played only a minor role in the establishment of the ECSC in 1957. The subsequent drafting of the ten equality Directives and the European Commission's strategic cooperation with and support of the women's movements on equal opportunities constituted further elements of frame bridging.

Secondly, the value amplification of gender mainstreaming was done by linking gender mainstreaming to positive values such as equality and to an important institution like the UN. The Commission also linked its position on gender mainstreaming up to academic discourses by referring to the term 'gender'.

Thirdly, the Commission extended its frame with gender mainstreaming by involving men in its implementation. With gender mainstreaming, both men and women are rendered responsible for incorporating equal opportunities in all policy areas, programmes and work organisation. Gender mainstreaming was also modified by including economic reasons in the explanation and its implementation.

Fourthly, gender mainstreaming transformed the frame of the European Commission by defining the necessity of a cultural change in the Commission as a pre-condition for its full implementation.

As it was shown in the book, the wide range of all four possible frame alignment processes were achieved in the case of gender mainstreaming in the Commission. This result is a strong indicator for the success of this concept, at least on a discursive level as the concept of framing mainly focusses on discursive processes.

Gender Mainstreaming as an Organisational Innovation

The definition of an organisational innovation used in this book is based on Hauschildt's (1993) definition of an innovation. The results of the empirical study will be briefly summarised here.

The first dimension of Hauschildt's definition, i.e. the subjective dimension, exists only to a limited extent in the Commission. Those interviewees who are part of the gender mainstreaming advocacy-network predominantly see gender mainstreaming as an innovation, whereas many of those outside such gender mainstreaming advocacy-network do not. One view of many of those outside the gender mainstreaming advocacy-network shows partly a lack of understanding of the concept. They themselves are in general aware of the concept but do not want to comment whether they regard gender mainstreaming as an innovation because they were unsure what it precisely means. In addition, they do not regard gender mainstreaming as different from the existing equal opportunities policies introduced by the Commission.

The second aspect of Hauschildt's subjective dimension of an innovation, i.e. to what extent an innovation is new for a particular organisational unit has been considered in respect of gender mainstreaming and the Commission. It emerged from the empirical study that gender mainstreaming is basically new for the European Commission, although some elements of gender mainstreaming have already been incorporated in the Second Action Programme for Equal Opportunities (European Commission 1994a). The Commission had implemented a proactive equal opportunities policy with its Second Action, however, no systematic inclusion of gender aspects was included in this policy. The most important change in the Commission's policy took place in 1996 when gender mainstreaming was defined as an organisational aim through its inclusion in the Commission Communication (European Commission 1996) and the Third Action Programme for Equal Opportunities (European Commission 1997a).

Furthermore, the Commissioners founded a group on gender mainstreaming. Even though this group has some serious flaws in its effectiveness, the impact on the Commission as a whole is repeatedly stressed by those involved with gender mainstreaming. In addition each DG is obliged to carry out an annual structural gender mainstreaming plan, in which progress since the last gender report is assessed and a plan for the coming year outlined. This forces each DG to systematise their activities relating to gender mainstreaming. Gender trainings are also offered for Directors and Heads of Units in DG Personnel and Administration and DG Employment and Socials Affairs. However its success has remained somewhat limited. This is partly because several Directors and Heads of Units do not attend the gender training personally but send female subordinates.

The processual dimension is particularly important with regard to gender mainstreaming. I consider the gender mainstreaming process in the concepts suggested by Hauschildt that is, idea, observation and discovery of a previously unknown subject, research, development, invention and intro-duction. The gender mainstreaming concept is new in the international arena. Even though the introduction of gender mainstreaming has been demanded by women's movements since the 1970s, it has only become a vibrant issue in the international arena following its inclusion in the UN Platform of Action in 1995. It was implemented in the Commission in 1996.

The normative aspect of Hauschildt's definition is the most difficult to assess. As discussed in chapter 4, some authors argue that only those products or processes are innovations which enable the improvement of the status quo. However, the assessment of this is very dependent on the norma-tive ideas of the different actors. The attempt to implement gender main-streaming has not yet succeeded in ensuring the diffusion of the concept throughout. Gender mainstreaming is basically understood by only a limited small group of people. One of the main reasons for this is that gender main-streaming is seen as only benefiting women. As a result, men are usually not committed to it.

Equality was an important norm for almost all actors interviewed regardless of their gender, status and DG. However, as emerged from other empirical studies, men tend to underestimate the actual extent of discrimina-tion in their own environment. Especially in their own working area, even though they see that women are disadvantaged, this is not interpreted as dis-crimination. Höyng and Puchert (1998) refer to this phenomenon as the non-perception by actors of interests which do not include their own interests. The conclusion that the non-perception on the part of various male actors persists with regard to the discrimination of women in society and in the Commission as an organisation, is reached in the empirical chapter.

The Institutionalisation/ Structuration of Gender Mainstreaming

On the macro-level, gender mainstreaming is institutionalised within the European Commission. The 1996 Communication of the European Commission (European Commission 1996) instructs its employees to implement gender mainstreaming in all their programmes and activities. The release of this Communication can be partly explained as being required further to the Platform for Action in Beijing in 1995. However, as was elaborated in chapter 6, it is impossible to judge whether its adoption was only a strategic response to the external requirements of the United Nations. Moving to the micro-level, it becomes obvious that the Commission is not only bound by the Platform for Action but also has been an active participant itself in making gender mainstreaming part of the Platform for Action (European Commission 1996, European Parliament 2003).

The term institution used in this book is based on Jepperson's definition as representing a 'social order or pattern that has attained a certain state or property [...] whereby order or pattern means standardised interaction sequences' (Jepperson 1991: 145). Jepperson stresses the importance of the environment in considering whether something is regarded as an institution.

The first assumption, that there is a connection between the level of understanding of the relevant actors about gender mainstreaming and the likelihood of organisational resistance to it can be confirmed as a result of the empirical investigation. The organisational understanding of the concept is relatively low except from the gender mainstreaming experts. Those who are not directly involved with gender mainstreaming adopted a rather active negative strategy to institutional processes. Transferring Oliver's typification of strategic responses of organisations to institutional processes (Oliver 1991: 152; see chapter 3) to the level of individual actors, the strategies displayed by most actors come closest to the 'defying strategy' which is the second most active approach in Oliver's typology. This is illustrated by the low degree of knowledge of gender mainstreaming even though all interviewed actors first are aware that gender mainstreaming ought to be implemented within the European Commission and second training opportunities and advice on gender mainstreaming is available. Even though gender mainstreaming should be taken into account by all actors, the norms and values of gender mainstreaming are often ignored. The rules and require-ments of gender mainstreaming are partly ignored and partly contested. The source of institutional pressure, that is the gender mainstreaming advocacy-network, is sometimes talked of in a pejorative way by actors not belonging to the gender mainstreaming advocacy-network.

However, it should be borne in mind that the actors interviewed only consisted of grade A-C actors (i.e. managers, assistants and secretaries) since a pre-test had shown that D grade staff who consist of qualified workers and couriers are not familiar with the gender mainstreaming concept. The D staff are not involved in any policy aspect of the Commission and thus one would expect that they know less of gender mainstreaming than other actors. Furthermore, their interaction with the other grades is relatively low. However, since gender mainstreaming is not only supposed to be implemented in the policies of the Commission but also in the Commission as an organisation, the lack of knowledge of D staff presents a serious flaw in the Commission's implementation of gender mainstreaming.

The second assumption that there is a correlation between the degree of vested interests that are opposed to the transformation of gender relations and the likelihood of organisational resistance to gender mainstreaming has also emerged to be correct from the empirical investigation. At the time of interviewing, few men could see advantages from gender mainstreaming. Most saw it as the same as equal opportunities policies and were afraid that they might be disadvantaged as a result of the implementation of gender mainstreaming, particularly due to the imposition of quota restrictions, even though quota are not an inherent part of the Commission's gender mainstreaming policy. Some saw it as clientele policies, one from which only women will gain.

The third assumption that there is a connection between social legitimacy derived from gender mainstreaming and the likelihood of organisational resistance to gender mainstreaming could be partly confirmed. Indeed, gender mainstreaming was first introduced in the European Commission because of the social legitimacy that was associated with the concept since it came from the UN Women's World Conference in Beijing. Inside the European Commission, none of the actors interviewed were openly against gender mainstreaming. However, shifting from the organisational level to the individual level a difference was perceived by some actors between how it is viewed if men as opposed to women are committed to gender mainstreaming. The statements of individual actors were contradictory, which reflects the fact that action by humans will always appear and might always be contradictory and that they can never be explained mono-causally or cannot be predicted.

The female actors interviewed, those who were directly involved in the implementation of gender mainstreaming, agreed that they have a perception that a commitment to gender mainstreaming hindered their careers. For men, some reinforced this view in that they were seen as weird if they championed gender mainstreaming. Others said that a commitment to gender mainstreaming was alleged to increase the prestige of a male actor and advance his career.

The implementation of gender mainstreaming within the Commission is an example of decoupling and confidence as described by Meyer and Rowan (1991 [1977]). To the outside world, the European Commission pretends to implement gender mainstreaming in order to be consistent with the norms of the UN. However, the internal implementation of gender mainstreaming is far from being institutionalised. Therefore, the structural elements of gender mainstreaming are decoupled from the daily routines and activities of the organisation.

The Institutionalisation of Gender Mainstreaming as an Innovation

In this book, gender mainstreaming is not seen as a state but rather as a process. Based on the micro-level approach developed by Zucker (1991 [1977]), the institutionalisation of gender mainstreaming has been examined as a process. In assessing to what extent gender mainstreaming can be seen as an institution, it is important to remember Zucker's contention that acts are not simply institutionalised or not institutionalised (Zucker 1991: 83-86). In Zucker's differentiation of high and low institutionalisation, gender mainstreaming has a low degree of institutionalisation because its implementation depends on the context of the gender mainstreaming advocacy-network. For there to be a high degree of institutionalisation within the European Commission it would presuppose that the majority of actors within the Commission be committed to gender mainstreaming since it is a transversal strategy. As regards Parson's definition of an institution, in which he differentiates institutions from norms in that the former are self-policing while the latter are not (Parsons 1951: 20), gender mainstreaming only constitutes an institution within the gender mainstreaming advocacy-network[125].

There are different kinds of rewards and sanctions in respect of gender mainstreaming. Firstly, the women's movement, especially the European Women's Lobby but also the EP and the Advisory Committee closely monitors the implementation of gender mainstreaming. This is facilitated by the Commission publishing an annual report on the implementation of gender mainstreaming. Both the EP and Advisory Committee also publish reports and opinions on the implementation of gender mainstreaming in the Commission. However, the rewards and sanctions only exist within the gender mainstreaming advocacy-network. The knowledge and commitment

---

125 This explanation on the gender mainstreaming advocacy-network and the rest of the Commission is based on Jepperson's distinction on centrality and core within organisations (Jepperson 1991: 145-7, see chapter 3).

of the great majority within the Commission is low. There are no sanctions and rewards for them, therefore the self-policing which Jepperson (1991) refers to of an institution has not occurred.

Even though the institutionalisation of gender mainstreaming within the Commission has remained limited, the inclusion of gender mainstreaming into the Treaty of Amsterdam (1997) has had enormous effects on the Member States of the European Union. All Member States of the EU have implemented gender mainstreaming in some form or another by now, most with the argument that it is legally necessary because of the Treaty of Amsterdam. The introductory articles of the Treaty of Amsterdam however only spell out general aims of the Union which are not legally enforceable. One of the research questions evolving from this book might thus points at whether the introduction of gender mainstreaming in the Member States can be seen as another example of legal coercion?

Annexe

Directives on Equal Opportunities

Overview on the Directives on Equal Opportunities

1975	Equal Pay Directive on equal pay for men and women
1976	Equal Treatment Directive with regard to employment, vocational training and promotion, and working conditions
1978	Equal Treatment Directive with regard to statutory social security schemes
1986	Equal Treatment Directive with regard to occupational social security
1986	Equal Treatment Directive with regard to agriculture and self-employment
1992	Maternity leave Directive
1996	Parental leave Directive
1997	Directive on the burden of proof in sex discrimination
1997	Part-Time work Directive
2002	Equal Pay Directive, amending the 1975 Equal Pay Directive on the application of equal pay for men and women Directive (Council of the European Union 2002a)

Description of the different Directives on Equal Opportunities[126]

1975   Equal Pay Directive on equal pay for men and women.

The most important principle of the equal pay directive is that for the same work or for work to which equal value is attributed, all discrimination on grounds of sex with regard to all aspects and conditions of remuneration is eliminated. Where a job classification system is used for determining pay, it must be based on the same criteria for both men and women. Employees wronged by failure to apply this principle must have the right of recourse to judicial process to pursue their claims. Member States shall abolish all discrimination between men and women arising from laws, regulations or administrative provisions which do not comply with the principle. They shall take the necessary measures to ensure that provisions appearing in collective agreements, wage scales, wage agreements or individual contracts of employment which are contrary to the equal pay principle may be declared null and void. They shall ensure that the equal pay principle is applied and that effective means are available to take care that it is observed. Employees shall be protected against dismissal by the employer as a reaction to a complaint within the undertaking or to any legal proceedings aimed at enforcing compliance with the equal pay principle. The provisions adopted pursuant to the Directive and relevant existing legislation shall be brought to the attention of employees.

The deadline for implementation of the legislation in the member states was 12.02.1976. In a report of 1980, the Commission summed up that no member state has implemented this directive in a totally satisfying way (Kattein 1994: 133). As a follow-up to the directive, the Commission adopted a Communication in 1996 on the code of conduct concerning the implementation of equal pay for women and men for work of equal value (European Commission 1996).

The Communication aims to provide concrete advice for employers and collective bargaining partners at business, sectoral or intersectoral levels in order to ensure the implementation of the principle of equality. In particular, it aims to eliminate sex discrimination where the pay structures are based on job classification and job evaluation schemes.

Essentially, the Code proposes that negotiators at all levels, whether on the side of the employers or the unions, should carry out an analysis of the

---

126 Parts of the following description of the Directives are closely linked to the Commission's summary of the legislation (European Commission 2003b).

remuneration system and evaluate the data required to detect sexual discrimination in the pay structures so that remedies can be found.

The Commission also instigated various infringement procedures against Luxembourg in 1982 (Court of Justice of the European Communities 1982a) the United Kingdom in 1982 (Court of Justice of the European Communities 1982b) and Denmark in 1985 (Court of Justice of the European Communities 1985).

1976 Equal Treatment Directive with regard to employment, vocational training and promotion, and working conditions (Council of the European Union 1976)

The principle of equal treatment means that there shall be no discrimination on the grounds of sex either directly or indirectly by reference in particular to marital or family status. Member States may, however, exclude from its field of application occupational activities for which, the sex of the worker constitutes a determining factor. The Directive shall be without prejudice to provisions concerning the protection of women like pregnancy or maternity, or to measures to remove existing inequalities which affect women's opportunities in the areas covered by the Directive. Application of the principle means that there shall be no discrimination in the conditions, including selection criteria, for access to all jobs or posts at all levels of the hierarchy. The deadline for implementation of the legislation in the member states was 12.2.1976. To follow up the implementation of the Directive, the Commission adopted a communication in 1996 to the Council and the European Parliament on the interpretation of the judgement of the European Court of Justice on 17 October 1995 in the case Kalanke vs. Freie Hansestadt Bremen (Court of Justice of the European Communities 1993; European Commission 1996a). The Kalanke judgement created uncertainty concerning the legitimacy of quotas and other forms of positive action aimed at increaseing the numbers of women in certain sectors or levels of employment. Through this communication, the Commission hoped to put a definitive end to the controversy arising as a result of the Kalanke case. In 2002, the 1976 Directive was amended (see later section on 2002 Directive).

1978 Equal Treatment Directive with regard to statutory social security schemes (Council of the European Union 1979)

The Directive applies to the working population including workers whose activity is interrupted due to illness, accident or unemployment, persons seeking employment, retired or invalidated workers and self-employed persons.

The principle of equal treatment means that there should be no discrimination on grounds of sex, in particular as concerns:

- the scope of the schemes and the conditions of access thereto;
- the obligation to contribute and the calculation of contributions;
- the calculation of benefits and the conditions governing the duration and retention of entitlement to benefit.

The principle of equal treatment is without prejudice to the provisions relating to the protection of women on the grounds of maternity.

The deadline for the implementation of the legislation in the member state was six years of notification. Even though this is one of the longest deadlines for the implementation of a directive, there were a number of infringement cases.

The Commission presented a proposal for a Council Directive completing the implementation of the principle of equal treatment for men and women in statutory and occupational social security schemes on 23 October 1987 (European Commission 1987) In addition, three reports were drawn by the Commission on the progression of the implementation of the Directive:

- Report on the implementation of Directive 79/7/EEC on the progressive implementation of the principle of equal treatment for men and women in matters of social security (European Commission 1988)
- report on the implementation of Directive 79/7/EEC of 19 December 1978 in Spain and Portugal (December 1994) (European Commission 1995c)
- report on the implementation of Directive 79/7/EEC of on the progressive implementation of the principle of equal treatment for men and women in matters of social security (European Commission 2003d).

1986 Equal Treatment Directive with regard to occupational social security (Council of the European Union 1986b)

The aim of this Directive is to define the meaning of Article 119 and the scope and ways of applying the principle of equal treatment for men and women in occupational social security schemes, otherwise the provisions are the same as in the 1978 Directive. The deadline for implementation of the legislation in the member states was 31.07.1989. The follow up work of the Commission consisted in sending out a questionnaire on the implementation of this Directive to the Member States, the results of which have not been published yet (European Commission 2003e).

1986 Equal Treatment Directive with regard to agriculture and self-employment (Council of the European Union 1986b)

The aim of this Directive is to pursue the implementation of the principle of equal treatment for persons engaged in an activity in a self-employed capacity and spouses participating in this activity. The aim is to protect pregnant women and women who have recently given birth engaged in such activities.

The deadline for implementation of the legislation in the member states was 30.06.1991. To follow up this Directive, the Commission wrote a report on the implementation of the Council Directive 86/613/EEC of 11 December 1986 (European Commission 1994b). The Commission itself commented on this Directive in the following way:

'Legally speaking this Directive can be considered to have been implemented in the Member States. However, in practice, the results are note entirely satisfactory in terms of the Directive's primary objective, which was to bring about a general improvement in the status of assisting spouses'. The first part of the comment is rather surprising, given that the self-defined primary objective is assessed not to have been implemented (European Commission 2003c).

1992 Maternity leave Directive (Council of the European Union 1992b)

The aim of this directive is to take minimum measures to protect the health and safety of pregnant workers, women workers who have recently given birth and women who are breastfeeding, considering them to be a specific risk group.

The deadline for the implementation of the legislation in the member states was 19.10.1994.

To implement this Directive, the Commission drafted a report on 15 March 1999 on the implementation of the Directive. The report provides a detailed breakdown of the rights of pregnant workers and workers who have recently given birth or are breastfeeding in the Member States of the Union. According to the report, the Directive has been well implemented by the Member States although problems persist. The report points to the marked variations across the EU in, among other things, the length of maternity leave, which ranges from 14 to 28 weeks, the proportion of this leave which is compulsory and the level at which it is paid. It also highlights specific implementing problems which have led to infringement proceedings which include the complete ban by several Member States on night work for pregnant workers, and the lack of any compulsory maternity leave. The report identifies other areas of concern such as differences over which type of workers fall within the scope of the Directive, the difficulty in squaring health and security considerations with women's entitlement to non-discriminatory treatment, and the right to return to a job. (European Commission 2003f)

Framework Agreements

Under the procedure laid down in the Agreement on social policy annexed to the Maastricht Treaty, the Commission set about consulting the social partners — the ETUC (European Trade Union Confederation), UNICE (the Union of Industries in the European Community) and the CEEP (European Centre of Public Enterprises) — which led to the signing of two framework agreements on parental leave and on part-time work. The purpose of these agreements is to reconcile professional and family life, prevent any form of discrimination against part-time workers – the majority of whom are women – and make working hours more flexible, taking account of employers' and workers' needs.

Following incorporation of the Agreement on social policy in the Treaty, after the Intergovernmental Conference and the Amsterdam European Council, the legal effect of the directives also applies to the United Kingdom.

1996 Parental leave Directive
(Council of the European Union 1996)

The aim of this Directive is to establish minimum requirements in respect of parental leave and unforeseeable absence from work, as an important means of reconciling professional and family responsibilities and promoting equal opportunities and treatment for women and men. The framework agreement on parental leave concluded on 14 December 1995 between the general cross-industry organisations (UNICE, CEEP and the ETUC), annexed to the Directive, is made obligatory.

The framework agreement provides for male and female workers to have individual entitlement to parental leave on the grounds of the birth or adoption of a child, enabling them to take care of the child for at least three months; the conditions of access to, and procedures for applying, parental leave to be defined by law and/or collective agreement in the Member States, subject to compliance with the minimum requirements of the agreement; the Member States and/or social partners to take the necessary measures to protect workers against dismissal on the grounds of an application for, or the

246

taking of, parental leave; workers to have the right to return to the same job at the end of parental leave or, if that is not possible, to an equivalent or similar job consistent with their employment contract or relationship; the maintenance of rights acquired or in the process of being acquired by the worker on the date on which parental leave starts; at the end of the period of leave, those rights will apply; the Member States and/or the social partners to take the necessary measures to allow workers to take time off from work, in accordance with national legislation, collective agreements and/or practice, for unforeseeable reasons arising from a family emergency in the event of sickness or accident making the immediate presence of the worker indispensable.

The deadline for implementation of the legislation in the member states was 03.06.1998 (European Commission 2003g).

1997 Directive on the Burden of Proof in Sex Discrimination (Council of the European Union 1997b)

Under the directive it is up to the defendants taken to court for direct or indirect discrimination to prove that they have not infringed the principle of equal treatment. Until that date, a person invoking a breach of the principle of equality in cases of discrimination of this kind normally had to assume the burden of proof on her own, even in cases where some facts would have been easier for the defendant to establish.

The deadline for implementation of the legislation in the member states was 01.01.2001 (European Commission 2003h).

1997 Part-Time work Directive (Council of the European Union 1997c)

The aim of the Directive was to ensure that workers concerned by the new forms of flexible working receive comparable treatment to full-time staff on open-ended contracts.

The deadline for implementation of the legislation in the member states was 20.01.2000, the Directive entered into force on 20.01.1998 (European Commission 2003i).

2002 Equal Pay Directive, amending the 1975 Equal Pay Directive
on the application of equal pay for men and women Directive

The aim of the Directive is to make it clear that positive action measures short of rigid quotas are permissible under Community law, and to ensure that the text of the Directive more clearly reflected the legal position as resulting from the Kalanke judgement (Council of the European Union 2002b).

12 Bibliography

Abel, Jörg (2000): *Netzwerke und Leitbilder Die Bedeutung von Leitbildern für die Funktionsfähigkeit von Forschungs- und Entwicklungs-Netzwerken.* In: Weyer, Johannes (ed.): *Soziale Netzwerke: Konzepte und Methoden der sozialwissenschaftlichen Netzwerkforschung.* Wien, Oldenburg (Oldenbourg Wissenschaftsverlag), pp.161-185.

Adorno, Theodor W. (1993): *Der Positivismusstreit in der deutschen Soziologie.* München (Deutscher Taschenbuch-Verlag).

Advisory Committee on Equal Opportunities for Women and Men (2002): *Opinion on the Implementation of Gender Mainstreaming in EU Policies.* Doc.Eqop 59-2001 (rev. 20.02.2002). Final. http://europa.eu.int/comm/employment_social/equ_opp/strategy/advcom09.pdf (Accessed 13.10.2002), Brussels.

Albertini-Roth, Hilde (1998): *Europa. Eine Chance für die Frauen. 20 Jahre Fraueninformation der Europäischen Kommission.* Köln (Omina).

Alvesson, Mats; Billing, Yvonne D. (1997): *Understanding Gender and Organizations.* London (Sage).

Aulenbacher, Brigitte; Goldmann, Monika (1993) (eds.): *Transformation und Geschlechterverhältnis.* Frankfurt a.m., New York (Campus).

Azzi, Giuseppe C. (1998): *Better Lawmaking: The Experience and the View of the European Commission.* In: Columbia Journal of European Law, pp.617-628.

Baccaro, Luccio (2001): *Decent Work Research Programme. Civil Society, NGOs, and Decent Work Policies: Sorting out the Issues.* Geneva (International Labour Organisation).

Barley, Stephen R.; Tolbert, Pamela S. (1997): *Institutionalization and Structuration: Studying the Links between Action and Institution.* In: Organization Studies, No.1, pp.93-117.

Barnard, Chester I. (1938): *The Functions of the Executive.* Cambridge, M.A. (Harvard University Press).

Baumgartner, Frank; Jones, Bryan D. (1991): *Agenda Dynamics and Policy Subsystem.* In: The journal of Politics, No. 4, pp.1044-73.

Bell, Daniel (1973): *The Coming of Post-Industrial Society. A Venture in Social Forecasting.* New York (Basic Books).

Bellier, Irène (2002): *In and Out, Fieldwork in Political Space: The Case of the European Commission.* In: ÖZP, No. 2, pp.205-16.

Belwe, Katharina (2002): *Editorial.* In: Aus Politik und Zeitgeschichte, No.34, p.2.

Berger, Ulrike (1993): *Organisationskultur und der Mythos der kulturellen Integration.* In: Müller-Jentsch, Walther (ed.) (1993): *Profitable Ethik – effiziente Kultur. Neue Sinnstiftungen durch das Management?* München, Mehring (Rainer Hampp Verlag) (=Schriftenreihe Industrielle Beziehungen; 5), pp.11-38.

Berger, Peter L.; Luckmann, Thomas (1966): *The Social Construction of Reality.* New York (Penguin).

Bergmann, Kristin (1999): *Die Gleichstellung von Frauen und Männern in der europäischen Arbeitswelt. Eine rechtsrelevante, empirisch-politikwissenschaftliche Untersuchung.* Opladen (Westdeutscher Verlag).

Bernstein, Basil (1971): *Class, Codes and Control.* Vol. 1, London (Paladin).

Beveridge, Fiona; Nott, Sue; Stephen, Kylie (2000): *Mainstreaming and the Engendering of Policy Making: a Means to an End?* In: Journal of European Public Policy, No.3, pp.385-405.

Bock, Gisela; James, Susan (1992): *Beyond Equality and Difference: Citizenship, Feminist Politics and Female Subjectivity.* London (Routledge).

Bogner, Alexander; Menz, Wolfgang (2002) *Das theoriegeleitete Experteninterview. Erkenntnisinteresse, Wissensformen, Interaktion.* In: Bogner, Alexander; Littig, Beate; Menz, Wolfgang (ed.): *Das Experteninterview.* pp.33-70. Opladen (Leske und Budrich).

Bourdieu, Pierre (1984*): Homo Academicus.* Paris (Les Editions de Minuit).

Braig, Marianne (1999): *Naueninteressen in Entwicklungstheorie und -politik. Von „Women in Development" zu „Mainstreaming Gender".* In: E+Z – Entwicklung und Zusammenarbeit, No. 10, pp.281-284.

Braunmühl, Claudia von (1997): *Mainstreaming Gender oder von den Grenzen, dieses zu tun.* In: Politische Vierteljahreszeitschrift. Sonderheft, No. 28, pp.475-490.

Braunmühl, Claudia von (2002): *Gender Mainstreaming: neue Konzepte – neue Chancen?* In: Nohr, Barbara, Veth, Silke (ed.) *Gender Mainstreaming. Kritische Reflexionen einer neuen Strategie.* pp.17-25. Berlin (Karl Dietz Verlag).

Bretherton, Charlotte (2001): *Gender Mainstreaming and EU Enlargement: Swimming against the Tide?* In: Journal of European Public Policy, No. 1, pp.60-81.

Brinkmann, Christian; Deeke, Axel; Völkel, Brigitte (eds.) (1995): *Experteninterviews in der Arbeitsmarktforschung. Diskussionsbeitrag zu methodischen Fragen und praktischen Erfahrungen.* Beiträge zur Arbeitsmarkt- und Berufsforschung 191, Nürnberg.

British Sociological Association (1989a): *BSA Guidelines on Anti-Sexist Language.* London.

British Sociological Association (1989b): *Anti-Racist Language: Guidance for Good Practise.* London.

British Sociological Association (1994): *Statement of Ethical Practise.* http://www.britsoc.co.uk/index.php?link_id=14&area=item1 (Accessed 05.01.2003).

Callenius, Carolin (2002): *Wenn Frauenpolitik salonfähig wird, verblasst die lila Farbe. Erfahrungen mit Gender Mainstreaming im Bereich internationaler Politik.* In: Bothfeld, Silke; Gronbach, Sigrid; Riedmüller, Barbara (ed.): *Gender Mainstreaming – eine Innovation in der Gleichstellungspolitik. Zwischenberichte aus der politischen Praxis.* Frankfurt (Campus).

Casscse, Sabino (ed.) (1987): *The European Administration.* Brussels (Institut International des Sciences Administratives).

Castells, Manuel (1997): *The Power of Identity. The Information Age: Economy, Society and Culture, Vol. 2.* Oxford (Blackwell).

CIA (2002): *World Fact Book.* Washington.

Cini, Michelle (1996): *The European Commission.* Manchester (Manchester University Press).

Cini, Michelle (2000): *Organizational Culture and Reform: The Case of the European Commission under Jacques Santer.* EUI Working Paper. RCS 2000/25. Florence.

Cini, Michelle (2001): *Reforming the European Commission: an Organisational Culture Perspective.* EUI Working Paper. RSC 11/2001. Florence.

Clegg, Steward R.; Hardy, Cynthia; Nord, Walter R. (eds.) (1996): *Handbook of Organization Studies.* London (Sage).

Cohen, Michael D., March, James G. (1974): *Leadership and Ambiguity: The American College President.* New York (McGraw-Hill).

Cohen, Michael, D.; March, James, G.; Olsen, Johan, P. (1972): *A Garbage Can Model of Organizational Choice.* In: Administrative Studies Quarterly, No. 17, pp.1-25.

Collins, Randall (1979): *The Credential Society.* New York (Academic Press).

Commission Européenne. Direction Générale Emploi et Affaires Sociales (2002): *Membres et Observateurs du Comité Consultatif pour L'Égalité des Chances entre les Femmes et les Hommes.* Empl/G/1/Ba/Amm D(1) Mise à jour 14.06.2002. http://europa.eu.int/comm/employment_social/equ_opp/strategy/advcom.pdf (Accessed 10.12.2002), Bruxelles.

Conrad, Yves (1992): *La Communauté Européenne du Charbon et de l'Acier et la Situation de ses Agents. Du règime Contractuel au Régime Statuaire (1952-1958).* In Heyen, Erk V. (ed.) (1992): *Jahrbuch für europäische Verwaltungsgeschichte. Die Anfänge der Verwaltung der Europäischen Gemeinschaft.* Baden-Baden (Nomos Verlagsgesellschaft), pp.59-74.

Costain, Anne N.; McFarland, Andrew (eds.) (1998): *Social Movements and American Political Institutions.* Lanham (Rowman and Littlefields).

Council of Europe, Rapporteur Group on Equality between Women and Men (1998): *Gender Mainstreaming: Conceptual Framework, Methodology and Presentation of Good Practices.* Strasbourg.

Council of the European Union (1976): *Council Directive 76/207/EEC of 9 February 1976 on the implementation of the principle of equal treatment for men and women as regards access to employment, vocational training and promotion, and working conditions* In:Official Journal L 039 14.02.76, p.40, Derogation in 194N, Incorporated by OJ L 001 03.01.94, p.484.

Council of the European Union (1979): *Council Directive 79/7/EEC of 19 December 1978 on the progressive implementation of the principle of equal treatment for men and women in matters of social security.* In: Official Journal L 006 10.01.79 p.24, incorporated by OJ L 001 03.01.94, p.484. Brussels.

Council of the European Union (1982): *Council Resolution of 12 July 1982 on the Promotion of Equal Opportunities for Women.* Brussels.

Council of the European Union (1984): *Council Recommendation of 13 December 1984 on the Promotion of Positive Action for Women.* In: Official Journal C 186, 21.07./1995.

Council of the European Union (1986a): *Second Council Resolution of 24 July 1986 on the Promotion of Equal Opportunities for Women.* Brussels.

Council of the European Union (1986b): *Council Directive 86/613/EEC of 11 December 1986 on the application of the principle of equal treatment between men and women engaged in an activity, including agriculture, in a self-employed capacity, and on the protection of self-employed women during pregnancy and motherhood.* In: Official Journal L 359 19.12.86, p.56, Incorporated by OJ L 001 03.01.94, p.484. Brussels.

Council of the European Union (1990): *Council Resolution of 29 May 1990 on the Protection of the Dignity of Women and Men at Work.* Brussels.

Council of the European Union (1992a): *Council Declaration of 19 December 1991 on the Implementation of the Commission Recommendation on the Protection of the Dignity of Women and Men at Work.* Brussels.

Council of the European Union (1992b): *Council Directive 92/85/EEC of 19 October 1992 on the introduction of measures to encourage improvements in the safety and health at work of pregnant workers and workers who have recently given birth or are breastfeeding (tenth individual Directive within the meaning of Article 16 (1) of Directive 89/391/EEC).* In: Official Journal L 348 28.11.92, p.1. Brussels.

Council of the European Union (1994): *Council Resolution of 22 June 1994 on the Promotion of Equal Opportunities for Men and Women through Action by the European Structural Funds.* Brussels.

Council of the European Union (1995a): *Council Resolution of 27 March 1995 on the Balanced Participation of Men and Women in Decision-making.* Brussels.

Council of the European Union (1995b): *Resolution of the Council and the Representatives of the Governments of the Member States, Meeting within the Council of 5 October 1995 on the Image of Women and Men portrayed in Advertising and the Media.* Brussels.

Council of the European Union (1996): *Council Directive 96/34/EC of 3 June 1996 on the framework agreement on parental leave concluded by UNICE, CEEP and the ETUC.* In Official Journal L 145, 19/06/1996 p. 0004-0009, CONSLEG-96L0034-16/01/1998-11 p., amended by OJ L 010 16.01.98, p.24. Brussels.

Council of the European Union (1997a): *Council Resolution of 4 December 1997 Concerning the Report on the State of Womens Health in the European Community.* Brussels.

Council of the European Union (1997b): *Council Directive 97/80/EC of 15 December 1997 on the burden of proof in cases of discrimination based on sex Official.* In: Journal L 014 20.01.98, p.6, Amended by OJ L 205 22.07.98, p.66. Brussels.

Council of the European Union (1997c): *Council Directive 97/81/EC of 15 December 1997 concerning the Framework Agreement on part-time work concluded by UNICE, CEEP and the ETUC-Annex: Framework agreement on part-time work.* In: Official Journal L 014, 20/01/1998, p.9-14. Brussels.

Council of the European Union (2000a): *Council Directive 2000/43/EC of 29/06/2000 Implementing the Principle of Equal Treatment Between Persons Irrespective of Racial or Ethnic Origin.* In: Official Journal L 180 19/97/2000, p. 22. Brussels.

Council of the European Union (2000b): *Council Directive 2000/78/EC of 27/11/2000. Establishing a General Framework for Equal Treatment in Employment and Occupation.* Official Journal L 303 of December 2, 2000, p.16. Brussels.

Council of the European Union (2002a): *Directive 2002/73/EC of the European Parliament and of the Council of 23/09/2002 Amending Council Directive 76/207/EEC on the Implementation of the Principle of Equal Treatment for Men* and Women as Regards access to Employment, Vocational Training and Promotion, and Working Conditions. Official Journal L 269, 05/10/2002, pp.15-20. Brussels.

Council of the European Union 2002b: Directive 2002/73/EC of the Eureopan Parliament and the Council of 23rd September 2002 amending Council Directive 76/207/EEC on the implementation of the principle of equal treatment for men and women as regards access to employment, vocational training and promotion, and working conditions. Official Journal L 269, 05/10/2002, pp.15-20. Brussels.

Court of Justice of the European Communities (1982a): 58/81 Commission vs. Luxembourg (1982) ECR, 2175-2186 61/81. Luxembourg.

Court of Justice of the European Communities (1982b): Commission vs. United Kingdom (1982) ECR, 2601-2625. Luxembourg.

Court of Justice of the European Communities (1985): 143/83 Commission vs. Denmark (1985) ECR, 427-437. Luxembourg.

http://europa.eu.int/scadplus/leg/en/cha/c10905.htm (Accessed 23.01.2003). Luxembourg.

Court of Justice of the European Communities (1993): C-450/93. Luxembourg.

Craig, Paul (2000): The Fall and Renewal of the Commission: Accountability, Contract and Administrative Organisation. In: European Law Journal, No. 2, pp.98-116.

Cram, Laura (1993): Calling the Tune without paying the Piper? Social Policy Regulation: the Role of the Commission in European Community Social Policy. In: Policy and Politics, No. 2, pp.135-146.

Crozier, Michel (1964): Le Phénomène bureaucratique. Paris (Edition du Seuil).

Cunningham, Susan (1992): The Development of Equal Opportunities Theory and Practise in the European Community. In: Policy and Politics, No. 3, pp.177-89.

Cyert, Richard M.; March, James G. (1963): A Behavioral Theory of the Firm. Englewood Cliffs (Prentice-Hall).

Dahlerup, Drude (1996): Demokratiets fremtid I et europaeisk kvindeperspektiv. In: KVINFO, Kvindeoffentlighed Europa, Copenhagen.

Davis, Kathy; Leijenaar, Monique; Oldersma, Jantine (eds.) (1991): The Gender of Power. London (Sage Publications).

Denzin, Norman K. (1989) [1970]: The Research Act. Chicago (Aldine).

Deutsche Gesellschaft für Soziologie (1992): Ethik Kodex. http://userpage.fu-berlin.de/~ifs/bds/ethkod.html (Accessed 23.05.2003).

Deutscher Bundestag (ed.) (2002): Gutachten für die Enquete-Kommission, Globalisierung der Weltwirtschaft – Herausforderungen und Antworten. Berlin.

Dexter, Lewis A. (1970): Elite and specialized Interviewing. Evanston (Northwestern University Press).

Die Grünen im Landtag NRW (ed.) (2000): Gender Mainstreaming. Eine Chance für Frauen. Dokumentation einer Veranstaltung am 26.10.2001. Düsseldorf.

Diekmann, Andreas (2002): Empirische Sozialforschung: Grundlagen, Methoden, Anwendungen. Reinbek bei Hamburg (Rowohlt-Taschenbuch).

DiMaggio, Paul, J. (1988): Interest and Agency in Institutional Theory. In: Zucker, Lynne G. (ed.) (1988) [1977]: Institutional Patterns and Organizations. Cambridge/Mass. (Ballinger), pp.3-21.

DiMaggio, Paul, J. (1998): The New Institutionalisms: Avenues of Cooperation. In: Journal of Institutional and Theoretical Economics, No. 154, pp.696-705.

DiMaggio Paul J.; Powell, Walter W. (1991a): *Introduction.* In: Powell, Walter W.; DiMaggio, Paul J. (eds.) (1991a): *The New Institutionalism in Organizational Analysis.* Chicago (University of Chicago Press), pp.1-40.

DiMaggio, Paul; Powell, Walter (1991b [1983]): *The Iron Cage Revisited: Institutional Isomorphism and Collective Rationality in Organizational Fields.* In: Powell, Walter W.; DiMaggio, Paul J. (eds.) (1991): *The New Institutionalism in Organizational Analysis.* Chicago (University of Chicago Press), pp.63-82.

Dinan, Desmond (1999): *Ever Closer Union.* Basingstoke (The Macmillan Press).

Doug, Imig; Tarrow, Sidney (eds.) (2001): *Contentious Europeans: Protests and Politics in an emerging Polity.* Lanham (Rowman & Littlefields).

Downs, George; Mohr, Lawrence B. (1976): *Conceptual Issues in the Study of Innovation.* In: Administrative Studies Quarterly, pp.700-14.

Durkheim, Emile (1950) [1901]: *The Rules of Sociological Method.* Glencoe/Ill. (Free Press).

Durkheim, Emile (1995 [1910]): *Die Regeln der soziologischen Methode.* Neuwied (Luchterhand).

Ebers, Mark (1985): *Organisationskultur. Ein neues Forschungsprogramm?* Wiesbaden (Gabler).

Educational Testing Service (2003): *Research.* http://www.ets.org/research/dif.html (Accessed 10.05.03).

Edwards, Geoffrey; Spence, David (eds.) (1997): *The European Commission.* London (Longman).

Elgstrom, Ole (2000): *Norm Negotiations. The Construction of new Norms regarding Gender and Development in EU Foreign Policy.* In: Journal of European Public Policy, No. 3, Special Issue, pp.457-76.

Equal Opportunities Commission (1997): *Mainstreaming Gender Equality in Local Government.* Manchester.

European Commission (1982): *Commission Decision 82/43/EEC of 9 December 1981 relating to the setting up of an Advisory Committee on Equal Opportunities for Women and Men.* In: European Journal L 020, 28.01.1982.

European Commission (1987): *Communication COM(87) 494 final.*

European Commission (1988): *Report on the implementation of Directive 79/7/EEC on the progressive implementation of the principle of equal treatment for men and women in matters of social security.* Brussels.

European Commission (1992): *Commission Recommendation of 27 November 1991 on the Protection of the Dignity of Women and Men at Work, including the Code of Practice to combat Sexual Harassment (92/131/EEC).* Brussels.

European Commission (1994a): Equal Oportunities Unit, Directorate-General for Personnel and Administration: *Second action programme for equal opportunities for women and men at the European Community (1994-1997).* Brussels.

European Commission (1994b): *Communication COM(94) 163 final.* Brussels.

European Commission (1995a): *Green Paper on Innovation.* Brussels, unpublished paper.

European Commission (1995b): *Commission Decision of 19 July 1995 amending Decision 82/43/EEC relating to the setting up of an Advisory Committee on Equal Opportunities for Women and Men.* In: Official Journal L 249, 17.10.1995.

European Commission (1995c): *Communication COM(95) 418 final.* Brussels.

European Commission (1996): *Commission Communication from the Commission of 21 February 1996: Incorporating equal Opportunities for Women and Men into all Community Policies and Activities.* COM(1996)67 final du 21.02.1996, Brussels.

European Commission (1997a): *Communication COM(96) 88 final.* Brussels.

European Commission (1997b): *Communication COM(96) 336 final.* Brussels.

European Commission (1997c) *Equal Oportunities Unit, Directorate – General for Personnel and Administration: Third action programme for equal opportunities for women and men at the European Community (1997-2000).* Brussels.

European Commission (1998a): *Progress Report COM (1998).* 122 final. http://europa.eu.int/comm/employment_social/equ_opp/com98122/com98122_en .pdf (Accessed 25.09.2002), Brussels.

European Commission (1998b): *One Hundred Words for Equality. A glossary of terms on equality between women and men.* European Commission, Brussels.

European Commission (1999a): *Designing Tommorow's Commission. A review of the Commission's Organization and Operation.* Brussels.

European Commission (1999b): *100 Words for Equality. A Glossary on Terms of Equality between Women and Men.* Brussels.

European Commission (1999c): *A Guide to Gender Impact Assessment.* Brussels.

European Commission (2000): *Commission Decision relating to Gender Balance within the Committees and Expert Groups established by it.* (2000/407/EC of 19/06/00) Official Journal L 154, 27/06/2000, p.34. http://europa.eu.int/comm/employment_social/equ_opp/news/balance_en.html (Accessed 25.09.2002), Brussels.

European Commission (2002a): *Staff Regulations of Officials of the European Communities, valid from 1 July 1991 to 30 June 2003.* Brussels

European Commission (2002b): *An administration at the Service of half a Billion Europeans. Staff Reforms at the European Commission.* Brussels.

European Commission (2003a): *Negotiations with Candidate Countries.* http://europa.eu.int/comm/enlargement_en.html (Accessed 04.07.2003, Brussels.

European Commission (2003b): *Scadplus Database.* http://europa.eu.int/scadplus (Accessed 23.01.2003). Brussels.

European Commission (2003c): *Scadplus Database.* http://europa.eu.int/scadplus/leg/en/cha/c10910.htm   (Accessed   23.01.2003). Brussels.

European Commission (2003d): Scadplus Database http://europa.eu.int/scadplus/leg/en/cha/c10907.htm   (Accessed   23.01.2003). Brussels.

European Commission (2003e): *Scadplus Communication.* http://europa.eu.int/scadplus/leg/en/cha/c10908.htm   (Accessed   23.01.2003). Brussels.

European Commission (2003f): *Scadplus Database.* http://europa.eu.int/scadplus/leg/en/cha/c10914.htm   (Accessed   23.01.2003). Brussels.

European Commission (2003g): *Scadplus Database.* http://europa.eu.int/scadplus/leg/en/cha/c10911.htm   (Accessed   23.01.2003). Brussels.

European Commission (2003h): *Scadplus Database.*
http://europa.eu.int/scadplus/leg/en/cha/c10913.htm (Accessed 23.01.2003).
Brussels.
European Commission (2003i): *Scadplus Database.*
http://europa.eu.int/scadplus/leg/en/cha/c10416.htm (Accessed 23.01.2003).
Brussels.
European Commission (2003j): *Directorates General and Services.*
http://europa.eu.int/comm/dgs_en.htm (Accessed 20.02.2003).
European Convention (2003): *Draft Treaty establishing a Constitution for Europe.*
http://european-convention.eu.int/docs/Treaty/cv00820-re01.en03.pdf (Accessed 03.07.2003), Brussels.
European Ombudsman (2000): *Draft Recommendation to the European Commission in Complaint 242/2000/GG.*
http://www.euro-ombudsman.eu.int/recommen/en/000242.htm
(Accessed 24.04.03). Brussels.
European Parliament (1996): Committee on Women's Rights. Rapporteur: Jessica Larive *A4-0283/96. Report on Implementation of equal Opportunities for Men and Women in the Civil Service*
http://www2.europarl.eu.int/omk/sipade2?PUBREF=-//EP//TEXT+REPORT+A4 -1996-0283+0+DOC+XML+V0//EN&L=EN&LEVEL=3&NAV=S&LSTDOC =Y (Accessed 20.05.2003), Brussels.
European Parliament (2003): *Resolution on Gender Mainstreaming in the European Parliament (2002/2025 (INI).* Rapporteur Lissy Gröner. A5-0060/2003, Brussels.
European Women's Lobby (2003): *What is the EWL?*
http://www.womenlobby.org/Document.asp?DocID=23&tod=133713 (Accessed 23.5.2003).
Evans, Judith (1995): *Feminist Theory Today: An Introduction to Second Wave Feminism.* London (Sage).
Expertenrat im Rahmen des Qualitätspakts (2001): *Abschlussbericht.* Münster.
Fielding, Nigel G.; Fielding, Jane L. (1986): *Linking Data.* Newbury Park (Sage).
Fischer, Frank Forester, John (eds.) (1993): *The argumentative Turn in Policy Analysis and Plannning.* Durham (Duke University Press).
Flick, Uwe (1998): *Qualitative Forschung Theorie, Methoden, Anwendung in Psychologie und Sozialwissenschaften.* Hamburg (Rowohlt).
Franzpötter, Reiner (1997): *Organisationskultur – Begriffsverständnis und Analyse aus interpretativ-soziologischer Sicht.* Baden-Baden (Nomos Verlagsgesellschaft).
Freeman, Christopher (1982): *The Economics of Industrial Innovation.* London (Pinter).
Friebertshäuscr, Barbara (ed.) (1997): *Handbuch qualitative Forschungsmethoden in der Erziehungswissenschaft.* Weinheim (Juventa).
Geppert, Jochen (2001): *Das Gender Mainstreaming- Konzept Der Landesregierung Sachsen-Anhalt.* In: Die Grüncn im Landtag NRW (ed.) 2001): Gender Mainstreaming. Eine Chance für Frauen. Dokumentation einer Veranstaltung am 26.10.2001. Düsseldorf, pp.28-30.
Giddens, Anthony (1979): *Central Problems in Social Theory Action, Structure and Contradiction in Social Analysis.* London (Macmillan).

Giddens, Anthony (1982): *Profiles and Critique in Social Theory.* London (Macmillan).

Giddens, Anthony (1984): *The Constitution of Society.* Cambridge (Polity Press).

Gjerding, Allan N. (1998): *Innovation Economics. Part II: The "New" Innovation Economics.* International Business Economy. Working Paper Series 1998, unpublished paper.

Glaser, Barney G.; Strauss, Anselm, L. (1975): *The Discovery of Grounded Theory. Strategies for Qualitative Research.* Chicago (Aldine).

Goffman, Erving (1974): *Frame Analysis.* Cambridge (Harvard University Press).

Goldmann, Monika (ed.) (1999): *Rationalisation, Organization, Gender. Proceedings of the International Conference.* Dortmund.

Goldmann, Monika (2001):*Das Konzept des Gender Mainstreaming: Ziele, Strategien, Instrumente.* In: Die Grünen im Landtag NRW (ed.) (2001): Gender Mainstreaming. Eine Chance für Frauen. Dokumentation einer Veranstaltung am 26.10.2001. Düsseldorf, pp.6-10.

Gottfried, Heidi; O'Reilly, Jacqueline (2000): *Flexibalization of Work and Gender Segregation in International Perspective (Germany – USA – Japan).* Paper presented at the International Conference on Gender and the Future of Work. 30th June – 1st July 2000. Bremen.

Gouldner, Alvin, W. (1979): *The Future of Intellectuals and the Rise of the New Class.* New York (Seabury).

Grant, Rebecca; Newland, Kathleen (eds.) (1991): *Gender in International Relations.* Bloomington/In.

Gregson, Nicky (1989): *On the (Ir)relevance of Structuration Theory to Empirical Research.* In: Held, David; Thompson, John B. (eds.) (1989): Social Theory of Modern Societies: Anthony (ed.): *Social Theory of Modern Societies: Anthony Giddens and his Critics.* Cambridge (Cambridge University Press), chapter 11, pp.235-248.

Griffiths, Phillips A. (1998) [1960]: *How Can One Person Represent Another?* In: Aristotelian Society. Supplementary, Volume 34, pp.187-208.

GTZ (1997): *Gender and Macro-Policy. Gender in Macro-Economic and Legal Policy. Advice in Technical Cooperation.* Social Policy Working Paper. Eschborn.

Hall, Peter A.; Taylor, Rosemary C. (1996): *Political Science and the Three New Institutionalisms.* In: Political Studies, pp.936-57.

Hantrais, Linda (2000): *Gendered Policies in Europe.* Basingstoke (Macmillan Press).

Hasse, Raimund; Krücken, Georg (1999): *Neo-Institutionalismus.* Bielefeld (transcript).

Hasse, Raimund; Krücken, Georg (2000): *Neo-Institutionalismus. Neo-Institutionalimus im Theorievergleich – Netzwerkansätze, Theorien der Strukturierung und Systemtheorie.* www.transcript-verlag.de (Accessed 17.04.2001).

Hatch, Mary J. (1997): *Organization Theory. Modern Symbolic and Postmodern Perspectives.* Oxford (Oxford University Press).

Hauschildt, Jürgen (1993): *Innovationsmanagement.* München (Vahlens).

Held, David; Thompson, John B. (1989) (eds.): *Social Theory of Modern Societies: Anthony Giddens and his Critics.* Cambridge (Cambridge University Press).

Helfferich, Barbara (1998): *Frauenpolitische Arbeit im Integrationsprozeß: Die Aktivitäten der Europäischen Frauenlobby im Kontext der Regierungskonferenz.* In: femina politica, No. 2, pp.35-44.

Helfferich, Barbara; Kolb, Felix (2001): *Multilevel Action Coordination in European Contentious Politics – The case of the European Women's Lobby.* In: Doug, Imig; Tarrow, Sidney (eds.) (2001): *Contentious Europeans: Protests and Politics in an emerging Polity.* Lanham (Rowman & Littlefields), pp.143-62.

Hennersdorf, Susan (1998): *Aufstiegsdiskriminierung von Frauen durch Mitarbeiterbeurteilungen.* Wiesbaden (Deutscher Universitätsverlag).

Heyen, Erk V. (ed.) (1992): *Jahrbuch für europäische Verwaltungsgeschichte. Die Anfänge der Verwaltung der Europäischen Gemeinschaft.* Baden-Baden (Nomos Verlagsgesellschaft).

Heyzer, Noeleen (ed.) (1997): *A Commitment to the World's Women: Perspectives on Development for Beijing and Beyond.* New York (UNIFEM).

Hoecker, Beate (1997): *Zwischen Macht und Ohnmacht: Politische Repräsentation von Frauen in den Staaten der Europäischen Union.* In: Aus Politik und Zeitgeschichte, No. 52, pp.3-14.

Höyng and Puchert (1998): *Die Verhinderung der beruflichen Gleichstellung. Männliche Verhaltensweisen und männerbündische Kultur.* Bielefeld (Kleine Verlag).

Hofstede, Geert (1998): *Attitudes, Values and Organizational Culture: Disentangling the Concepts.* In: Organization Studies, No. 3, pp.477-92.

Honegger, Claudia; Arni, Caroline (eds.) (1999): *Gender – die Tücken einer Kategorie. Joan W. Scott, Geschichte und Politik.* Zürich (Chronos).

Hooghe, Lisbeth (1998a): *Supranational Activists or Intergovernmental Agents? Explaining the Orientations of Senior Commission Officials towards European Integration.* EUI Working Papers. RSC 98/36. Florence.

Hooghe, Lisbeth (1998b): *Images of Europe. Orientations to European Integration among Senior Commission Officials.* EUI Working Paper. RSC 98/48. Florence.

Hooghe, Lisbeth (2001): *The European Commission and the Integration of Europe Images of Governance.* Cambridge (Cambridge University Press).

Hoskyns, Catherine (1996): *Integrating Gender: Women, Law and Politics in the European Union.* London (Verso).

Hughes, Everett C. (1936): *The ecological aspect of institutions.* In: American Sociological Review, 1, pp.180-89.

Hummer, Waldemar; Obwexer, Walter (1999): *Der „geschlossene" Rücktritt der Europäischen Kommission: Von der Nichtentlastung für die Haushaltsführung zur Neuernennung der Kommission.* In: Integration, No. 2, pp.77-94.

Ikenberry, John G. (1988): *Conclusion: an Institutional Approach to American Foreign Policy.* In: Ikenberry, John et al. (eds.) (1988): *The State and the American Foreign Policy.* Ithaca (Cornell University), pp.219-243.

Ikenberry, John G. et al. (eds.) (1988): *The State and the American Foreign Policy.* Ithaca (Cornell University).

ILO (2003): *Definition of Gender Mainstreaming.* http://www.ilo.org/public/english/bureau/gender/newsite2002/about/defin.htm (Accessed 31.01.2003).

Interparliamentary Union (2003): *Parline Database.* http://www.ipu.org/english/home.htm (Accessed 22.02.3003), Geneva.

Jansen, Mechthild; Baringhorst, Sigrid; Ritter, Martina (1995): *Perspektiven aktueller Frauenforschung,* Vol. 2., Münster (LIT Verlag).

Jary, David; Jary, Julia (1995): *Dictionary of Sociology.* Glasgow (HarperCollins).

Jepperson, Ronald L. (1991): *Institutions, Institutional Effects and Institutionalism.* In: Powell, Walter W.; DiMaggio, Paul J. (eds.) (1991): *The New Institutionalism in Organizational Analysis.* Chicago (University of Chicago Press), pp.143-63.

Jewson, Nick (ed.) (1995): *Formal Equal Opportunities Policies and Employment Best Practise.* London (Routledge).

Jónasdóttir, Anna (1988): *Does Sex Matter to Democracy?* In: Scandinavian Political Studies, No. 4, pp.299-327.

Jung, Dörthe, Küpper, Gunhild (2001): *Gender Mainstreaming und betriebliche Veränderungsprozesse.* Bielefeld (Kleine Verlag).

Kaspersen, Lars B. (2000): *Anthony Giddens – An Introduction to a Social Theorist.* Oxford (Blackwell).

Kattein, Martina (1994): *Frauenerwerbstätigkeit in der EG. Perspektiven für die 90er Jahre.* Frankfurt a.M. (Campus).

Keck, Margaret E.; Sikkink, Kathryn (1998): *Activists beyond Borders. Advocacy Networks in International Politics.* Ithaca, London (Cornell University Press).

Keeler, John (1993): *Opening the Window for Reform Mandates, Crises, and Extraordinary Policy-Making.* In: Comparative Political Studies, No. 4, pp.433-86.

Kieser, Alfred (2001a): *Max Webers Analyse der Bürokratie.* In: Kieser, Alfred (ed.) (2001): *Organisationstheorien.* Stuttgart (Kohlhammer), pp.39-64.

Kieser, Alfred (2001b): *Institutionalistische Ansätze in der Organisationstheorie.* In: Kieser, Alfred (ed.) (2001): *Organisationstheorien.* Stuttgart (Kohlhammer) (= 4. Aufl.), pp.319-54.

Kieser, Alfred (ed.) (2001): *Organisationstheorien.* Stuttgart (Kohlhammer).

Kimmel, Michael (2002): *Bye, Bye Feminism, Hello Gender.* State University of New York. Keynote presentation at conference on 'Implementation of Gender Mainstreaming in Europe – a Challenge to Political Education' Leipzig, Germany, 8 September 2002.

Kluckhohn, Florence R.; Strodtbeck, Fred L. (1961): *Variations in Value Orientations.* Evanston/Ill. (Row, Peterson).

Knapp, Gudrun-Axeli (1997): *Gleichheit, Differenz, Dekonstruktion: vom Nutzen theoretischer Ansätze der Frauen- und Geschlechterforschung für die Praxis.* In: Krell, Getraude (ed.) (1997): *Chancengleichheit durch Personalpolitik. Gleichstellung von Frauen und Männern in Unternehmen und Verwaltungen. Rechtliche Regelungen, Problemanalysen, Lösungen.* Wiesbaden (Gabler), pp.73-83.

Krafft, Alexander; Ulrich, Günter (1995): *Akteure in der Sozialforschung.* In: Brinkmann, Christian; Deeke, Axel; Völkel, Brigitte (eds.) (1995): *Experteninterviews in der Arbeitsmarktforschung. Diskussionsbeitrag zu methodischen Fragen und praktischen Erfahrungen.* Beiträge zur Arbeitsmarkt- und Berufsforschung 191, Nürnberg, pp.23-33.

Kreisky, Eva; Sauer, Birgit (eds.) (1997): *Geschlechterverhältnisse im Kontext politischer Transformation.* In: Politische Vierteljahresschrift. Sonderheft.

Krell, Getraude (ed.) (1997): *Chancengleichheit durch Personalpolitik. Gleichstellung von Frauen und Männern in Unternehmen und Verwaltungen. Rechtliche Regelungen, Problemanalysen, Lösungen.* Wiesbaden (Gabler).

Krell, Gertraude (2001): *Gleichstellung aus der Perspektive der Managementlehre und der Organisationstheorie.* In: WSI Mitteilungen, No. 8, pp.520-24.

Larson, Magali S. (1977): *The Rise of Professionalism: A Sociological Analysis.* Berkeley (University of California Press).

Layder, Derek (1993): *New Strategies in Social Research.* Cambridge (Polity Press)

Leitner, Andrea; Wroblewski, Angela (2000): *Chancengleicheit und Gender Mainstreaming.* Institut für Höhere Studien, Wien, Reihe Soziologie 41 (= Soziologie 41), unpublished paper.

Lenz, Ilse (2001): *Globalisierung, Frauenbewegungen und internationale Regulierung.* In: Zeitschrift für Frauenforschung und Geschlechterstudien, No. 1+2, pp.8-28.

Lenz, Ilse (2002): *Geschlechtsspezifische Auswirkungen der Globalisierung in den Bereichen Global Governance, Arbeitsmärkte und Ressourcen.* In: Deutscher Bundestag (ed.) (2002): *Gutachten für die Enquete-Kommission „Globalisierung der Weltwirtschaft – Herausforderungen und Antworten".* Berlin, pp.309-23.

Lenz, Ilse (2005 forthcoming): *Globalization, Varieties of Gender Regimes, and Regulations for Gender Equality at Work.* In: Gottfried, Heidi et al. (eds.): *The New Economy, Globalisation and Gender.* London (Palgrave).

Lenz, Ilse; Mae, Michiko; Klose, Karin (eds.) (2000): *Frauenbewegungen weltweit.* Opladen (Leske und Budrich).

Lequesne, Christian (2000): *The European Commission: A Balancing Act between Autonomy and Dependence.* In: Neunreither, Karlheinz; Wiener, Antje (eds.) (2000): *European Integration after Amsterdam: Institutional Dynamics and Prospects for Democracy.* Oxford (Oxford University Press), pp.36-51.

Liebert, Ulrike (1999): *Gender Politics in the European Union: The Return of the Public.* In: European Societies. The Journal of the European Sociological Association, No. 2, pp.191-232.

Liebert, Ulrike (ed.) (2002): *Gendering Europeanisation.* Brussels (Peter Lang).

Liff, Sonia (1996): *Managing Diversity: New Opportunities for Women.* Warwick Papers in Industrial Relations, No. 57. Warwick: University of Warwick School of Industrial and Business Studies, Industrial Relations Research Unit, unpublished paper.

Lobby européen des femmes (2002): *Rapport annuel 2001. Les Femmes en Europe, l'Europe dans le Monde.* Bruxelles.

Lorber, Judith (1994): *Paradoxes of gender.* New Haven (Yale University Press).

Lovenduski, Joni (1998): *Gendering Research in Political Science.* In: Annual Review of Political Science, No. 1, pp.333-56.

Lovenduski, Joni; Stephenson, Susan (1998): *Overview State of the Art Study of Research on Women in Political, Economic and Social Decision Making in Europe.* Final Report. Brussels.

Maastricht Treaty (1992): *Treaty on European Union – Text of the Treaty* http://europa.eu.int/abc/obj/treaties/en/entoc01.htm (Accessed 01.06.2003), Brussels.

Macauley, Peter Duncan (2001): *Doctoral Research and Scholarly.* Communication: *Candidates, Supervisors and Information Literacy.*

http://tux.lib.deakin.edu.au/adt-VDU/uploads/approved/adt-VDU20020913.
133614/public/ (Accessed 05.05.2003), Deakin University, Philosophy Faculty of Education. Doctoral Thesis, unpublished paper.

Mackay, Fiona; Bilton, Kate (2000): *Learning from experience: lessons in mainstreaming equal opportunities.* Edinburgh (Governance of Scotland Forum).

Maier, Friederike (1997): *Entwicklung der Frauenerwerbstätigkeit in der Europäischen Union.* In: Aus Politik und Zeitgeschichte, No. 52, pp.15-27.

Majone, Giandomenico (ed.) (1996): *Regulating Europe. The European Commission as a Regulator.* London (Routledge).

March, James G. and Johan P. Olsen (1976): *Ambiguity and Choice in Organizations.* Bergen (Universitetsforlaget).

March, James G.; Olsen Johan P. (1998): *The Institutional Dynamics of International Political Orders.* In: International Organization, No. 4, pp.943-69.

March, James G.; Simon, Herbert A. (1958): *Organizations.* New York (John Wiley & Sons, Inc.).

Maruani, Magaret (ed.) (1998): *Les nouvelles Frontières de l'Inégalité.* Paris (La Découverte).

Marx, Karl (1969) [1869]: *Der 18. Brumaire des Louis Bonaparte.* Frankfurt a.M. (Insel-Verlag).

Marx, Karl (1999) [1869]: *Works of Marx & Engels 1852. The Eighteenth Brumaire of Louis Napoleon.* Translated by Saul K. Padover from the German edition of 1869. (Marx/Engels Internet Archive).
http://www.marxists.org/archive/marx/works/1852/18th-brumaire/index.htm
(Accessed 23.12.2002).

Mason, David; Jewson, Nick (1994): *"Race", Employment and Equal Opportunities: towards a Political Economy and an Agenda for the 1990s.* In: Sociological Review, No. 4, pp.591-617.

Maturana, Humberto R. (1985): *Erkennen: Die Organisation und Verkörperung von Wirklichkeit. Ausgewählte Arbeiten zur biologischen Epistemologie.* Braunschweig (Viehweg).

Mayer, Zald, N.; McCarthy, John D. (ed.) (1986): *Social Movements and Resource Mobilization in Organizational Society: Collected Essays.* New Brunswick (Transaction Books).

Mayntz, Renate; Scharpf, Fritz W. (1995a): *Der Ansatz des akteurzentrierten Institutionalismus.* In: Mayntz, Renate; Scharpf, Fritz W. (eds.) (1995): *Gesellschaftliche Selbstregelung und politische Steuerung* Frankfurt a.M., New York (Campus), pp.39-72.

Mayntz, Renate; Scharpf, Fritz W. (eds.) (1995b): *Gesellschaftliche Selbstregelung und politische Steuerung.* Frankfurt a.M., New York (Campus).

Mayring, Philipp (2000): *Qualitative Content Analysis. [28 paragraphs]* In: Forum: Qualitative Social Research [On-line Journal]. Available at:
http://www.qualitative-research.net/ (Accessed 16.05.2003).

Mazey, Sonia (1992): *Conception and Evolution of the High Authority's Administrative Service (1952-1956): from Supranational Principles to Multinational Practices.* In: Heyen, Erk V. (ed.) (1992): *Jahrbuch für europäische Verwaltungsgeschichte. Die Anfänge der Verwaltung der Europäischen Gemeinschaft.* Baden-Baden (Nomos Verlagsgesellschaft), pp.31-47.

Mazey, Sonia (1995): *The development of EU equality policies: bureaucratic expansion on behalf of women?* In: Public Administration, No. 4, pp.591-610.

Mazey, Sonia; Richardson, Jeremy J. (1997): *Policy Framing: Interest Groups and the 1996 Inter-Governmental Conference.* In: West European Politics, 20 (3) pp.111-33.

Mazey, Sonia (1998): *The European Union and Women's Rights: from the Europeanization of National Agendas to the Nationalization of a European agenda?* In: Journal of European Public Policy, No. 59(1), pp.131-52.

Mazey, Sonia (2000): *Introduction: Integrating gender – intellectual and 'real world' Mainstreaming.* In: Journal of European Public Policy, No. 3 Special Issue, pp.333-45.

Mazey, Sonia (2001): *Gender Mainstreaming in the European Union.* London (Kogan Page).

McAdam, Doug (1998): *On the International Origins of Domestic Political Opportunities.* In: Costain, Anne N.; McFarland, Andrew (eds.) (1998): Social Movements and American Political Institutions. Lanham (Rowman and Littlefields), pp.251-67.

McAdam, Doug; McCarthy, John D.; Zald, Mayer N. (1996): *Comparative Perspectives on Social Movements: Political Opportunities, Mobilizing Structures, and Cultural Framings.* New York (Cambridge University Press).

McCarthy, John D. (1986): *Prolife and Prochoice Movement Mobilization: Infrastructure Deficits and New Technologies.* In: Mayer, Zald, N.; McCarthy, John D. (ed.) (1986): Social Movements and Resource Mobilization in Organizational Society: Collected Essays. New Brunswick (Transaction Books), pp.67-98.

McDonald, Maryon (1998): *Anthropological Study of the European Commission.* Cambridge.

Meehan, Elizabeth M. (1990): *Sex equality policies in the European Community.* In: Journal of European Integration, Weidenfeld, Werner; Wessels, Wolfgang (eds.) (1999): *Jahrbuch der Europäischen Integration (1998/99).* Bonn (Europa Union Verlag). Vol. 13, No. 2-3, pp.185-196.

Merkle, Judith A. (1980): *Management and Ideology The Legacy of the International Scientific Management Movement.* Berkeley (University of California Press).

Meulemann, Heiner (1993): *Befragung und Interview. Über soziale und soziologische Situationen in der Informationssuche.* In: Soziale Welt, No. 1, pp.98-119.

Meuser, Michael (1989): Gleichstellung auf dem Prüfstand. Frauenförderung in der Verwaltungspraxis. Pfaffenweiler (Centaurus-Verlagsgesellschaft).

Meuser, Michael; Nagel, Ulrike (1997): *Das ExpertInneninterview – Wissenssoziologische Voraussetzungen und methodische Durchführung.* In: Friebertshäuser, Barbara (ed.) (1997): Handbuch qualitative Forschungsmethoden in der Erziehungswissenschaft. Weinheim (Juventa), pp.481-91.

Meuser, Michael; Nagel, Ulrike (2002): *ExpertInneninterviews – vielfach erprobt, wenig bedacht. Ein Beitrag zur qualitativen Methodendiskussion.* In: Bogner, Alexander; Littig, Beate; Menz, Wolfgang (eds.) (2002): Das Experteninterview. Theorie, Methode, Anwendung. Opladen (Leske und Budrich), pp.71-94.

Meyer, John; Rowan, Brian (1991) [1977]: *Institutionalized Organizations: Formal Stucture as Myth and Ceremony.* In: Powell, Walter W.; DiMaggio, Paul J. (eds.)

(1991): *The New Institutionalism in Organizational Analysis.* Chicago (University of Chicago Press), pp.41-62.

Meyer, John W.; Scott, Richard, W. (eds.) (1992) [1983]: *Organizational Environments: Ritual and Rationality.* Newbury Park, London, New Delhi (Sage).

Minssen, Heiner (1999): *Von der Hierarchie zum Diskurs? Die Zumutungen der Selbstregulation.* München (Reiner Hampp Verlag).

Moe, Terry (1984): *The new Economics of Organization.* In: Journal of Political Science, No. 29, pp.739-77.

Mohr, Lawrence B. (1982): *Explaining organizational Behaviour: The Limits and Possibilities of Theory and Research.* San Fransisco (Jossey-Bass).

Möller, Simon (1999): *Sexual Correctness: die Modernisierung antifeministischer Debatten in den Medien.* Opladen (Leske und Budrich).

Monnet, Jean (1976): *Mémoires d'Europe.* Paris (Editions Fayard).

Moore, William L.; Tushman, Michael L. (1982): *Managing Innovation over the Product Life Cycle.* In: Tushman, Michael L.; Moore, William L. (eds.): *Readings in the Management of Innovation.* Boston, pp.131-50.

Müller, Ursula (1993): *Sexualität, Organisation und Kontrolle.* In: Aulenbacher, Brigitte; Goldmann, Monika (eds.) (1993): *Transformation und Geschlechterverhältnis.* Frankfurt a.M., New York (Campus), pp.97-114.

Müller-Jentsch, Walter (ed.) (1993): *Profitable Ethik – effiziente Kultur. Neue Sinnstiftungen durch das Management?* München, Mehring (Rainer Hampp Verlag) (Schriftenreihe Industrielle Beziehungen, Bd.5).

Munters, Quirinus J.; Meijer, E.; Mommaas, H.; Giddens, Anthony (eds.) (1985): *Anthony Giddens: een Kennismaking met de Structuratietheorie.* Wageningen (Landbouwhogeschool).

Neuberger, Oswald (1995): *Mikropolitik Der alltägliche Aufbau und Einsatz von Macht in Organisationen.* Stuttgart (Lucius & Lucius).

Neunreither, Karlheinz; Wiener, Antje (eds.) (2000): *European Integration after Amsterdam: Institutional Dynamics and Prospects for Democracy.* Oxford (Oxford University Press).

Newland, Kathleen (1991): *From Transnational Relationships to International Relations. Women in Development and the International Decade of Women.* In: Grant, Rebecca; Newland, Kathleen (eds.) (1991): Gender in International Relations. Bloomington/In., pp.122-132.

Nietzsche, Friedrich (1980) [1910]: *Zur Genealogie der Moral.* München (Deutscher Taschenbuch-Verlag) Vol. 2).

Niskanen, William A. (1971): *Bureaucracy and Representative Government.* New York (Aldine-Atherton).

Noël, Emile (1992): Témoignage: l'Administration de la Communauté Européenne dans la Rétrospective d'un ancien haut Fonctionnaire. In: Heyen, Erk V. (ed.) (1992): *Jahrbuch für europäische Verwaltungsgeschichte. Die Anfänge der Verwaltung der Europäischen Gemeinschaft.* Baden-Baden (Nomos Verlagsgesellschaft), pp.145-58.

Nordic Council of Ministers (2000): *Implementation: Gender Mainstreaming in the Nordic Council of Ministers. Address delivered on 23rd November 2000 by Soren Christensen, Secretary General at the Conference arranged by OECD in association with the Nordic Council of Ministers.*

Nutt, Paul C. (1984): *Types of Organizational Decision Processes*. In: Administrative Science Quarterly, pp.414-50.

Oakley, Ann (1972): *Sex, Gender and Society*. London (Temple Smith).

OECD (1998): *DAC Source Book on Concepts and Approaches linked to Gender Equality*. http://www.oecd.org/dataoecd/36/47/1887561.pdf (Accessed 23.5.2001).

OECE (2001): *Office for Democratic Institutions and Human Rights. Gender Action Plan*. http://www.osce.org/odihr/documents/gender_ap2001.php3#22 (Accessed 10.12.2002), Warsaw.

Oliver, Christine (1991): *Strategic Responses to Institutional Processes*. In: Academy of Management Review, No. 1, pp.145-79.

Ortmann, Günther (1995): *Formen der Produktion, Organisation und Rekursivität*. Opladen (Westdeutscher Verlag).

Ortmann, Günther; Sydow, Jörg; Türk, Klaus (eds.) (2000): *Theorien der Organisation*. Wiesbaden (Westdeutscher Verlag).

Ostner, Ilona; Lewis, Jane (1998): *Geschlechterpolitik zwischen europäischer und nationalstaatlicher Regelung* In: Pierson, Paul (ed.) (1998): *Standort Europa Sozialpolitik zwischen Nationalstaat und europäischer Integration*. Frankfurt a.M. (Suhrkamp), pp.196-239.

Parsons, Talcott (1951): *The Social System*. Glencoe (Free Press).

Pfau-Effinger, Birgit (1996): *Analyse internationaler Differenzen in der Erwerbsbeteiligung von Frauen. Theoretischer Rahmen und empirische Ergebnisse*. In: Kölner Zeitschrift für Soziologie und Sozialpsychologie, No. 3, pp.462-92.

Phillips, Anne (1998): *Feminism and Politics*. Oxford (Oxford University Press).

Pierce, Jon L; Delbecq, André L. (1977): *Organization Structure, Individual Attitudes and Innovation*. In: Academy of Management Review, No. 2, pp.27-37.

Pierson, Paul (ed.) (1998): *Standort Europa Sozialpolitik zwischen Nationalstaat und europäischer Integration*. Frankfurt a.M. (Suhrkamp).

Pinl, Claudia (2002): *Gender Mainstreaming – ein unterschätztes Konzept*. In: Aus Politik und Zeitgeschichte, No. 34, pp.3-8.

Pijpers, Alfred; Edwards, Geoffrey (eds.) (1997): *The European Union and the Agenda of 1996*. London (Pinter).

Pollack, Mark A.; Hafner-Burton, Emilie (2000): *Mainstreaming Gender in the European Union*. In: Journal of European Public Policy, No. 1, pp.432-456.

Powell, Walter W. (1988): *Institutional Effects on Organisational Structure and Performance*. In: Zucker, Lynne G. (ed.) (1988) [1977]: *Institutional Patterns and Organisations*. Cambridge/Mass. (Ballinger), pp.115-36.

Powell, Walter W.; DiMaggio, Paul J. (eds.) (1991): *The New Institutionalism in Organizational Analysis*. Chicago (University of Chicago Press).

Ranson, Stewart; Hinings, Robert; Greenwood, Royston (1980): *The Structuring of organizational Structures*. In: Administrative Science Quarterly, Vol. 28, pp.314-337.

Rantalaiho, Liisa. (1993) *The Gender Contract* in H. Vasa (ed.) (1993): *Shaping Structural Change in Finland: the Role of Women*. Helsinki (Ministry of Social Affairs and Health).

Rasmussen, Hjalte (1986): *On Law and Policy in the European Court of Justice*. Dordrecht, Boston (Nijhoff).

Razavi, Shahra; Miller, Carol (1994): *Gender Mainstreaming: A Study of Efforts by the UNDP, the World Bank and the ILO to Institutionalize Gender Issues.* Occasional Paper No. 4. UN Fourth World Conference on Women, Geneva.

Rees, Theresa (1998): *Mainstreaming Equality in the European Union.* London (Routledge).

Reihlen, Markus (1998): *Die Heterarchie als postbürokratisches Organisationsmodell der Zukunft?* (Working paper No. 96 of the Department of General Management, Business Planning and Logistics of the University of Cologne). Cologne.

Rein, Martin; Schön, Donald (1993): *Reframing Policy Discourse.* In: Fischer, Frank Forester, John (eds.) (1993): *The Argumentative Turn in Policy Analysis and Plannning.* Durham (Duke University Press), pp.144-166.

Reinicke, Wolfgang H. (ed.) (1998): *Global Public Policy: Governing without Government.* Washington (Brookings).

Richardson, Jeremy (1996): *European Union. Power and Policy-Making.* London (Routledge).

Rickards, Tudor (1985): *Stimulating Innovation: A Systems Approach.* London (Frances Pinter).

Riley, Patricia (1983): *A Structurationist Account of Political Culture.* In: Administrative Studies Quarterly, pp.414-37.

Risse Kappen, Thomas (1995): *Bringing Transnationalism Back.* Cambridge (Cambridge University Press).

Ritchie, Ella (1992): *The Model of French Ministerial Cabinets in the Early European Commission.* In: Heyen, Erk V. (ed.) (1992): *Jahrbuch für europäische Verwaltungsgeschichte. Die Anfänge der Verwaltung der Europäischen Gemeinschaft.* Baden-Baden (Nomos Verlagsgesellschaft), pp.95-106.

Ritti, Raymond Richard; Gouldner, Fred H. (1979): *Professional Pluralism in an Industrial Organization.* In: Management Science, No. 16, pp.233-246.

Robson, Colin (1993): *Real World Research A Resource for Social Scientists and Practitioner-Researchers.* Oxford (Balckwell).

Rogalla, Dieter (2003): *Die Auswirkungen des Elysée Vertrages.* Vortrag auf Einladung der deutsch-französischen Association in Bochum, unpublished paper.

Rogers, Everett M. (1962): *Diffusion of Innovations.* New York (New Press).

Rometsch, Dietrich (1999): *Die Europäische Kommission.* In: Weidenfeld, Werner; Wessels, Wolfgang (eds.) (1999): *Jahrbuch der Europäischen Integration (1998/99.)* Bonn (Europa Union Verlag), pp.71-78.

Rowan-Campbell, Dorienne (1997): *National Machineries for Women: A Balancing Act.* In: Heyzer, Noeleen (ed.9 (1997): *A Commitment to the World's Women: Perspectives on Development for Beijing and Beyond.* New York (UNIFEM), pp.141-147.

Rubery, Jill (1998): *Equal Pay in Europe.* Basingstoke (Macmillan Press).

Sanjuán, Teresa F. (1998): *Women in the New European Society.* In: Women of European Newsletter, No. 79, p. 3.

Sauer, Birgit (1994): *Gleichstellungspolitik – Totem und Tabus. Eine feministische Revision.* Frankfurt/New York (Campus).

Schaeffer-Hegel, Barbara (1995): *Frauen mit Macht. Zum Wandel der politischen Kultur durch die Präsenz von Frauen in Führungspositionen.* Pfaffenweiler (Centaurus-Verl. Ges.).

Schein, Edgar (1992): *Organizational Culture and Leadership*. San Francisco (Jossey-Bass).

Schmidt, Verena (1998): *Teutonic vs. Tartan Sexual Equality in Politics: A Comparative Analysis of the Treatment of the Equal Representation Issue by the Labour Party in Scotland and the Greens in Germany*. University of Edinburgh, Social Science Department, M.Sc. Dissertation, unpublished paper.

Schmidt, Verena (2000): *Zum Wechselverhältnis zwischen europäischer Frauenpolitik und europäischen Frauenorganisationen*. In: Lenz, Ilse; Mae, Michiko; Klose, Karin (eds.) (2000): Frauenbewegungen weltweit. Opladen (Leske und Budrich), pp.199-232.

Schmidt, Verena (2001a): *The Evolution of Gender Inequalities in the European Union: Labour Market Participation, Wage Inequalities and Unemployment in cross-national Comparison*. Jean-Monnet-Working-Paper 2001/1. http://www.hbs.ruhr-uni-bochum.de/schmidt1.htm (Accessed 27.04.2001).

Schmidt, Verena (2001b): *Gender Mainstreaming als Leitbild für Geschlechtergerechtigkeit in Organisationsstrukturen*. In: Zeitschrift für Frauenforschung und Geschlechterstudien, No. 1, pp.45-62.

Schmidt, Verena (2003a): *The Conception and Implementation of Gender Mainstreaming in the European Commission*. In: Serrano, Amparo; Mósesdóttir, Lilja; Leitner, Andrea (eds.) (2003): *Equal Pay and Gender Mainstreaming: Monitoring the European Employment Strategy*. European Trade Union Institute (ETUI) Brussels, pp.125-152.

Schmidt, Verena (2003b): *The Institutionalisation of Gender Mainstreaming in the European Commission. The Implementation of an Innovation in a complex Organisation*. Original version of the doctoral thesis as handed in to the doctoral committee. Doctoral Thesis, unpublished paper.

Schratzenstaller, Margit (2000): *Durch die Geschlechterbrille gesehen – Haushalt und Finanzen im Überblick,* Vortrag am 29.05.2000 im Rahmen des Kommunalpolitischen Frauenforums „Kommunale Finanzen und Geschlechtergerechtigkeit", (Veranstalterin: Niedersächsische Landeszentrale für politische Bildung).

Schumpeter, Joseph A. (1931): *Theorie der wirtschaftlichen Entwicklung – Eine Untersuchung über Unternehmergewinn, Kapital, Kredit, Zins und den Konjunkturzyklus*. München, Leipzig (Duncker u. Humblot).

Schunter-Kleemann, Susanne (ed.) (1992): *Herrenhaus Europa: Geschlechterverhältnisse im Wohlfahrtsstaat*. Berlin (Edition Sigma).

Scott, Richard W. (ed.) (1995): *Institutions and Organizations*. Thousand Oaks, London, New Delhi (Sage).

Scott, Joan W. (1999): *Millenial Fantasies The Future of "Gender" in the 21st Century*. In: Honegger, Claudia, Arni, Caroline (ed.) (1999): *Gender- die Tücken einer Kategorie Joan W. Scott, Geschichte und Politik*. Zürich (Chronos), pp.19-37.

Scott, Richard W.; Meyer, John W. (1991*): The Organization of Societal Sectors: Propositions and Early Evidence*. In: Powell, Walter W.; DiMaggio, Paul J. (ed.) (1991): *The New Institutionalism in Organizational Analysis*. Chicago (University of Chicago Press), pp.108-40.

Selznick, Philip (1949): *TVA and Grass Groots*. Berkeley (University of California Press).

Selznick, Philip (1957): *Leadership in Administration: A Sociological Interpretation.* Evanson (Row Peterson).

Selznick, Philip (1996*): Institutionalism "Old" and "New".* In: Administrative Studies Quarterly, pp.270-277.

Sensi, Dina (1997): *Mécanismes et Indicateurs de Suivi de Mainstreaming.* Dossier/ SOC97- 102512 05 DOO, Bruxelles.

Serrano, Amparo; Behning, Ute (eds.) (2001): *Gender Mainstreaming in the European Employment Strategy.* Brussels (European Trade Union Institute).

Serrano, Amparo; Mósesdóttir, Lilja; Leitner, Andrea (2003) (eds.): *Equal Pay and Gender Mainstreaming: Monitoring the European Employment Strategy.* Brussels (European Trade Union Institute; to be published).

Silvera, Rachel (1998): *Les Salaires: toutes choses inégales par ailleurs?* In: Maruani, Magaret (ed.) (1998): *Les nouvelles Frontières de l'Inégalité.* Paris (La Découverte), pp.127-38.

Simon, Herbert A. (1957): *Models of Man.* New York (John Wiley & Son).

Simon, Herbert A. (1976) [1945]: *Administrative Behaviour – A Study of Decision-Making Processes in Administrative Organisations.* New York (Free Press).

Singh, Rina (1998): *Gender Autonomy in Western Europe.* Basingstoke (Macmillan Press).

Slappendel, Carol (1996): *Perspectives on Innovation in Organizations.* In: Organization Studies, No. 1, pp.107-29.

Smireich, L. (1983): *Concepts of Culture and Organisational Analysis.* In: Administrative Studies Quarterly, No. 28, pp.339-58.

Smyrl, Marc (1998): *When (and How) Do the Commission's Preferences Matter?* In: Journal of Common Market Studies, No. 1, pp.79-99.

Snow, David; Rochford, Burke E. Jr.; Worden, Steven K. et al. (1986): *Frame Alignment Processes, Micromobilization, and Movement Participation.* In: American Sociological Review, pp.464-481.

Spence, David (1997): *Staff and Personnel Policy in the Commission.* In: Edwards, Geoffrey; Spence, David (eds.) (1997): *The European Commission.* London (Longman), pp.97-114.

Spence, David (2000): *Plus ca Change, plus c'est la meme Chose? Attempting to reform the European Commission.* In: Journal of European Public Policy, No. 1, pp.1-25.

Spitzley, Helmut (1980): *Wissenschaftliche Betriebsführung, REFA, Methodenlehre und Neuorientierung der Arbeitswissenschaft.* Köln (Bund-Verlag).

Squires, Judith (1994*): Beyond the Liberal Conception of Equal Opportunity.* Paper delivered to the Equity, Labour and Social Divisions Initiative.

Squires, Judith (1996*): Quotas for Women: Fair Representation?* In: Parliamentary Affairs, No. 1, pp.71-88.

Steinmo, Sven et al. (eds.) (1992): *Structuring Politics: Historical Institutionalism in Comparative Analysis.* Cambridge et al. (Cambridge University Press).

Stetson, Dorothy M.; Mazur, Amy (eds.) (1995): *Comparative State Feminism.* London: Sage.

Stevens, Anne; Stevens, Handley (2001): *Brussels Bureaucrats? The Administration of the European Union.* Basingstoke (Palgrave).

Strauss, Anselm L. (1991): *Grundlagen Qualitativer Sozialforschung.* München (Fink).

Sverdrup, Ulf (2000): *Precedents and Present Events in the European Union. An Institutional Perspective on Treaty Reform.* In: Neunreither, Karlheinz; Wiener, Antje (eds.) (2000): *European Integration after Amsterdam: Institutional Dynamics and Prospects for Democracy.* Oxford (Oxford University Press), pp.241-65.

Tarrow, Sidney (1998): *Power in Movement. Social Movements and Contentious Politics.* Cambridge and New York (Cambridge University Press).

Taylor, Frederick W. (1967) [1911]: *The Principles of Scientific Management.* New York (W. W. Norton).

Thelen, Kathleen (1999): *Historical Institutionalism in Comparative Politics.* In: Annual Review of Political Science, No. 2, pp.369-404.

Thelen, Kathleen; Steinmo, Sven (1992): *Historical institutionalism in comparative politics.* In: Steinmo, Sven et al. (eds.) (1992): *Structuring Politics: Historical Institutionalism in Comparative Analysis.* Cambridge et al. (Cambridge University Press), pp.1-32.

Tolbert, Pamela; Zucker, Lynne G. (1996): *The Institutionalization of Institutional Theory.* In: Clegg, Steward, R.; Hardy, Cynthia; Nord, Walter R. (eds.) (1996): *Handbook of Organization Studies.* London (Sage), pp.175-90.

Tondorf, Karin (2001): *Gender Mainstreaming – verbindliches Leitprinzip für Politik und Verwaltung.* In: WSI Mitteilungen, No. 4, pp.271-77.

Tondorf, Karin; Krell, Gertraude (1999): *An den Führungskräften führt kein Weg vorbei.* Düsseldorf (Hans-Böckler-Stiftung).

Treaty of Amsterdam (1997): *Consolidated Version of the Treaty on European Union.* http://europa.eu.int/eur-lex/en/treaties/dat/eu_cons_treaty_en.pdf (Accessed 01.06.2003), Brussels.

Treaty of Rome (1957): *Treaty establishing the European Coal and Steel Community.* http://europa.eu.int/abc/obj/treaties/en/entoc29.htm (Accessed 01.06.2003), Brussels.

True, Jacqui; Mintrom, Michael (2001): *Transnational Networks and Policy Diffusion: The Case of Gender Mainstreaming.* In: ISQ, No. 1, pp.27-57.

Türk, Klaus (1989): *Neuere Entwicklungen in der Organisationsforschung. Ein Trendreport.* Stuttgart (Enke).

Türk, Klaus (2000): *Organisation als Institution der kapitalistischen Gesellschaftsform.* In: Ortmann, Günther; Sydow, Jörg; Türk, Klaus (eds.) (2000): *Theorien der Organisation.* Wiesbaden (Westdeutscher Verlag), pp.124-76.

Tushman, Michael L.; Moore, William L. (eds.) (1982): *Readings in the Management of Innovation.* Boston.

UN (1985): *Nairobi Forward-looking Strategies for the Advancement of Women* http://www.un.org/womenwatch/confer/nfls.htm (Accessed 20.02.2003).

UN (1995): *Report Of The Fourth World Conference On Women.* Beijing, *4-15 September 1995.* http://www.un.org/esa/gopher-data/conf/fwcw/off/a--20.en (Accessed 23.04.2002), New York.

UN Inter-agency Committee on Women and Gender Equality (1997): *Working Bibliography Gender Mainstreaming.* Geneva.

UN Economic and Social Council (2002): *Mainstreaming a Gender Perspective into all Policies and Programmes in the United Nations System.* E/2002/L.14. New York.

UN (2000): *Beijing + 5 and Beyond.*
http://www.un.org/womenwatch/daw/followup/bfbeyond.htm   (Accessed
09.03.2002), New York.

Van de Ven, Andrew H.; Angle, Harold L.; Poole, Scott (eds.) (1989): *Research on the Management of Innovation The Minnesota Studies.* New York (Harper and Row).

Verband der Europäischen Beamten (2001): *250 Fragen über Europa und die Europäische Politik. Eine Ausgabe – 2001 des SFE Brüssel.* Brüssel (SFE).

Verloo, Mieke (1999): *On the Conceptual and Theoretical Roots of Gender Mainstreaming.* ESRC Seminar Series "The Interface between Public Policy and Gender Equality".

Verloo, Mieke (2000): *Gender Mainstreaming: Practise and Prospects.* EG (99) 13.

Verloo, Mieke; Roggeband, Connie (1996): *Gender Impact Assessment: The Development of a new Instrument in the Netherlands.* In: Impact Assessment, H. March, pp.3-20.

Volmerg, Birgit; Leihäuser, Thomas; Neuberger, Oswald et al. (eds.) (1995): *Nach allen Regeln der Kunst. Macht und Geschlecht in Organisationen.* Freiburg (Kore).

Walgenbach, Peter (2001): *Giddens' Theorie der Strukturierung.* In: Kieser, Alfred (ed.) (2001): *Organisationstheorien.* Stuttgart (Kohlhammer)), pp.355-75.

Walk, Heike; Brunnengräber, Achim; Altvater, Elmar (2000): *Einleitung* In: Walk, Heike; Brunnengräber, Achim; Altvater, Elmar (eds.) (2000): *Vernetzt und verstrickt. Nicht-Regierungs-Organisationen als gesellschaftliche Produktivkraft.* Münster (Westfälisches Dampfboot), pp.10-27.

Walk, Heike; Brunnengräber, Achim; Altvater, Elmar) (eds.) (2000): *Vernetzt und verstrickt. Nicht-Regierungs-Organisationen als gesellschaftliche Produktivkraft.* Münster (Westfälisches Dampfboot).

Warner, Harriet, R. (1984): *Social Policy in Practice: Community Action on Behalf of Women and its Impact in the Member-States.* In: Journal of Common Market Studies, pp.141-67.

Weber, Max (1946 [1919]): *Science as a Vocation. Essays in Sociology.* New York (Oxford University Press).

Weber, Max (1976) [1921]: *Wirtschaft und Gesellschaft. Grundriss der verstehenden Soziologie.* Fünfte, revidierte Auflage, besorgt von Johannes Winckelmann. Tübingen (Mohr Siebeck).

Weber, Max (1976 [1934]): *Die protestantische Ethik I – Eine Aufsatzsammlung.* Published by Winckelmann, Johannes, Gütersloh (Mohn).

Weber, Max (1979 [1921]): *Economy and Society – An Outline of Interpretative Sociology.* Berkeley (University of California Press).

Weber, Max (1988) [1921]: *Gesammelte politische Schriften.* Tübingen (Mohr).

Weber, Max (1994 [1919]) *Wissenschaft als Beruf.* In: Winckelmann, Johannes (ed.): *Gesammelte Aufsätze zur Wissenschaftslehre.* Tübingen (UTB).

Weidenfeld, Werner; Wessels, Wolfgang (eds.) (1999): *Jahrbuch der Europäischen Integration (1998/99).* Bonn (Europa Union Verlag).

Weingast, Barry; Marshall, William (1988): *The Industrial Organization of Congress.* In: Journal of Political Economy, No. 96, pp.132-163.

Wenander, Karin (2000): *Umsetzung des Gender Mainstreaming Auftrages in Schweden: JämKom-Projekt der Schwedischen Kommunen und Gender*

Mainstreaming in den Bereichen des kommunalen Wirkens – Jämtegrering in der Kommune. Stuttgart (ÖTV).

Wendon, Bryan (1998): *The Commission as image-venue Entrepreneur in EU Social Policy.* In: Journal of European Public Policy, No. 2, pp.339-353.

Westie, Frank R. (1957): *Toward Closer Relations Betweeen Theory and Research: A Procedure and an Example.* In: American Sociological Review, Vol. 22, pp.149-154.

Wetterer, Angelika (2002): *Strategien rhetorischer Modernisierung Gender Mainstreaming, Managing Diversity und die Professionalisierung der Gender-Expertinnen.* In: Netzwerk Frauenforschung NRW Journal, No. 14, pp.24-38.

WIDE (2003): *Positions and Structure of WIDE.* http://www.eurosur.org/wide/home.htm. (Accessed 23.05.2003)

Wiener, Antje; Neunreither, Karlheinz (eds.) (2000): *European Integration after Amsterdam.* Oxford (Oxford University Press).

Willis, Paul (1977): *Learning to Labour.* Farnborough (Saxon House.

Wirtschafts- und Sozialausschuss (2000): Selbstdarstellung. http://www.esc.eu.int/de/org/presentation.htm (Accessed 02.04.2000), Brussels.

Wirtschafts- und Sozialausschuss (2000): Members of Groups. http://www.esc.eu.int/en/org/fr_org_groups.htm (Accessed 02.04.2000), Brussels.

Witte, Eberhard (1973): *Organisation für Innovationsentscheidungen.* Göttingen (Schwartz).

Wolffensperger, Joan (1985): In: Munters, Quirinus J.; Meijer, E.; Mommaas, H.; Giddens, Anthony (eds.) (1985): Anthony Giddens: een Kennismaking met de Structuratietheorie. Wageningen (Landbouwhogeschool), pp.134-156.

Wolffensperger, Joan (1991): *Engendered Structure: Giddens and the Conceptualization of Gender.* In: Davis, Kathy; Leijenaar, Monique; Oldersma, Jantine (eds.) (1991): *The Gender of Power.* London (Sage Publications), pp.87-108.

Women in Decision-making (2003): *European Database. Employees by Sex and Grade within the Administration of the European Commission.* http://www.db-decision.de/english/eu/ECAdmin.htm (Accessed on 24.8.03), Frauen Computer Zentrum Berlin.

Women Ministers of EU Countries (1996): *Women for the Renewal of Politics and Society. Rome, 18 May 1996.* Rome.

Woodward, Alison E. (1999a): *Mainstreaming as European Policy Innovation: speaking the Language of Power to Gender Test the State.* Kolloquiumspaper, Wissenschaftszentrum Berlin für Sozialforschung.

Woodward, Alison (1999b): *Women Acting Rationally: Speaking the Language of Power to Gender Test the State.* In: Beiträge aus der Forschung, Vol. 111. Rationalisation, Organisation, Gender. Sozialforschungsstelle Dortmund. pp.133-43.

Woodward, Alison E. (2001a): *Gender Mainstreaming in European Policy: Innovation or Deception?* Wissenschaftszentrum Berlin für Sozialforschung. Discussion Paper No. FS101-103. http://skylla.wz-berlin.de/pdf/2001/i01-103.pdf (Accessed 05.07.2003), Berlin.

Woodward, Alison E. (2001b): *Die McDonaldisierung der internationalen Frauenbewegung: Negative Aspekte guter Praktiken.* In: Zeitschrift für Frauenforschung und Geschlechterstudien, No. 1+2, pp.29-44.

Woodward, Alison (2003): *Mainstreaming and Equal Pay: A Logical Partnership?* In: Serrano, Amparo; Mósesdóttir, Lilja; Leitner, Andrea (eds.) (2003): *Equal Pay and Gender Mainstreaming: Monitoring the European Employment Strategy.* European Trade Union Institute (ETUI) Brussels, (to be published).

World Bank (2002): *Annual Report 2002.* http://www.worldbank.org/annualreport/2002/Overview.htm#Resources (Accessed 28.06.2002), Washington.

Young, Brigitte (1998) *Genderregime und Staat in der globalen Netzwerkökonomie.* PROKLA 111, Juni 1998, pp.175-98.

Zaltman, Gerald; Duncan, Robert; Holbek, Jonny (1973): *Innovations and Organizations.* New York (Wiley).

Znaniecki, Florian (1934): *The Method of Sociology.* New York (Farrar and Rinehart).

Zucker, Lynne G. (1986): *Production of Trust: Institutional Sources of Economic Structure, 1840-1920.* In: Research in Organisational Behaviour, pp.53-112.

Zucker, Lynne, G. (1987): *Institutional Theory of Organization.* In: Annual Review of Sociology, pp.443-64.

Zucker, Lynne G. (ed.) (1988) [1977]: *Institutional Patterns and Organizations.* Cambridge/Mass. (Ballinger).

Zucker, Lynne G. (1991 [1977]): *The Role of Institutionalization in Cultural Persistence.* In: Powell, Walter W.; DiMaggio, Paul J. (eds.): *The New Institutionalism in Organizational Analysis.* Chicago (University of Chicago Press), pp.83-115.